THE **GUINNESS** BOOK OF
WEATHER
FACTS AND FEATS

THE GUINNESS BOOK OF
WEATHER
FACTS AND FEATS

Ingrid Holford

GUINNESS SUPERLATIVES LIMITED
2 CECIL COURT, LONDON ROAD, ENFIELD, MIDDLESEX

© Ingrid Holford
and Guinness Superlatives Ltd 1977

Published in Great Britain by
Guinness Superlatives Ltd, 2 Cecil Court,
London Road, Enfield, Middlesex

ISBN 0 900424 75 3

Guinness is a registered trade mark of
Arthur Guinness Son & Co Ltd

Set in 'Monophoto' Plantin Series

Manufactured in the United States of America

OTHER GUINNESS SUPERLATIVES TITLES

CONTENTS

ACKNOWLEDGEMENTS

This book could not have been written without the ready co-operation from people in all parts of the world, and I wish in particular to give thanks to the following: In the USA – J Aldrich, J Cooley, D Douglas, D C Gaby, G Gutheridge, P J Herbert, Dr S B Idso and D Ludlum; in Canada – W F J Evans; in Australia – R J Gourlay and Dr S C Mossop; in India – S Kumar and Dr A K Mukherjee; in New Zealand – M J Hammersley and A I Tomlinson; in the Canary Isles – F Blanco.

In Great Britain, many people have spared valuable time to talk to me about their work, and in particular I gratefully acknowledge help from R McAllen, R Ogden, R A S Ratcliffe and F Singleton, all of the Meteorological Office, Bracknell; W R Richardson of Kew Observatory; Lt Cdr R Browne of HMS *Endurance*; Dr G T Meaden of the Tornado and Storm Research Association; C Swithinbank of the Polar Antarctic Survey; L Holland of the Scott Polar Research Institute; D L Day of Negretti & Zambra, S W Richardson of C F Casella & Co; Dr R Griffiths and R White.

Amongst many people in Great Britain who have corresponded with me, and whom I thank for information, are S Burt, C G Collier, Dr R Harwood, W Herbert, T R Hughes, D Imrie, L Draper, Prof G Manley, Dr D H McIntosh, A J Thomas and J M Walker.

All photographs, except those taken by myself, are acknowledged in the captions and many of them were published previously in *Weather*.

My greatest debt, however, is to authors, too numerous to list individually, who have contributed fascinating information to the following weather journals, which the Editors have kindly permitted me to use:

> *Weather*, journal of the Royal Meteorological Society, James Glaisher House, Grenville Place, Bracknell, Berks.
> *Meteorological Magazine*, the journal of the Meteorological Office, London Road, Bracknell, Berks.
> *Journal of Meteorology*, Cockhill House, Trowbridge, Wilts.
> *Weatherwise*, 230 Nassau St, Princeton NJ 08540 USA.
> *Climatological Observers Link Bulletin*, 2 School St, Long Lawford, Rugby, Warwick.

I also wish to thank the Director General of the Meteorological Office, Bracknell, and to the Controller of Her Majesty's Stationery Office, for permission to use statistics and charts.

In compiling this book, I have been greatly assisted by Diana Davies who interpreted my sometimes complicated ideas into diagrams; Barbara Prower who deciphered and typed my manuscript; Karin Bianchi who helped with the index, and Phil Defries who relieved me of many photographic tasks. My husband endured most tolerantly my preoccupation with this book and consequent neglect of domestic chores, but nothing would have come to fruition without the encouragement and advice from everyone at Guinness Superlatives Ltd, especially Beatrice Frei.

INTRODUCTION

Weather is a dictator which distributes favours and penalties impartially and it is no respecter of persons.

Countless observant people without any instruments other than their own senses originally laid the foundations of meteorology, which has progressed since the 17th century into the highly technical science of today. Satellites and electronic instruments relay endless weather information with a minimum of delay, computers solve in minutes obstruse mathematical sums at a speed beyond the capability of the human brain. Meteorological theory is peppered with long words which have little meaning to the non-professional. It sometimes seems that there is no room left for simple weather wisdom, but nothing could be further from the truth. Human experience is still the vital ingredient which turns computed data into weather forecasts and which gives to a general forecast the detail necessary for assessing local weather. Human observations can still provide unusual evidence which is of great help to the professionals who are trying to unravel mysteries of the atmosphere. This book is written not merely for amateur and professional meteorologists but for all who take a lively interest in or chronicle the weather locally, nationally or globally.

While this book lists all the recorded absolute weather extremes, these have doubtless been surpassed in regions which are so inhospitable that they remain uninhabited. Moreover, even electronic equipment cannot monitor the whole atmosphere all the time and much of what happens remains unrecorded. What impinges on everyone, however, are weather excesses which overstep the average conditions in which people live because it is these which cause discomfort or disaster. This book has concentrated on such facts.

CHAPTER 1

THE RADIATING SUN

Helios, sun god
Earth's solstices and equinoxes

The Sun has been revered throughout history as the source of light and warmth and life itself, and has brought about the most complex mythologies. Until rational explanations evolved the Sun was usually personified as a god, whose routine appearances and disappearances were foibles of his personality. Some of the better known names for the Sun god were *Helios* (Greek), *Sol* (Roman), *Mithras* (Iranian), *Shamash* (Assyrian), *Surya* (Indian), *Ormuzd* (Persian) and *Tezcatlipoca* (Mexican).

However, there were races who symbolised and worshipped objects instead; the Egyptian reverence of the scarab beetle was probably an allusion to the way the god *Ra* rolled the Sun around the sky as that beetle rolls its ball of dung ahead of itself. Even the orientation of Christian churches according to the position of the Sun are remnants of sun-worship.

Preoccupation with the Sun and its benefits led to extraordinarily accurate observations of its behaviour long before scientific explanations evolved. All over the world apparently useless monuments turn out to be accurate instruments for measuring the time of year according to the position of the Sun.

Claudius Ptolemaeus, said to have been born in Ptolemais Hermii, Egypt, was a Greek astronomer at Alexandria between AD 127 and AD 151. He was the first to propound an explanation of observed facts about the Sun. Ptolemy, as he became known, thought the Earth was stationary and that the Sun, Moon and planets revolved around it. On this basic assumption, astronomers of succeeding centuries built an elaborate concept of the paths of the heavenly bodies, a theory in fundamental sympathy with Christian belief in God's preoccupation with man and Earth.

Nicholas Copernicus (1473–1543), was born in Prussia, studied medicine at Padua, Italy, became doctor of canon law at Ferara in 1503 and then devoted himself to astronomy. He was the first to dare to contradict Ptolemy's theory and thought the Earth and planets revolved round the Sun – a revolutionary idea which was considered subversive and banned by the Church. However, scientists such as the Danish astronomer Tycho Brahe (1546–1601), the German astronomer Johann Kepler (1571–1630) and the Italian astronomer and physicist Galileo Galilei (1564–1642) defied disapproval and even persecution, to develop the Copernican theory and lay down the principles of modern astronomy.

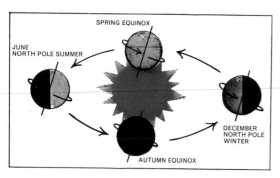

The Earth revolves around the Sun and also
rotates about its own axis.

We now know that the Sun is a radiant globe,
composed mainly of gases which whirl in
vortex around an axis. It has a mean diameter
of 865 thousand miles (1392 thousand km) and
provides a luminosity of 3×10^{27} candlepower.

The Earth traces an elliptical path round the
Sun, so the distance between the two varies,
but on average is 93 million miles (150 million
km).

The Perihelion is that position in the Earth's
orbit at which it is nearest to the Sun, 91·4
million miles (147·1 million km); it occurs in
early January.

The Aphelion is the occasion when the Earth
is furthest from the Sun, 94·5 million miles
(152·1 million km), which happens in early
July.

Day and night occur because the Earth
rotates about its own axis once in 24 hours, and
every place on Earth alternately faces and turns
away from the Sun.

The seasons happen because the Earth's axis
is tilted at $66\frac{1}{2}°$ to the plane in which it travels
round the Sun, and each hemisphere alter-
nately leans towards or away from the Sun.

The longest night takes place at the North
Pole, which is at sea level, when the spherical
bulk of the rest of the Earth obscures the Sun
for 186 continuous days during the winter.

During this time the South Pole is continually
turned towards the Sun and has its polar day.
The polar night at the South Pole is slightly
shorter than it is at the North Pole because the
high elevation of the mountainous continent
of Antarctica allows it to catch sight of the Sun
sooner.

Day glow, or day sky, are terms for the very
pale glow in the sky which lingers after sunset,
indicating that 'just round the corner' the
atmosphere is still fully illuminated by the Sun.
One of the first people to draw attention to this
fact was Erasmus Darwin (1731–1802) grand-
father of Charles Darwin the famous naturalist. Erasmus was a country doctor and a
keen weather observer, and his frequent
journeys outdoors at night, in an era when
there was little artificial street lighting to
confuse the eye, enabled him to detect day
glow. The duration of day glow varies with
latitude. Jersey, in the Channel Isles, experiences a pale light in the sky towards the north
west for a few hours between the months of
May and August. The Shetland Isles, however,
have a semblance of almost continual day between 26 April and 22 August, which the inhabitants call 'simmer dim' (*simmer* being a
Scottish form of the word summer). In suitable
weather there is enough light at midnight on
21 June to take a photograph.

Equinox means equality of day and night. It
occurs all over the world when the Sun crosses
the equator – from south to north on 21 March,
and from north to south on 22 September.

Solstices are the two occasions, about 21 June
and 21 December, when the Earth's equator is

RANGE OF AVERAGE HOURS OF POSSIBLE SUNSHINE IN BRITAIN				
	Mar	June	Sept	Dec
Shetlands (60°N)	11·8	18·6	12·9	6·1
Liverpool, Merseyside, (54°N)	11·8	17·0	12·7	7·5
Land's End, Cornwall (50°N)	11·9	16·3	12·6	8·2

furthest from the Sun. The Sun then appears to be stationary while the Earth swings back again into the opposite side of its elliptical track.

The Tropics of Cancer and Capricorn, 23° 27′ north and south of the equator respectively, encompass the only regions of the Earth on which the Sun shines directly overhead at some time of the year.

The Sun provides heat and no one who has ever basked in the sunshine has doubted the fact.

Galileo was the first person to make a problem of what seemed too obvious to comment about. He wrote in 1640 to Prince Leopold of Tuscany that he thought the Sun's rays were only transformed into heat when they encountered obstructions to their passage, and so it has been proved.

The Sun's energy is transmitted by electromagnetic waves of various wave lengths. Approximately 12 per cent are short wave ultra violet rays, 37 per cent are visible light rays and the remaining 51 per cent are still longer infra red rays. About 40 per cent of all this radiation is reflected by the atmosphere surrounding the Earth, without benefit to us, 15 per cent is absorbed directly by the atmosphere en route to Earth and the remaining 45 per cent reaches the lower levels in which weather forms. There, the rays may be further reflected or absorbed

by cloud or smoke, or reach the Earth unimpeded. At the surface, absorbed energy is converted to heat, and reflected energy imparts colour to the reflecting body.

The albedo of any substance is its ability to reflect the Sun's radiation. This is usually expressed as a percentage. Forests and wet earth reflect 5–10 per cent, rock and dry earth 10–25 per cent, sand and grass 20–30 per cent, clouds 50–65 per cent, old snow 55 per cent and new snow as much as 80 per cent.

A water surface acts like a mirror when the Sun's rays strike it obliquely and may reflect as much as 70 per cent of radiant energy. When the Sun is high in the sky, as little as 5 per cent of the energy may be reflected and the rest will be absorbed.

People walking over a clean snow surface absorb radiant energy from the Sun and also reflected rays from the snow. Hence skin can get sunburnt even though snow itself absorbs too little energy to cause melting.

The amount of reflection from the colour bands of the light spectrum varies according to the substance. Those which reflect all the colours appear white, those which reflect one or several colours acquire the colour of the light reflected, and substances which absorb all the visible rays appear black.

Smooth substances reflect more radiant energy than rough ones, which trap the energy between adjacent faces of the uneven contours. A polished metal surface can reflect 94 per cent of radiant energy falling upon it.

A black-body is a term used to describe a surface which absorbs all radiant energy falling upon it. A perfect black body exists in theory only, since everything reflects some energy, but a surface coated with lampblack may absorb as much as 97 per cent.

Absorbed rays are converted to heat and raise the temperature of any substance according to the material of which it is made. A given mass of water requires more heat than the same mass of rock to raise its temperature by the

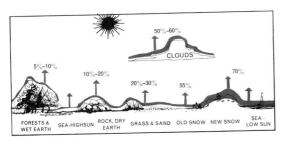

FORESTS & WET EARTH   SEA-HIGHSUN   ROCK, DRY EARTH   GRASS & SAND   OLD SNOW   NEW SNOW   SEA - LOW SUN

The albedo of any surface is its ability to reflect the Sun's radiation and it is usually expressed as a percentage of incoming radiation.

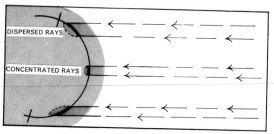

DISPERSED RAYS

CONCENTRATED RAYS

Radiant energy reaching unit area of the Earth's surface is greatest at the equator when the Sun is overhead, and least at the Poles when the Sun just skirts the horizon.

same amount. Moreover the Sun's rays penetrate a considerable depth into clear water, spreading the heat throughout. Hence large stretches of water heat up only imperceptibly from one day to another, reaching maximum temperature in late summer.

Soil, which is made up of tiny rock particles,

heats quickly in the sunshine. When soil is dry, the insulating air pockets prevent heat being conducted downwards. The heat is all devoted to raising the temperature of the surface. When soil is wet, heat is conducted more easily downward and the temperature of the surface does not rise in such a disproportionate way.

Glass is almost transparent to the Sun's rays which warm up everything *under* glass rather than the glass itself.

Concentration of radiant energy reaching a unit area of the Earth's surface is greatest at the equator when the Sun is vertically overhead and the radiant waves travel through the smallest depth of atmosphere. Radiant energy over a unit area is least at the poles when the Sun just skirts the horizon, and the rays travel obliquely through a long distance of atmos-

Curved sundial at Herculaneum, Italy, uncovered from the volcanic ash which buried the town in AD 79. Pen held in position formerly occupied by an indicator arm.

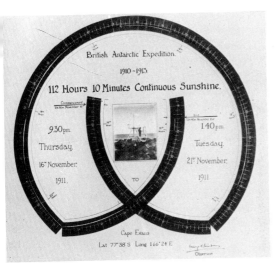

Suncard from the British Antarctic Expedition 1910–13, showing more than 112 hours of continuous sunshine. (P Defries; courtesy Kew Observatory, London)

The Campbell-Stokes sunshine recorder consists of a glass sphere that focuses the Sun's rays on a card; as the Sun moves across the sky, it burns a line into the card. It is attributed to two men. In 1853 John Francis Campbell, (1821–85) better known as 'Campbell of Islay', collector of traditional Gaelic ballads, mounted a spherical bowl of water in a round wooden frame and placed it where it received unimpeded sunlight. The Sun's rays penetrated the bowl which was left in place for six months at a stretch and focused on the wood, making a scorch trace, thus measuring the length of time that the surface received sunshine. In 1875 Campbell started to place paper behind the bowl in order to get a daily record of sunshine. In 1876 Sir George Stokes (1819–1903), Irish physicist, improved the instrument by using a solid glass sphere and supporting it between clamps on a curved metal mounting, holding a paper chart.

phere, to spread out over a large surface area on arrival.

Some small increase in heat can be engineered by presenting a sloping surface to a low altitude Sun so that the rays impinge more nearly to the perpendicular. South facing terraced vineyards in Europe's mountainous areas, or south facing slopes of Jersey's potato fields therefore make the most of available sunshine.

A pyrheliometer is an instrument for measuring the direct radiation from the Sun. A normal | incidence / pyrheliometer| consists / of metal plates exposed at right angles to the Sun's rays and the means of converting the energy received into a measurable electric current.

A sun-dial measures the time of day by the position on a graduated surface of a shadow cast by the Sun behind a projecting rod or obstruction. The most usual variety used in a garden consists of a horizontal flat plate with an inclined arm set in the centre, but curved or angled dials have been used throughout history.

Sunshine totals have considerable publicity value to seaside resorts, and a minor scandal arose in 1900 when observers at an English resort were discovered to have joined up intermittent burns on their charts by means of a hot wire in order to augment their totals! The reason for this was to improve the position of the seaside resort in the list of monthly sunshine records in the southern area.

RECORD HOURS OF SUNSHINE IN GREAT BRITAIN FOR EACH MONTH SINCE 1890		year	hours
Jan	Bournemouth, Dorset	1959	115
Feb	Jersey, Channel Isles	1891	167
Mar	Aberystwyth, Dyfed	1929	253
Apr	Westbourne, W Sussex	1893	302
May	Worthing, W Sussex	1909	353
June	Pendennis Castle, Cornwall	1925	382
July	Hastings, E Sussex	1911	384
Aug	Guernsey, Channel Isles	1899	325
Sept	Jersey, Channel Isles	1959	281
Oct	Felixstowe, Suffolk	1920	207
Nov	Falmouth, Cornwall	1923	145
Dec	Eastbourne, E Sussex	1962	117

The sunniest place in the world is the eastern Sahara desert with a mean annual sunshine of 4300 hours, 97 per cent of the possible total.

Average hours of sunshine at a particular place provide a valuable standard by which to gauge the actual sunshine in a particular year at the same place.

HOURS OF SUNSHINE DURING TWO MONTHS, JUNE AND AUGUST			
Selected stations in Great Britain	Average	Actual 1976	1976 as percentage of average
Plymouth, Devon	622	822	132
Kew, London	594	829	140
Lowestoft, Suffolk	602	896	149
Birmingham, West Midlands	500	737	147
Valley, Gwynedd	590	732	124
Durham, Durham	474	691	146
Eskdalemuir, Dumfries and Galloway	432	541	125
Abbotsinch, Strathclyde	483	611	127
Dyce, Grampian	465	613	132
Stornaway, Western Isles	440	512	116
Aldergrove, Antrim	449	611	136

Absence of bright sunshine denotes cloud, dust or physical obstruction. No sunshine was recorded at Westminster, London during the whole of December 1890.

No sunshine was reported from any of 50 reporting stations in Great Britain on 10 January 1965.

The eruption of the volcano Laki in Iceland in June 1783 was followed by colder than usual months in Great Britain, partly due to dust in the upper air which dimmed the Sun.

Lochranza, a village on the Isle of Arran stretches for $1\frac{1}{4}$ miles (2 km) along a NW-SE axis, and has three hills rising steeply between 750 ft and 1600 ft high (229 m–488 m). These block the sight of the Sun from the landward part of the village between 18 November and 8 February each year.

Distribution of heat absorbed by materials is achieved in three ways:

● **conduction** through their own mass or to anything with which they are in contact, always from the warmer surface to the colder.

Air is a poor conductor of heat, water a good one. Hence heat acquired by the top layer of dry sand or soil is conducted very slowly downwards because of the insulating air pockets between the particles. Wet soil, however, conducts heat much more quickly from the surface downwards.

● **re-radiation** (on long wave-length) to anything nearby which is colder. A person sitting on a sunny terrace, for instance, receives direct radiation from the Sun and also re-radiation from the terrace.

Once the Sun sets, the Earth cannot benefit from incoming radiation from that source. The Earth itself and everything upon it become the only effective radiators of heat. When there is no cloud in the sky to trap the Earth's long-wave emissions of energy then all temperatures fall considerably. A cloud cover, however, acts like a protective blanket, reflecting back again much of the radiant energy from the ground and preventing excessive falls in temperature.

Short wave radiation from the Sun warms everything on Earth, which in turn re-radiates heat on long wave length.

● **convection** – a heat distribution method only available to fluids such as air and water. Air in immediate contact with a surface warmer than itself warms by conduction. This causes it to become less dense; it acquires buoyancy and rises. Colder air from above or alongside moves in to take its place and after warming on the heating agent, rises in turn. Thus an air circulation forms, either in the horizontal plane or in the vertical but always with heavier cold air replacing lighter warm air. This is how warmth circulates in a centrally heated room, how warm air gradually spreads to the shady parts of a garden and how the major winds of the world circulate warmth from one place to another.

Windows in Sorrento, Italy, shuttered against summer sunshine and the 'greenhouse effect'.

Water is able to re-radiate heat, conduct heat and also distribute heat within itself by **upside-down-convection.** As soon as the top layer of water cools because of re-radiation it becomes heavier than the warmer water below and sinks beneath it. That warmer water then cools in turn and sinks in consequence. The important result, as far as weather formation is concerned, is that a river, lake or sea surface cools only very slowly during any one night and only appreciably by the end of winter. It is often warmer than adjacent land during the winter even though it is usually colder than adjacent land in summer.

Glass is peculiar because it is transparent to short wave radiation from the Sun, but only partly transparent to the long wave re-radiation from substances heated under glass.

The Greenhouse Effect is the name given to the accumulation of heat under closed glass on a sunny day, because more short wave energy can pass through the glass than can pass out again when re-radiated as long-wave energy. The Earth gains a similar 'greenhouse' benefit by being cocooned in the atmosphere, which is more transparent to incoming short wave solar radiation than it is to out-going long wave radiation from the Earth. The Earth and the atmosphere therefore remain warmer than they would be if the Earth radiated heat as efficiently as it receives it from the Sun.

Convection of air over a warming surface. Upside-down convection below a cooling water surface.

CHAPTER 2

THE INVENTION OF THERMOMETERS

STATE OF QATAR دولة قطر

Weather observing ship.

Philo of Byzantium, physicist and philosopher who lived in the 1st century BC was probably the first person to prove that air expands on heating. He inserted a bent tube into the top of a hollow leaden globe and dipped the open end of the bent tube into a flask of water. Then he set the apparatus in the Sun. As the air in the lead flask warmed, bubbles were seen coming from the tube and escaping upwards through the water in the flask. Philo concluded that the air must have expanded on warming. Then he took the apparatus into the shade so that the lead globe

A thermometer measures the temperature of any substance, which is determined by the internal energy of the molecules; the faster the molecules move the hotter is the substance. Temperature is a difficult abstract concept, but is a familiar and practical measurement nowadays because of the ubiquitous thermometer. It is hard to appreciate the problems of scientists who had none and could only measure in terms of comparative warmth, ie – *this* feels hotter than *that*.

By the end of the 16th century scientists knew from observation that many substances, like metal, expand when heated and contract when cooled. The search commenced for substances which had a constant temperature under normal conditions, and which could be used as standards for measuring the temperature of other materials.

Galileo Galilei 1564–1642. (Courtesy Negretti & Zambra Ltd)

Reconstruction of Philo's thermoscope, in the Science Museum, London. (Crown copyright; courtesy Negretti & Zambra Ltd)

cooled, and he noticed that the level of the water in the open flask fell. He deduced that the water must have risen in the tube because of shrinkage of the inside air caused by cooling. Little development of the idea took place for 15 centuries.

Galileo Galilei (1564–1642), Italian physicist and astronomer, made a similar instrument in 1593 when trying to measure the temperature of air, and he called it a **thermoscope**. It was a tube with a bulb at one end but open at the other end and therefore contained air. Galileo warmed the bulb by holding it in his hand, and then inverted the tube in a container of coloured water. As the air in the tube cooled again the coloured water moved up the small bore tube for a distance proportional to the amount of cooling. This thermoscope had no scale and its limitation was that it took no account of atmospheric pressure acting on the water in the open container (p. 40).

Francesco Sagredo, Italian scientist, corresponded with Galileo on the subject of temperature and mentioned his experiments which indicated that a mixture of snow and salt is colder than snow alone.

Sanctorius Justipolitanus Sanctoria (1561–1636), another contemporary of Galileo and physician at the University of Padua, was particularly interested in body temperature as an indication of fever. He was the first to appreciate that there is a 'normal' temperature of good health. He attempted to make a scale for the thermoscope by dividing into degrees the range between the temperature of snow and the heat of a candle flame.

The first sealed thermometer, known as the 'Florentine' thermometer, was made by Ferdinand II, Grand Duke of Tuscany, in 1641. He used alcohol, which we now know has a freezing point of $-175°F$ $(-115°C)$,

Copy of Galileo's thermoscope, in the Science Museum, London. (Crown copyright; courtesy Negretti & Zambra Ltd)

well below normal air temperature, and he sealed the tip of the glass tube so as to exclude the influence of atmospheric pressure. The scale was divided between the temperature of snow in deepest winter and the blood temperature of animals. Alcohol, however, was discovered to boil at a temperature below that at which water boiled, which made the liquid unsuitable in thermometers for general use.

Mercury thermometers were introduced in 1657 by the Academia del Cimento at Florence. Mercury is a silver-white liquid metal which is a good conductor of heat and therefore expands and contracts quickly when warmed or cooled. (It freezes at $-39°F$ ($-38°C$) and boils at $673°F$ ($357°C$), which is well above the upper limit of air temperature.) There were initial problems with the mercury which tended to cling to the side of the glass,

but nevertheless mercury thermometers gained in popularity throughout Europe.

Robert Boyle (1627–91), Irish chemist and natural philosopher, visited Florence and studied the work of Galileo. In 1664 he conducted experiments with thermometers at the request of the Royal Society. He suggested using the freezing point of oil of aniseed as the lower fixed point of the scale of thermometers, because he realised there was something not quite consistent about the freezing point of water (p. 91). The first English thermometer based on the expansion of alcohol in a hermetically sealed glass tube was made under Boyle's direction.

Robert Hooke (1635–1703), English physicist and associate of Boyle, developed a thermometer scale in 1665 which used the temperature of freezing water as zero.

Ferdinand II, Grand Duke of Tuscany. (Courtesy Negretti & Zambra Ltd)

Carlo Renaldini of Pisa suggested in 1694 that the upper fixed point of the thermometer scale should be the boiling point of water and the lower fixed point should be the melting point of ice, the whole scale to be divided into 12 degrees.

Sir Isaac Newton (1642–1727), English scientist and mathematician, also favoured the division of the temperature scale into 12 units, and suggested that the lower point be the temperature of freezing salt water and the upper fixed point be the temperature of the normal healthy human body.

Gabriel Daniel Fahrenheit (1686–1736), German physicist who settled in Holland, was the first to consolidate disjointed ideas into a thermometer scale which gained permanent popularity. Fahrenheit decided not to use alcohol as his thermometer liquid because it boiled at too low a temperature to be generally useful; he experimented with a mixture of alcohol and water, but this contracted and expanded at too uneven a rate when temperature altered. In 1714 he settled for mercury, after having invented a cleaning method which prevented the liquid from sticking to the walls of the tube. He approved of the 12 degree scale because of its divisibility into whole numbers, but since he felt the need for smaller units he multiplied the basic 12 degrees by 8 and spread them between zero (the lowest temperature he could reach with a mixture of water and sal ammoniac) and normal blood heat of the human body, which therefore became 96 degrees. Interpolating and extrapolating around, these fixed points gave 32 degrees for the melting point of ice and 212 degrees for the boiling point of water. Degrees Fahrenheit, abbreviated °F, still has many adherents.

René-Antoine Ferchault de Réaumur (1683–1757), French physicist, was meanwhile working independently on the matter of temperature scale and in 1730 suggested a scale divided into 80 degrees. He chose this figure because he used alcohol in his thermometer stem, and he noted that its volume increased by 8 per cent between measurements taken in melting ice and boiling water. The scale was used for a time but never really established itself.

Anders Celsius (1701–44), Swedish astronomer, published his idea of temperature scale in 1742: zero for the boiling point of water and 100 degrees for the melting point of ice. This was a curious reversal of the usual instinctive principle of giving the highest numerals to the warmest temperatures, and many people reacted against it. The scale was therefore soon turned upside down. Amongst claimants to have been the first to allocate zero to the melting point of ice and 100 degrees to the boiling point of water were Jean Pierre Christen (1683–1755) of France and Marten Stromer of Sweden in 1743. Some people even think that the Swedish botanist, Carl von Linné (Linnaeus) (1707–78), already had a thermometer graduated in the present 0 to 100° centigrade manner as early as 1737. This reversed Celsius scale was adopted by the scientific world at once because of the simplicity of the metric system for complicated mathematics. Recently it was adopted as the international unit by the World Meteorological Organisation, which then had to decide whether to honour any particular name or not. It decided that the scale should be attributed to Celsius, despite other claimants.

Degrees Celsius is abbreviated °C. 0°C is the temperature of a mixture of pure ice and water at an atmospheric pressure of 1013·25 millibars. 100°C is the temperature of boiling water at an atmospheric pressure of 1013·25 millibars.

Centigrade remains a popular name for the Celsius scale, denoting simply that there are 100 degrees between the two fixed points. It is possibly a fairer way of spreading credit amongst the many people who puzzled the question of thermometer scales to a successful conclusion.

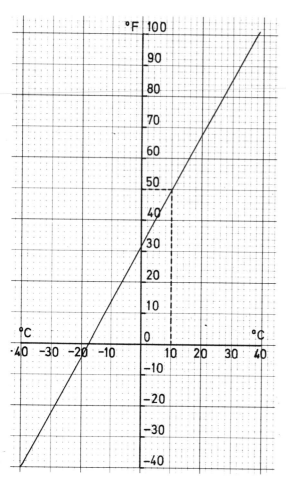

Temperature conversion graph. The co-ordinates of every point on the line give equivalent temperatures in Celsius and Fahrenheit degrees.

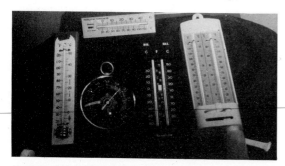

A selection of inexpensive thermometers suitable for domestic or garden use.

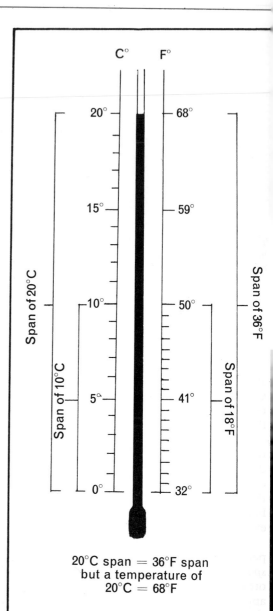

20°C span = 36°F span
but a temperature of
20°C = 68°F

The conversion of a temperature reading of 20°C is 68°F. The conversion of a temperature span of 20°C is 36°F.

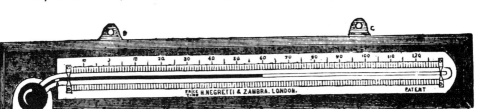

FIG. 34.

Report of the Astronomer Royal, May, 1852.

" We have for several years been very much troubled by the failures of the Maximum Self-Registering Thermometers, especially those exposed to the sun: the part of the tube in which the index ought to slide becomes foul, apparently lined with a coat of metal, and the index is immoveable. A construction invented by Messrs. Negretti and Zambra appears likely to evade this difficulty. The mercury in its expansion is forced past an obstruction in the tube, and does not return past in its contraction. No index is required in this construction. The specimens of this instrument which we have tried answer well."

An early maximum and minimum thermometer made by Negretti & Zambra Ltd, with the report on it by the Astronomer Royal in May 1852.

The conversion of temperatures from one scale to another is a necessary chore in a world still divided in loyalty to Fahrenheit and Celsius. However, the arithmetic is complicated by the fact that the two scales do not have the same zero.

On any particular thermometer graduated with both scales, the *length* of every Celsius degree is $\frac{9}{5}$ times the *length* of every Fahrenheit degree, whatever the particular reading of the thermometer. Similarly, the length of every Fahrenheit degree is $\frac{5}{9}$ times the length of every Celsius degree.

Therefore, the *span* between any two temperatures read on one scale converts into the *span* between the same temperatures on the other scale by simple multiplication of the appropriate factor; as the following example shows:

A change in temperature of 18°F = a change of $(18 \times \frac{5}{9})$°C = 10°C

or a change in temperature of 15°C = a change of $(15 \times \frac{9}{5})$°F = 27°F

It makes no difference if the span of 18°F occurs in the tropics or the Antarctic, it will always convert into 10°C.

However, the conversion of actual temperature readings has to take account of the fact that zero on the Celsius scale is not zero on the Fahrenheit scale but 32, which must be added or subtracted at an appropriate stage before or after applying the 9:5 ratio.

To convert Fahrenheit to Centigrade
Deduct 32 from a Fahrenheit reading before multiplying the result by $\frac{5}{9}$

eg A temperature of 68°F:
subtract 32 from 68 = 36
multiply 36 by $\frac{5}{9}$ = 20°C

To Convert Centigrade to Fahrenheit
Multiply Centigrade reading by $\frac{9}{5}$; then add 32 to the result

eg A temperature of 25°C:
multiply 25 by $\frac{9}{5}$ = 45
add 32 = 77°F

These conversion formulae indicate that although the span between one degree Fahrenheit and one degree Celsius is always the same, there is only one particular temperature where both scales read the same, and that is −40°:
subtract 32 from −40°F = −72
multiply −72 by $\frac{5}{9}$ = −40°C.

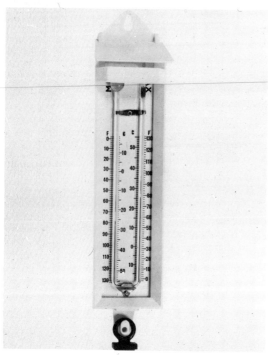

Six's maximum and minimum thermometer.
(CF Casella & Co Ltd)

pulled down by magnet to rest on the surface of the mercury below. When temperature rises, the liquid in the upper arm which is filled right up to the top, expands and pushes the mercury column down so that the index in the other arm is forced upwards, remaining at the highest point reached. When the temperature falls, the liquid in the filled arm contracts, the mercury is forced upwards by the weight of the liquid in the other arm and the index is carried along with the mercury to register the lowest temperature reached. The indices are re-set each day by magnet.

The self registering clinical thermometer was patented by Negretti and Zambra of London in 1852. The capillary tube containing mercury has a constriction near the bulb which prevents the flow of mercury back to the bulb except by shaking.

Precision maximum meteorological thermometers also have a constriction near the bulb and require shaking to re-set.

Precision minimum meteorological thermometers contain alcohol because of its low freezing point. They contain an index that is able to slide within the liquid but that cannot break through the miniscus of the alcohol. The index is re-set by tilting the tube.

Correct exposure of thermometers is crucial if air temperatures read at different

Early thermometers were liable to be inaccurate even after a sensible scale had evolved. There were imperfections in glass manufacture, difficulties in getting a consistent bore in the tubes and problems of applying graduations accurately to the glass. Modern instruments for precision work are graduated directly on to the glass, but cheaper thermometers, quite adequate for popular use, have graduations marked upon the board on which the thermometer is mounted.

Six's maximum and minimum thermometer was invented by James Six, of Cambridge University, in 1780, and the self-recording instrument is still popular. A U-shaped tube contains mercury in the lower part and a transparent liquid in the upper arms, completely filling one arm but only partially filling the other. A small index with an iron core grips the sides of each upper arm by means of a small spring, but the index can be

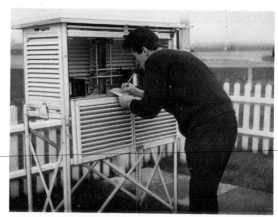

Observer at London Airport reading instruments in a Stevenson Screen.

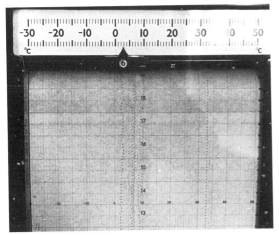

Electrical resistance thermometers record continuously as a series of dots on a rotating roll of graph paper. (P Defries, courtesy Kew Observatory)

places are to be comparable. Thermometers must be screened from direct sunshine and from radiation from the ground. An acceptable position for a domestic thermometer is 4 ft (1·2 m) high on a north facing wall.

The Stevenson Screen is a standard meteorological housing for thermometers. It was designed by Thomas Stevenson (1818–87), father of the famous author Robert Louis, and consists of a screen with louvred sides to permit a regulated through-flow of air. It has a double roof as insulation against direct sunshine and stands 4 ft (1·2 m) above ground, well away from any building or obstruction. Stevenson Screens are frequently mistaken for beehives by the uninitiated!

Grass minimum temperatures are read from a thermometer resting horizontally on supports so that its bulb just touches short cut grass and is freely exposed to the sky.

A black bulb thermometer is a mercury thermometer with a blackened bulb, encased in an outer sheath evacuated of air and exposed horizontally to the Sun. It attempts to measure direct radiation heat from the Sun, but exposures are difficult to standardise, the black coating to the bulb deteriorates quickly

and it is difficult to eliminate the effect of the temperature of the outside air. A pyrheliometer is now usually used instead (p.15).

A bent stem soil thermometer measures the temperature of soil, the length of bent stem depending upon the depth of insertion required. The bulb is adequately insulated against the temperature of the outside air and of other layers of soil.

Non-liquid thermometers measure temperature in various ways, such as:
a) electrical resistance of a metal wire, varying in known fashion according to temperature.
b) amount of curl in a bimetallic strip whose materials have different coefficients of expansion.
c) current induced in a closed circuit of dissimilar metals, where one joint remains at standard temperature and the other changes.

A Marine Thermometer Screen, so called because it was first developed for use on Weather Ships, houses electrical thermometers. It looks rather like five inverted soup plates stacked on top of each other!

A thermograph is a self registering thermometer. The thermometer is connected to a pen which records the temperature by making a continuous trace on a drum rotating by

A Marine Screen housing electrical resistance thermometers. (P Defries, courtesy of Kew Observatory)

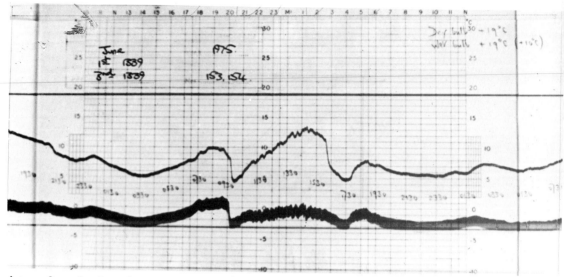

A trace from the photothermograph still in use at Kew Observatory. The overlay grid serves to determine temperature, which is read at the lower edge of the traces. The one trace is much thicker than the other because the air gap in the mercury through which light passes is greater in one thermometer than in the other. It is unlikely that the two thermometers are the same pair which were originally installed. (P Defries; courtesy Kew Observatory)

clockwork. The temperature element is usually a coil of two dissimilar metals with different coefficients of expansion.

The photothermograph is an elaborate thermograph, designed for the Meteorological Office in 1867, using mirrors and beams of light. Two bent stem thermometers are fixed

Beckley's photothermograph, as illustrated in a late 19th century catalogue of CF Casella & Co. Robert Beckley was an assistant at Kew Observatory from 1853 until 1872.

to an outside, north-facing wall and are long enough to enter a hole in the wall and bend upwards again to an indoor table. One thermometer has a wet bulb. The mercury in the tubes contains an air gap within their vertical length indoors. A series of lenses and a mirror on the table directs light from a gas lamp between vertical plates in front of the air gaps, and the resulting light beam focuses on to photosensitive paper attached to a rotating drum. An illustration from Casella's catalogue of that era shows only one lamp and mirror, but sometimes the light system on the table was duplicated, one set for each thermometer. Such a photothermograph which used to be at the Radcliffe Observatory, Oxford, is now in the Science Museum, London, complete with the Stevenson Screen which housed the thermometers on the outside wall. A photothermograph was first installed at Kew Observatory, London, in October 1867 and has been in continuous use ever since, apart from a few months at the beginning of 1969 when it was being serviced.

nfra-red thermography is the most recent development for measuring long wave radiation from the Earth, whereby heat radiated is converted into a photograph. In day-time adiation from the Earth is confused by eflected solar radiation, and therefore the most accurate infra-red thermography is done at night. Experiments indicate that surface temperatures can be measured accurately to the nearest degree from a height of about 25 miles (40 km) by this method.

CONVERSION OF FAHRENHEIT AND CENTIG SCALES OF TEMPERATURE

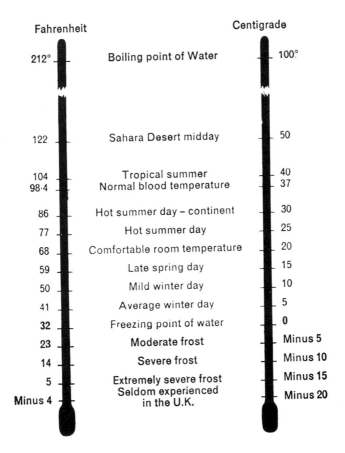

Fahrenheit		Centigrade
212°	Boiling point of Water	100°
122	Sahara Desert midday	50
104	Tropical summer	40
98·4	Normal blood temperature	37
86	Hot summer day – continent	30
77	Hot summer day	25
68	Comfortable room temperature	20
59	Late spring day	15
50	Mild winter day	10
41	Average winter day	5
32	Freezing point of water	0
23	Moderate frost	Minus 5
14	Severe frost	Minus 10
5	Extremely severe frost	Minus 15
Minus 4	Seldom experienced in the U.K.	Minus 20

Diagram available to the general public from Anglia Television's Weather Service

CHAPTER 3

SURFACE TEMPERATURES

Island observing station

Surface air temperature is a measure of the warmth of air as indicated by a thermometer in a Stevenson screen or other acceptable exposure (p. 25). It took many years to invent the thermometer, it takes only a second to take one reading, but the accumulation of statistics which results from regular daily observations all over the world provides a full-time exercise of interpretation for many meteorologists. Air temperature refers to one particular place only and to one moment of time; temperature elsewhere in the same locality may differ considerably. Therefore a decimal point difference between two temperatures is useful as a comparative guide but gives a somewhat false impression of the accuracy with which local air temperature can be defined.

Maximum and minimum temperatures can only be the highest and lowest *recorded* under acceptable meteorological conditions. Nobody can disprove any personal conviction that greater extremes have been experienced in some place where there is no thermometer.

An average temperature, often called a mean temperature, is the result of adding a series of individual readings and dividing these by the number of readings. It gives a good indication of a typical temperature, but it camouflages individual extremes within the averaging period.

Comparison of air temperatures over long periods is hindered by the fact that genuinely comparable temperature records only go back about 100 years. Nevertheless, weather conditions can be traced back much further by means of letters and books giving factual evidence of cold and heat. For instance:

July 975 was very hot in Eastern England. The Abbey of Croyland recorded that 'the lord abbat Turketul caught a fever from the intense heat of the Dog-star in that year'. (The Dog days are those preceding and following the rise and set of the Canicula, Dog star, two or three weeks either side of 11 August.)

The winter of 1435 in Great Britain was cold enough for the Thames to bear waggons as far as Gravesend and for wine to freeze in Scotland.

In 1619, an explorer writing from what is now Churchill, Canada, reported all glass bottles containing beverages burst in a sudden frost and on 25 January 1620 a cannon burst on firing because the iron had become brittle.

In 1684 a bottle of ink froze indoors at Oxford, and more than 3 in (76 mm) thickness of ice formed on a pond in one night.

Weather diaries became a hobby of the intelligentsia soon after thermometers were generally available to the public. The Royal Society, London, founded in 1660 for the exchange and promotion of philosophical and scientific information, gave the seal of its approval to the habit of making regular weather observations. As the quality of instruments improved and the necessity of consistent observations became understood, these isolated diaries improved and have become invaluable to research workers tracing back weather conditions through past centuries. Holland probably has the best series, allowing reliable records of weather to be traced back continuously to 1706. France, Italy, Germany and England can trace back weather as far as 1700 or a little earlier, but some gaps have to be filled by estimation. London weather is known for every day since 1668.

Thomas Barker of Rutland kept one of the most valuable series of weather diaries in Great Britain between 1736 and 1798. They were well set out and legibly written in ink, a page of which is illustrated.

The Manley records are realistic temperatures for central England traced back to 1659 by Professor Gordon Manley of Cambridge. His research continues to extend the data and the figures are widely used for comparative purposes.

Extract from Thomas Barker's diary. (Courtesy Lancing College)

Dallol, Ethiopia, the hottest place in the world. (D E Pedgley, Anti Locust Research Centre)

The hottest place in the world is Dallol, Ethiopia, which has hardly any seasonal relief from high temperatures.

Weather records were kept by a prospecting company on the edge of the Danakil Depression near the southern end of the Red Sea for a sequence of six years 1960–66:

The mean daily maximum temperature was more than 100°F (37·8°C) every month of the year except December when it was 98°F (36·7°C), and January when it was 97°F (36·1°C).

The mean daily minimum temperature was between 75°F and 89°F (24·4°C and 31·7°C).

The mean annual temperature (average of the mean maximum and mean minimum) was 94°F (34·4°C)

In comparison, the highest mean annual temperature, averaged over the years 1931–60, in Great Britain was 52·7°F (11·5°C) at Penzance, Cornwall, and on the Isles of Scilly.

Consistently long sequences of high daily maxima are characteristic of places in low latitudes and removed from the moderating influence of the sea. For example:

Yuma, Arizona, USA		°F	°C	consecutive days	year
Maxima	>	110	43·3	14	1955
Maxima	>	100	37·8	101	1937
Maxima	>	90	32·2	152	1956
Minima	>	85	29·4	16	1959

HIGHEST RECORDED MAXIMUM AIR TEMPERATURES

		°F	°C	
In the world:	Al'azizyah, Libya	136·4	58·0	13 Sept 1922
In N America:	Death Valley, California	134·0	56·7	10 July 1913
In Australia:	Cloncurry	127·5	53·1	13 Jan 1889
In Greenland:	Fvitgut	86·1	30·1	23 June 1915
In Antarctica:	Hope Bay	53·0	11·7	23 Mar 1946
In Great Britain:	Tonbridge, Kent	100·5*	38·1*	22 July 1868
In 1976:	Plumpton, Sussex	96·8	36·0	28 June 1976
(unconfirmed)	Henfield, Sussex	98·0	36·7	27 June 1976

* Recorded in a Glaisher stand. Probably equivalent of 98°F (36·7°C) if it had been recorded in a Stevenson Screen.

LONGEST SEQUENCES OF HIGH MAXIMUM AIR TEMPERATURES

		°F	°C	days	
In the world:	Death Valley, California	120·0	48·9 or more,	43	6 July–17 Aug 1917
	Marble Bar, W Australia	100·0	37·8 or more,	160	31 Oct–7 April 1924
	Wyndham, W Australia	90·0	32·2 or more,	333	1946
In Great Britain:	Cheltenham, Gloucestershire	89·6	32·0 or more,	7	1–7 July 1976
			11 out of 12		26 June–7 July 1976

HIGHEST MONTHLY MAXIMUM TEMPERATURES IN GREAT BRITAIN

		°F	°C	
Jan	Aber, Gwynedd	65·0	18·3	10 Jan 1971
Feb	Barnstaple, Devon	67·0	19·4	28 Feb 1891
	Cambridge, Cambridgeshire	67·0	19·4	28 Feb 1891
Mar	Wakefield, South Yorkshire	77·0	25·0	29 Mar 1929
	Cromer, Norfolk	77·0	25·0	29 Mar 1968
	Santon Downham, Norfolk	77·0	25·0	29 Mar 1968
Apr	London (Camden Square)	85·0	29·4	16 Apr 1949
May	Tunbridge Wells, Kent	91·0	32·8	29 May 1944
	Horsham, Sussex	91·0	32·8	29 May 1944
	London (various)	91·0	32·8	29 May 1944
June	Southampton, Hampshire	96·0	35·6	28 June 1976
	London (Camden Square)	96·0	35·6	29 June 1957
July	Tonbridge, Kent	100·5	38·1	22 July 1868
Aug	London (Ponders End, Middlesex)	98·8	37·1	9 Aug 1911
Sept	Barnet, Herts	96·0	35·6	2 Sept 1906
	Epsom, Surrey	96·0	35·6	2 Sept 1906
	Bawtry, West Yorkshire	96·0	35·6	2 Sept 1906
Oct	London (various)	84·0	28·9	6 Oct 1921
Nov	Prestatyn, Clwyd	71·0	21·7	4 Nov 1946
Dec	Achnashellach, Highland	65·0	18·3	2 Dec 1948

MEAN MAXIMUM TEMPERATURES, SUMMER 1976,
at selected stations in the northern hemisphere.

		June °F	July °F	Aug °F	June °C	July °C	Aug °C
Belgium	Leuven	78·3	79·7	77·0	25·7	26·5	25·0
Greece	Athens	82·5	85·6	83·7	28·1	29·8	28·7
Malta	Luqa	79·5	85·1	84·0	26·4	29·5	28·9
Sweden	Valla	70·0	74·5	73·5	21·1	23·6	23·1
Rep. of Ireland	Straide	67·5	68·4	73·0	19·7	20·2	22·8
England	Penryn	70·8	72·5	74·8	21·6	22·5	23·8
	Brighton	74·5	78·0	77·2	23·6	25·6	25·1
	London	77·9	78·2	74·8	25·5	25·7	23·8
	Leigh-on-Sea	77·0	76·8	74·5	25·0	24·9	23·6
	Sheffield	71·6	74·0	73·5	22·0	23·8	23·1
Scotland	Braemar	65·1	69·9	68·9	18·4	20·8	20·5
Shetland	Whalsay	56·6	58·6	61·5	13·7	14·8	16·2
N Ireland	Armagh	68·4	68·9	72·2	20·2	20·5	22·3
Wales	Swansea	68·5	71·6	73·7	20·3	22·0	23·2
Canada	Halifax	70·7	70·1	73·0	21·5	21·2	22·8
USA	San Francisco	73·5	70·4	71·8	23·1	21·3	22·1
Jamaica	Kingston	88·0	89·8	89·8	31·1	32·1	32·1

The summer season officially comprises the months June, July and August in the northern hemisphere, while in the southern hemisphere, summer comprises the months December, January, February and takes its year date as that in which January and February occur.

An isotherm is a line on a map which joins places having equal temperature for the particular period specified. The quality of summers throughout the world is indicated on maps by mean July isotherms for the northern hemisphere and mean January isotherms for the southern hemisphere.

The hottest summer in central England, which is remote from the moderating influence of the sea, was 1976, when highest temperatures occurred in June and July. 1975 was also hot, but the heat wave was later, in the first fortnight of August, so that maximum temperatures were slightly lower than in 1976.

It was without parallel in the history of British meteorological records to have two consecutive hot summers within the six hottest. The summer of 1976 rather spoilt a popular theory that warm summers occur in *odd* date years and cool summers in *even* date years!

Mean daily temperature					
Hottest				Coolest	
	°F	°C		°F	°C
*1976	63·6	17·6	1907	56·5	13·6
1947	63·0	17·0	1888	56·5	13·6
1933	63·0	17·0	1879	56·7	13·7
1911	62·5	16·9	1922	56·7	13·7
1899	62·5	16·9	1909	57·0	13·9
1975	62·2	16·8	1890	57·2	14·0
1959	61·9	16·6	1920	57·2	14·0
1955	61·7	16·5	1954	57·3	14·1
1949	61·7	16·5	1956	57·3	14·1
1893	61·7	16·5	1903	57·5	14·2

* *Summer of 1826 also estimated 17·6°C in the Manley Records*

Consistently widespread high daily maxima was a particular characteristic of the 1976 heat wave in Great Britain. Daily maxima reached or exceeded 89·6°F (32°C) every day between 23 June and 8 July at one or more reporting stations using approved thermometers in Stevenson Screens. Although the highest temperatures naturally occurred in the south of England and the Midlands, exceptionally high maxima were recorded in north England and Scotland. For instance:

°F	°C		
89·6	32·0	Marple, Greater Manchester	1976 29 June
89·6	32·0	Liverpool, Merseyside	30 June
90·0	32·2	St Helens, Merseyside	30 June
89·6	32·2	Squires Gate, Lancashire	1 & 5 July
86·0	30·0	Braemar, Grampian	8 July
84·2	29·0	Lossiemouth, Grampian	9 July
84·2	29·0	Kinloss, Grampian	9 July

Long winter nights, especially when there is no insulating blanket of cloud in the sky, cause land masses to cool faster than the sea. Therefore the lowest air temperatures occur over continents in high latitudes, with particularly low temperatures in valleys into which cold air drains.

Air frost is the name given to air with a temperature at or below 32°F (0°C). It is often accompanied by hoar frost (p. 108).

A frost hollow is low lying ground into which cooling, dense air drains and from which there is no natural outlet, thus making it prone to air frost.

A notable frost hollow in England is at Rickmansworth, Herts, where a natural valley is further blocked by a railway embankment which acts as a dam against the free flow of cold air. Minimum temperature fell to 17°F (−8·3°C) as late as 17 May in 1935.

A freezing day is one in which the temperature never rises above 32°F (0°C). Places in the centre of continents in high latitudes such as Yukon, Alaska, USA consider a freezing day with this upper limit 'warm' compared with the many much colder days they experience. Freezing days never occur on islands (such as Hawaii, Pacific Ocean) set in the middle of warm seas. The British Isles have mild winters with very few freezing days when the wind brings air from the Atlantic, and have cold winters when the wind blows persistently from the Arctic or from the interior of Europe.

The longest continuous period of freezing days in England this century was 34 days at Moor House, Cumbria, 23 December 1962–25 January 1963, and 31 continuous days throughout January of the same year at Great Dun Fell. Both these stations are exposed high level stations, and the cold at Kew, London, during the same period was probably more representative of a wider area. Kew had nine continuous freezing days, 17–25 January 1963, out of a total 18 freezing days, a record only broken by a total of 21 freezing days in 1891.

Continental sequences of freezing days are much more dramatic, even in temperate latitudes. One of the longest cold waves in the USA gave the following consecutive days of frost between 17 October 1935 and 10 April 1936.

176 days, min. <32°F (0°C) 17 Oct–10 Apr
92 days, max. <32°F (0°C) 30 Nov–29 Feb
67 days, min. <0°F (−17·8°C) 31 Dec–6 Mar
41 days, max. <0°F (−17·8°C) 11 Jan–20 Feb

The coldest night in Great Britain in recent years was 21 January 1940 when 14 stations over a wide area reported temperatures below 0°F (−17·8°C) and Rhayader, Powys, reported −10°F (−23·3°C).

The lowest annual minimum temperature in Great Britain occurs at Braemar, Scotland, where it was less than 0°F (−17·8°C) in 11 years out of the 40 years between 1930–69.

LOWEST MINIMUM AIR TEMPERATURES

		°F	°C	
In the world:	Vostok, Antarctica	−126·9	−88·3	24 Aug 1960
In N Hemisphere:	Verkhoyansk, USSR	−90·4	−68·0	5 & 7 Feb 1892
In Canada:	Snag, Yukon	−81·0	−63·0	3 Feb 1947
*In Scotland:	Braemar	−17·0	−27·2	11 Feb 1895
In Greece:	Kavalla	−13·0	−25·0	27 Jan 1954
In England:	Haydon Bridge	−10·0	−23·3	21 Jan 1881
In Wales:	Rhayader	−10·0	−23·3	21 Jan 1940
In Australia:	Charlotte Pass	−8·0	−22·2	22 Aug 1947
In Ireland:	Market Castle	−2·0	−18·9	16 Jan 1881
In South Africa:	Carolina	5·5	−14·7	23 July 1926

* −23·0°F (−30·5°C) has been claimed for Blackadder, Borders, 4 Dec 1879. The temperature was read on an official instrument but the exposure was suspect.

LOWEST MONTHLY MINIMUM AIR TEMPERATURES IN GREAT BRITAIN

		°F	°C	
Jan	Kelso, Borders	−16	−26·7	17 Jan 1881
Feb	Braemar, Grampian	−17	−27·2	11 Feb 1895
Mar	Logie Coldstone, Grampian	−9	−22·8	14 Mar 1958
Apr	Eskdalemuir, Dumfries & Galloway	4	−15·6	2 Apr 1917
May	Ben Nevis, Highland	14	−9	17 May 1891
June	Dalwhinnie, Highland	22	−5·6	9 June 1955
July	Ben Nevis, Highland	26	−3·3	10 July 1888
Aug	Inverdruie, Grampian	26	−3·3	21 Aug 1973
Sept	Ben Nevis, Highland	18	−7·8	23 Sept 1893
Oct	Braemar, Grampian	11	−11·7	20 Oct 1880
Nov	Braemar, Grampian	−10	−23·3	14 Nov 1919
Dec	Kelso, Borders	−16	−26·7	2 Dec 1879

MEAN DAILY TEMPERATURE, IN THREE COLDEST WINTERS, CENTRAL ENGLAND

	°F	°F	°F	Average for Winter	°C	°C	°C	Average for Winter
	Dec	Jan	Feb	Winter	Dec	Jan	Feb	Winter
1963	35·3	28·2	30·8	31·5	1·8	−2·1	−0·7	−0·3
1740	37·7	27·0	29·1	31·3	3·2	−2·8	−1·6	−0·4
1684	26·6	30·2	32·9	29·9	−3·0	−1·0	0·5	−1·2

Vostok, Antarctica, the coldest place in the world. (Novosti Press)

The coldest area of the world is inland of Antarctica. Vostok, at 78° 26′ S, 106° 52′ E, is 11 500 ft (3505 m) above sea level and is known as the pole of cold, having a mean annual temperature of −72°F (−57·8°C) and a mean July temperature of −130°F (−90°C).

At the geographical south pole, where an American scientific station has been keeping records for 20 years, the mean July temperature is −105°F (−75°C), and the mean annual temperature is −56°F (−49·2°C). The coldest year was 1976, which had a mean temperature of −58°F (−50°C).

In the northern hemisphere the coldest area is Siberia, where the village of Oymyakon (63° 16′ N, 143° 15′ E) claims to be the coldest permanently inhabited place, recording −96°F (−71·1°C) in 1964.

Winter in the northern hemisphere is considered to be the three consecutive months December, January and February, and is commonly ascribed the date year in which January and February occur. **In the southern hemisphere** winter comprises the months June, July and August. The coldness of any winter cannot be measured in terms of individual very low minimum temperatures, because these often occur under clear skies and the Sun next day raises air temperatures to more agreeable levels. Persistent cold occurs when air streams arrive from colder parts of the world, often accompanied by cloud so that temperatures do not rise appreciably during the day.

Mean minimum temperatures in winter tend to be lower with increasing distance from the sea, as indicated by the following mean January minimum temperatures:

	°F	°C
Latitudes 45°–60°N		
London, GB	34	1·7
Paris, France	32	0
Berlin, Germany	26	−3·3
Moscow, USSR	−9	−12·8
Omsk, USSR	−14	−25·5
Winnipeg, Canada	−13	−25·0
Vancouver, Canada	32	0
Latitudes higher than 60°, N or S		
Fairbanks, Alaska	−21	−29·5
Yakutsk, USSR	−53	−47·0
S Pole, Antarctica	−81	−62·8
McMurdo Sound, Antarctica	−24	−31·2
Spitzbergen, Arctic Ocean	−4	−20·0

The coldest winter in Great Britain this century was 1963 when many temperature records were broken. Amongst others, Southampton had its coldest winter of the century, Manchester the coldest since 1888, and Edinburgh, Aberdeen and Wick the coldest since 1895. Winter 1963 probably rates as cold as winter 1740 but not as cold as 1684, the coldest in instrumental history in Great Britain.

The longest sequences of cold winters in central England, with mean daily temperature of less than 38·3°F (3·5°C), is three years. Such sequences have occurred on only four occasions: from 1879–81, 1886–88, 1891–93 and 1940–42.

The longest sequence of mild winters in central England, with mean daily temperature above 39°F (3·9°C), was eleven years, from 1918 to 1928. Similarly mild winters occurred for eight years, from 1932 to 39, for seven years, from 1910 to 1916 and for six years, from 1971 to 76.

There has only been one sequence of five winters since 1873, when mean daily temperature was above 40·1°F (4·5°C), and that was

1972–76. However, there were five four-year periods which reached this temperature during winter: 1736–39, 1866–69, 1882–85, 1911–14 and 1920–23.

The coldest and mildest winters in central England since 1873 are given below.

	Mean daily temperature				
	Coldest			Mildest	
	°F	°C		°F	°C
1963	31·5	−0·3	1975	43·1	6·2
1897	33·2	0·7	1935	43·0	6·1
1947	34·0	1·1	1943	42·6	5·9
1895	34·1	1·2	1877	42·6	5·9
1940	34·7	1·5	1925	42·5	5·8

Perpetually cold winters, with mean temperature of 32°F (0°C) or less in the midwinter month are indicated by the isotherm maps for January in the northern hemisphere and for July in the southern hemisphere. Nearly all the inhabited lands with cold winters are in the Northern hemisphere, though the southern tip of Argentina just enters the appropriate isotherm band in the southern hemisphere.

Two notorious cold winters, from different centuries and on opposite sides of the world, experienced similar minimum temperatures.

In 1812, Napoleon's retreat from Moscow was made in bitterly cold weather. The following temperatures were recorded on a thermometer with non-standard exposure, being attached to the buttonhole of a uniform. En route from Moscow to Smolensk minimum temperatures recorded were:

	°F	°C
9 November	5	−15
30 November	−13	−25
3 December	−22	−30
6 December	−35	−37

In 1977, the eastern half of the United States of America had its coldest winter for 200 years, and by the end of January at least 100 people had died of cold. Temperatures of −31°F (−35°C) were reported from North Dakota and Minnesota. Indianapolis had a mean January temperature of 10°F (−12°C),

which was 18°F (10°C) *lower* than average. The mean January temperature in these states was the same as the mean January temperature at Fairbanks, Alaska, where the temperature was 20°F (12°C) *higher* than average. Cold weather continued in the eastern states until the last week in February.

Extreme ranges of temperature may occur throughout the whole time scale.

The greatest seasonal fluctuations occur in the centre of land masses with long cold winters but short hot summers. Verhoyansk, NE Siberia, with a lowest temperature of −90·4°F (−68°C) has also recorded a summer maximum of 98°F (36·7°C), a range of 188·4°F (101·7°C).

The smallest fluctuations occur on small islands where air temperature is determined by surrounding sea temperature. Garapan on Saipan, one of the Mariana Islands in the Pacific Ocean, had an extreme range of only 21·2°F (11·8°C) during nine years, 1927–35. Lowest temperature was 67·3°F (19·6°C) and the highest 88·5°F (31·4°C).

Over a longer period of 55 years, 1911–66, the Island of Fernando de Noronha had an extreme temperature range of only 24·1°F (13·3°C) the lowest being 65·6°F (18·7°C) and the highest 89·6°F (32°C).

A recent spectacular weekly range of temperature in England occurred in the first week of June 1975. On 2 June several screen temperatures fell to below 35·6°F (2°C) and snow fell in various places from Scotland to south of England. Ground frost was widespread in many places between 2 June and 4 June. On 6 June, temperature climbed to over 70°F (21·1°C) in various places, starting a long hot summer.

The greatest daily range of temperature recorded in the world was 100°F (55·5°C), from 44°F (6·7°C) down to −56°F (−48·8°C) at Browning, Montana, USA, from 23–24 January 1916.

The greatest daily range in England occurred at Rickmansworth on 29 August 1936, when temperature rose 50·9°F (28·3°C) in nine hours from 34·0°F (1·1°C) to 84·9°F (29·4°C).

In Scotland, 24–25 January 1958, temperature rose 46·6°F at Kincraig from −5·8°F (−21°C) to 39·8°F (4·3°C).

The most abrupt change in temperature recorded in the world was at Spearfish, South Dakota, when temperature rose 49°F (27·2°C) in *2 minutes*, from −4°F (−20°C) to 45°F (7·2°C) between 7·30 am and 7·32 am on 22 January 1943.

Sea surface temperature determines the temperature of air moving over it for any appreciable distance. Sea temperature varies from 28·5°F (−2°C) in the White Sea and near polar ice, to 96°F (35·6°C) which was once recorded in the Persian Gulf.

Mean February and September sea temperature in European waters varies between the following:
54°F and 66°F (12°C and 19°C) in southern Bay of Biscay
46°F and 61°F (8°C and 16°C) in Irish Sea
42°F and 50°F (6°C and 10°C) near Faroes

Land surface temperature is hottest near the equator, in places where the ground material is receptive to the Sun's radiation, and dry so that air pockets deter conduction of the heat down into the subsoil. 183°F (84°C) was recorded in sand on the coastal plain north of Port Sudan on 24 September 1960. The temperature of a black cloth laid near the ground at Khartoum on 31 May 1918, was 194°F (90°C), at a time when the shade temperature of air was 109°F (42·8°C). Even in temperate latitudes extremely high surface temperatures can be reached. A black glass exposed fully to the Sun has been known to reach a temperature of 160°F (71·1°C) at Watford, Herts, when the air temperature was only 70°F (21·1°C).

Permafrost is the name given to permanently frozen land, which occurs wherever the mean annual air temperature is about 16°F (−9°C). Any cover such as moss or tundra insulates the soil against the benefit of the sun-

rays, so that there may be an appreciable rise in air temperature during the short summer without much affect upon the frozen ground.

In Canada about 50 per cent of the total land surface is permanently frozen, to a depth of about 6 ft (2 m) at the southern limit, and to about 900 ft (300 m) at the northern limit.

The greatest measured depth of frozen ground is 4920 ft (1500 m) on April 1968 in the basin of the river Lena, Siberia.

1620 ft (494 m) permafrost was measured on Melville Island, NW Territory, Canada, in July 1963 by the Jacobsen-McGill Arctic Research Expedition.

The human body produces heat from food and physical activity. It then has to dissipate similar amounts of heat in order to maintain the balance required for comfort.

A normally clothed adult dissipates heat at a rate of:
  115 watts when at rest
  160 watts when walking slowly
  265 watts when jiving
  440 watts when doing heavy physical work.

One person can raise the temperature of an unventilated room measuring 10 ft³ (3 m³) by 15°F (8°C). Hence, large assemblies of people in confined surroundings can create uncomfortably hot conditions without the need for artificial heat.

Radiation is the basic method of dissipating heat from the body. Heat from the core is brought by the blood to the surface of the skin, which acts as a radiator. The greater the temperature difference between air and skin, the more rapidly heat is dissipated. In order to 'draw' the heat from inside the body, the skin maintains a temperature gradient with the core.

Normal core temperature of a healthy person is 98·6°F (37°C).

Normal skin temperature for comfort is 91·4°F (33°C).

Shivering starts when skin temperature falls to 86°F (30°C).

Winter scene on Mount Rigi, Switzerland.
Temperature often falls very low at night under
clear skies but the Sun raises air temperature to
more agreeable levels during the day. (Dr G Frei)

Thermal equilibrium is the comfortable balance of internal heat production and dissipation. An unclothed person may be in thermal equilibrium when at rest in still air having a temperature of 86°F (30°C).

A lightly clothed person may be in thermal equilibrium when at rest in still air having a temperature of 70°–75°F (21°–24°C).

At air temperatures above 90°F (32°C) even bare skin cannot radiate enough heat to maintain normal body temperature and the sweat glands take over (see p. 104).

A marathon runner cannot dissipate all the heat necessary even by radiation and sweating, and his body temperature may rise to over 105°F (41°C).

Irreversible damage to the body is liable to occur when core temperature rises above 106°F (41°C) though two patients have been known to survive a temperature of more than 110°F (43°C).

Very low air temperatures can be endured by the human body provided it is adequately insulated against heat loss. Several layers of clothing with cellular structure to retain warm air pockets are better insulation than one thick non-cellular layer, through which heat may be lost by conduction. In Arctic conditions a person needs 5 times as much insulation when at rest than he needs when working.

Hypoaesthesia is the loss of sense of pain or touch which occurs when skin temperature falls to about 50°F (10°C).

Frostbite is the injury caused to body tissue at sub-freezing air temperatures, partly due to formation of ice crystals within the tissue and partly due to constriction of the blood vessels and impaired circulation. The skin then appears white, serving as visual warning that first aid treatment is urgently required. Frost-bitten gloved hands and booted feet cannot be seen and do not send pain signals to the brain, so they suffer more frequently from permanent damage than the face, which can be seen by other people.

Hypothermia is a condition of abnormally low core temperature and often has fatal consequences. The body loses thermal control when core temperature falls below 90°F (32°C) and coma follows. Death occurs any time after core temperature falls to 79°F (26°C) but two casualties have been known to survive core temperatures of 60°F (16°C).

The human body can endure very low air
temperatures when sufficiently insulated against
the cold. (Mt Washington Observatory)

Conduction of heat from the body when immersed in water may occur 23 times faster than it does in air, especially for people without a substantial layer of fat serving as protection. The sea temperature, 180 miles from Madeira, was 64°F (18°C) on 24 December 1963 when the cruise ship Lakonia caught fire; 128 deaths resulted and the majority were caused by hypothermia from prolonged immersion in water.

Immersion in water at temperatures of less than 35°F (2°C) leads to death within 7–15 minutes.

A wet suit is a close fitting garment of neoprene which only permits a thin layer of water to exist between the body and the impervious material. This layer of water quickly warms to body temperature and remains undiluted by colder water in which a person may be emerged. Wet suits are necessary protection for those whose sports, such as dinghy sailing or water skiing, make emersion in cold water likely.

Modern double-lined wet suits (Typhoon).

°F (to nearest whole degree)					°C (to nearest half degree)			
JANUARY		JULY			JANUARY		JULY	
Max	Min	Max	Min		Max	Min	Max	Min
87	73	81	73	Accra, Ghana	30·5	23·0	27·0	23·0
59	49	83	70	Algiers, Algeria	15·0	9·5	28·5	21·0
97	70	67	39	Alice Springs, Australia	36·0	21·0	19·5	4·0
48	36	88	65	Athens, Greece	9·0	2·0	31·0	18·5
90	68	90	76	Bangkok, Thailand	32·0	20·0	32·0	24·5
55	44	82	69	Barcelona, Spain	13·0	6·5	28·0	20·5
43	35	65	52	Belfast, N. Ireland	6·0	1·5	18·5	11·0
35	26	74	56	Berlin, Germany	1·5	−3·5	23·5	13·5
35	26	73	55	Berne, Switzerland	1·5	−3·5	23·0	13·0
83	67	85	77	Bombay, India	28·5	19·5	29·5	25·0
34	19	86	61	Bucharest, Rumania	1·0	−7·0	30·0	16·0
85	63	57	42	Buenos Aires, Argentina	29·5	17·0	14·0	5·5
65	47	96	70	Cairo, Egypt	18·5	8·5	35·5	21·0
70	53	50	35	Christchurch, N. Zealand	21·0	11·5	10·0	1·5
49	41	96	76	Chungking, China	9·5	5·0	35·5	24·5
86	72	85	77	Colombo, Ceylon	30·0	22·0	29·5	25·0
36	28	72	56	Copenhagen, Denmark	2·0	−2·0	22·0	13·5
90	77	87	67	Darwin, Australia	32·0	25·0	30·5	19·5
41	32	67	52	Dundee, Scotland	5·0	0·0	19·5	11·0
−2	−20	72	48	Fairbanks, Canada	−19·0	−29·0	22·0	9·0
26	17	71	54	Helsinki, Finland	−3·5	−8·5	21·5	12·5
34	20	77	55	Innsbruck, Austria	1·0	−6·5	25·0	13·0
46	37	81	65	Istanbul, Turkey	8·0	2·5	27·5	18·5
78	58	63	39	Johannesburg, S. Africa	25·5	14·5	17·0	4·0
83	65	77	62	Kampala, Uganda	28·5	18·5	25·0	16·5
86	67	90	73	Kingston, Jamaica	30·0	19·5	32·0	23·0
57	46	81	63	Lisbon, Portugal	14·0	8·0	27·5	17·0
44	35	73	55	London, England	6·5	1·5	23·0	13·0
47	35	88	64	Madrid, Spain	8·5	1·5	31·0	17·5
88	75	89	75	Manaus, Brazil	31·0	24·0	31·5	24·0
50	35	84	63	Marseille, France	10·0	1·5	29·0	17·0
78	57	56	42	Melbourne, Australia	25·5	14·0	13·5	5·5
87	75	81	71	Mombasa, Kenya	30·5	24·0	27·0	21·5
21	6	78	61	Montreal, Canada	−6·0	−14·5	25·5	16·0
15	3	73	55	Moscow, USSR	−9·5	−16·0	23·0	13·0
77	65	88	75	Naussa, Bahamas	25·0	18·5	31·0	24·0
37	24	82	66	New York, USA	3·0	−4·5	28·0	19·0
59	42	98	70	Nicosia, Cyprus	15·0	5·5	36·5	21·0
28	19	70	54	Oslo, Norway	−2·5	−7·5	21·0	12·0
57	44	84	67	Palma, Majorca	14·0	6·5	29·0	19·5
43	34	76	58	Paris, France	6·0	1·0	24·5	14·5
86	63	63	48	Perth, Australia	29·5	17·0	17·0	9·0
36	28	57	48	Reykjavik, Iceland	2·0	−2·5	14·0	9·0
52	40	87	67	Rome, Italy	11·0	4·5	30·5	19·5
69	58	83	69	Santa Cruz, Tenerife	20·5	14·5	28·5	20·5
85	53	59	37	Santiago, Chile	29·5	11·5	15·0	3·0
19	5	60	47	Stockholm, Sweden	−7·5	−15·0	15·5	8·5
33	16	90	73	Tientsin, China	0·5	−9·0	32·0	23·0
47	29	83	70	Tokyo, Japan	8·5	−1·5	28·5	21·0

AVERAGE AIR TEMPERATURES AT SELECTED PLACES THROUGHOUT THE WORLD

CHAPTER 4

THE PRESSURE AND CHARACTER OF THE ATMOSPHERE

Weather observing satellite.

It is not surprising that the pressure of the atmosphere had to be *discovered*. It is imperceptible by the human body under normal conditions because pressure acts both inwards and outwards on everything containing air.

Hero of Alexandria, Greek engineer of the 2nd century BC, was probably the first to demonstrate that air was a substance with weight. He inverted an open ended vessel full of air downwards on to the surface of water and showed that the water would not fill the vessel unless air escaped as bubbles rising to the surface. He deduced that air was a material substance, probably composed of particles, but the idea was too advanced for the era in which he lived and he was merely laughed at. The question was taken up again in a serious manner in the 17th century.

Evangelista Torricelli (1608–47), Italian mathematician and physicist, became a pupil of Galileo in 1641. Galileo set him the problem of why water would not rise in a pump more than about 33 ft (10 m) above its natural level. In seeking the answer Torricelli experimented in 1643 with a glass tube 4 ft (1·2 m) long. He filled it with mercury, the heaviest known liquid, and inverted the open end under the surface of mercury in another container. The level of mercury in the tube fell but not so far as to equalise with the level in the container. Since there was nothing but mercury vapour in the top of the tube he had created the first sustained vacuum, thereafter called the Torricellian vacuum. He concluded that the only thing that could be pushing the mercury in the tube higher than the level in the container must be the pressure of the atmosphere on the surface of mercury in the container.

Blaise Pascal (1623–62), French mathematician and physicist, repeated Torricelli's experiment but used red wine instead of mercury. Since wine is even lighter than water which in turn is 13·6 times lighter than mercury, Pascal's tube had to be 46 ft (14 m) tall to prove that the atmosphere exerted a pressure. In order to confirm the existence of atmospheric pressure, Pascal persuaded his young brother to walk with a Torricelli tube to the 3458 ft (1054 m) summit of Puy de Dôme, in the Auvergne mountains near Clermont Ferrand where he lived. (Pascal himself always suffered from ill health.) The level of mercury in the

Von Guerike's experiment to demonstrate the 'force of vacuum'. (Courtesy Negretti & Zambra Ltd)

tube fell 3·33 in (84 mm), showing that 1000 ft (300 m) depth of atmosphere near the surface exerts a pressure of approximately 1 in (25 mm) mercury.

Similar falls in atmospheric pressure are recorded wherever a modern ship rises through the locks of a canal, or an aeroplane climbs into the air.

Otto von Guerike (1602–86), German Physicist and the Mayor of Magdeburg for 35 years, demonstrated the logical consequences of atmospheric pressure with a flamboyant experiment in 1651. He made two hollow hemispheres of metal, 20 in (500 mm) in diameter and evacuated the air in between by means of an air pump of his own invention.

He then caused two teams of eight horses to pull on each hemisphere, but they could not be separated until some air was admitted between the two parts by a valve. They had been firmly clamped together by atmospheric pressure alone.

Variation in atmospheric pressure, as recorded by the daily fluctuations in the level of mercury in a Torricelli tube, was a very puzzling fact for scientists of the 17th century.

Giovanni Borelli (1608–79), Italian mathematician at Pisa and friend of Galileo, was sent a Torricelli tube by the Grand Duke Ferdinand II of Tuscany, and instructed to make constant observations with it. Correspondence between Borelli and the Duke's brother, Prince Leopold, contained the following wild theories.

Pressure might be caused by the weight of clouds or rain; that idea was contradicted when it was observed that pressure usually *fell* during wet weather.

The clouds might actually support the air above; but that suggestion was dismissed as improbable.

Air might pile up like water waves; but Borelli did not like the analogy with transient water waves, because high atmospheric pressure often lasted for several days.

Even Erasmus Darwin, a century later, confessed that he could not imagine how one fifteenth of the atmosphere could apparently 'disappear' and cause a corresponding fall in atmospheric pressure. Nevertheless, Prince Leopold remained convinced, even without explanations, that pressure was an important factor in the weather process and suggested that the Torricelli tube should be given a special name.

René Descartes (1596–1650), French mathematician and philosopher, was probably the first person to apply a scale to a Torricelli tube and use it for measuring pressure. He wrote a letter to a colleague called Mersenne on 13 December 1647, saying

'So that we may also know if changes of weather and of location make any difference to it, I am sending you a paper scale two and a half feet long, in which the third and fourth inches above two feet are divided into lines; and I am keeping an exactly similar one here, so that we may see whether our observations agree.'

Robert Boyle (1627–91), English chemist, is accredited with being the first to call an instrument measuring atmospheric pressure a barometer (Greek *báros*: weight, *métron*: measure).

Barometer manufacture encountered many problems. Mercury is very heavy, and glass is susceptible to breakage. The mercury cistern

John Patrick's household assembly, incorporating one of Sir Samuel Morland's angled barometers, as displayed in the Science Museum, London. (Crown Copyright; courtesy Negretti & Zambra Ltd)

had to be closed against spillage but remain susceptible to atmospheric pressure, and leather proved the most suitable material. At first it was just tied down over the top of a wooden cistern. Later the whole cistern was made of leather, enclosed in a wooden case and cemented to the neck of the glass tube. A screw device at the bottom could reduce the volume of the wooden box and force mercury to the top of the tube so that it did not sway dangerously during travel. In 1738, Charles Orme (1688–1747) became the first instrument maker to boil mercury in order to expel all air and make a better vacuum within the baro-

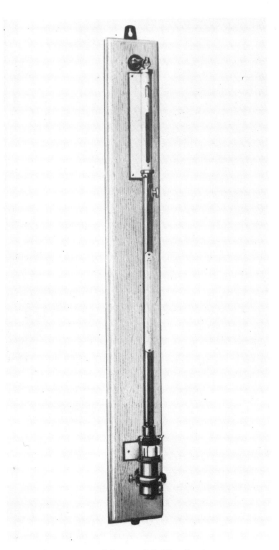

Aneroid barometer in ornate carved frame from the old Royal Yacht *Victoria and Albert*, *c* 1899. (Negretti & Zambra Ltd)

Fortin barometer. (Negretti & Zambra)

meter. Mercury miniscus (curvature) is very pronounced and there were initial difficulties about detecting small changes in mercury level.

The angled barometer was invented in 1670 by Sir Samuel Morland, master mechanic to Charles II, as an attempt to get greater accuracy of measurement. The tube was bent at 28 in (700 mm) above the cistern and a remaining possible 3 in (75 mm) vertical rise

in mercury was accommodated in an angled arm 18 in (450 mm) long. These sloping arms were even more liable to break than the vertical barometers, a problem which Charles Orme tried to overcome by mounting three angled barometers with *short* sloping arms at staggered heights on a board. Each barometer recorded within certain barometric pressure ranges only.

The wheel barometer was invented in 1665 by Robert Hooke, secretary to the Royal Society, London. A float attached to a silk cord rested on the mercury in the cistern and the cord passed round a pulley, being kept taut by a counterweight. A needle was attached to the pulley and revolved over a graduated dial as the mercury level changed.

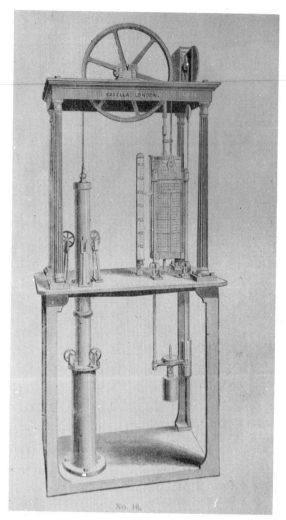

The King's Barograph, an early self recording mercury barometer from a 19th century catalogue of C F Casella & Co Ltd.

Barograph, showing aneroid pressure capsule and the trace made on the rotating drum chart.

Popular demand for barometers increased enormously during the 18th century and the design of barometer cases became a prestige trade on a par with clockmaking. One of the most popular designs was the banjo wheel barometer.

Amongst the many weather enthusiasts who owned a barometer was Daniel Defoe (1660–1731), English author, who was living in London at the end of 1703. He experienced the most disastrous storm ever suffered in southern England and wrote a detailed report about it afterwards (p. 88).

Not all barometer owners could afford to treat their instruments with the reverence they deserved as is apparent from Thomas Hutchins' letter from Manitoba in 1771:

'The surgeon being in great need of quicksilver, we were obliged to borrow some from the barometer, consequently no observations can be taken from the instrument for some time.'

Mercury was apparently used as a purgative!

The Fortin barometer takes its name from the man who, in 1810, first applied a device to the barometer for setting the zero of the instrument. A screw action adjusts an ivory point so that it just rests on the surface of the mercury in the cistern.

The aneroid barometer was invented in 1843 by Lucien Vidie (1805–66), French scientist, as a result of pressure gauge research by E. Bourdon of France. It has the advantage of being easily transportable and is quite accurate enough for most practical purposes. The aneroid consists of corrugated capsules evacuated of air, with the faces kept apart either by the rigidity of the metal or by a separate spring. Changes in atmospheric pressure cause the capsules to expand or contract and the movement is recorded by a needle over

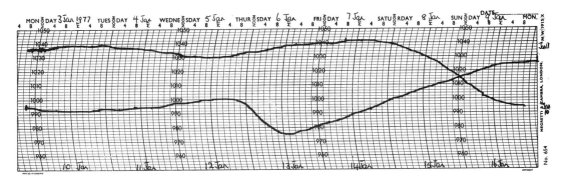

Barogram recorded in south west London for two consecutive weeks beginning 3 January 1977 and showing typical atmospheric pressure.

a dial. Aneroid movements frequently replaced the mercury columns inside old barometers when repairs were needed. Modern aneroid barometers are often housed in banjo shapes for old times' sake.

A barograph is an instrument which connects a barometer to an inked pen resting on a chart wound round a drum, which rotates by clockwork. This gives a continuous trace of pressure. Self-recording mercury barometers were made but were cumbersome, and modern barographs nearly always use aneroid mechanisms.

An altimeter measures height above ground by the difference in atmospheric pressure at that height and at ground level. Altimeters are used in aircraft and have to be re-set each day to accord with surface pressure.

Barometric correction to mean sea level is necessary before pressure readings at different places can be compared. Correction is achieved by adding an imaginary column of air equivalent to the height above sea level at which the barometer is read.

The millibar, abbreviated mb, is the modern international unit in which atmospheric pressure is measured, and it can be defined in terms of Pascals (Pa) in honour of Blaise Pascal.

$$1 \text{ mb} = 100 \text{ Pa} = 100 \text{ Newtons per square metre}$$

1000 mb = the pressure exerted by 29.53 in or 750.06 mm of mercury under standard conditions at $32°F$ ($0°C$).

A standard atmosphere at mean sea level is considered to exert a pressure of 1013.2 mb.

The character of the upper air, beyond the reach of ground based instruments, became of crucial interest to scientists discussing the phenomenon of atmospheric pressure. The only way to investigate was to send instruments aloft.

Dr Alexander Wilson of Glasgow made the first serious attempt to measure upper air temperature in 1749 when he flew a thermometer from a kite, but naturally this method was restricted to a fairly shallow layer of atmosphere.

The Montgolfier brothers, French inventors Joseph Michel (1740–1810) and Jacques Etienne (1745–99), invented a hot air balloon which suggested to the scientists that they might ascend into the atmosphere themselves and make observations. The French physicist **Jacques Alexandre Charles** went aloft in a hydrogen balloon on 15 October 1783, taking a barometer with him to measure altitude. The first ascent specifically to obtain

James Glaisher, FRS. (*Travels in the Air* by James Glaisher)

Glaisher and Coxwell get into trouble because of lack of oxygen during an ascent.
(*Travels in the Air* by James Glaisher)

meteorological data was made in 1784 by **Dr John Jeffries** and the aeronaut **Jean Pierre François Blanchard**, when they measured temperature, humidity and pressure up to an altitude of 9000 ft (2740 m).

Joseph Louis Gay Lussac (1778–1850), French chemist, and **Jean Biot** (1774–1862), French physicist, made an ascent to 23 000 ft (7000 m) in 1804 and found that the atmosphere became drier with altitude, but that the chemical composition was the same as that at the surface.

James Glaisher (1809–1903), English meteorologist, usually with Coxwell as pilot, made the most important series of ascents between 1862 and 1866 at the request of the British

Association. Glaisher made 28 flights, in the most famous of which he and Coxwell recorded 29 000 ft (8840 m) on 5 September 1862 before Glaisher became unconscious and Coxwell became so paralysed that he could only open the control valve with his teeth. It seems churlish to quibble at their *estimated* maximum height of 37 000 ft (11 300 m).

Research in the subsequent years showed that the stress on their bodies was due to diminished partial pressure of oxygen (see p. 100). The human body can adapt to this only slowly over time and people living at an altitude of 18 000 ft (4486 m) in the Andes, the highest inhabited area of the world, have a deep and rapid breathing system which results in barrel-like chests.

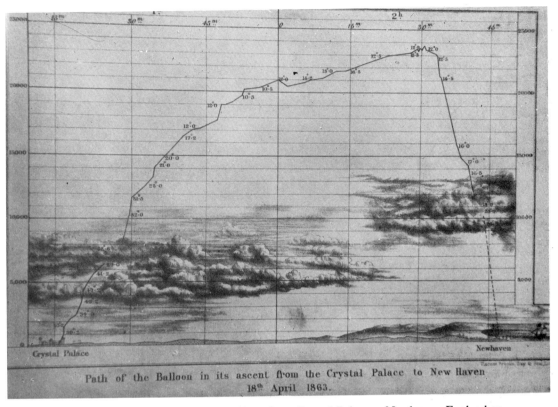

Path of the Balloon in its ascent from the Crystal Palace to New Haven 18ᵗʰ April 1863.

Recorded temperatures during an ascent by balloon from Crystal Palace to Newhaven, England on 18 April 1863. (*Travels in the Air* by James Glaisher)

Professor A. Berson and R. Suring made a higher ascent still on 30 June 1901 in an open gondola suspended beneath the balloon but carrying a supply of oxygen. They reached a height of 35 435 ft (10 800 m) and this remained a record for some years while Finvielle, Tissandier and Flammarion all continued gleaning material by manned ascents.

Professor Auguste Piccard, Swiss physicist, broke the record in 1931 when he travelled in an airtight capsule suspended beneath a balloon, with an inside air supply at ordinary pressure of 30·6 in (775 mm) mercury. He reached a height of 53 153 ft (16 201 m) where outside atmospheric pressure was only 3·1 in (78 mm) of mercury.

(The current record for the highest balloon flight is held by Commander Ross of the US Navy Reserve who reached 113 740 ft (34 668 m) over the gulf of Mexico on 4 May 1961.)

Meanwhile, these dramatic but cumbersome ascents aloft to obtain information did not blind people to the fact that invaluable information could be acquired on high mountains. These observations referred to more modest levels but could have greater continuity.

The highest weather observatory in Great Britain used to be on top of Ben Nevis at 4400 ft ASL (1341 m). It was built by public subscription, opened in December 1883 and was administered by the Scottish Meteorological Society. It provided regular hourly

The Observatory on top of Ben Nevis, Scotland, at the end of the 19th century. (Meteorological Office, Bracknell)

observations until September 1904. The highest weather station at present is at the top of the Cairngorms ski lift, at 3575 ft ASL (1089 m).

The observatory exposed to the most extreme weather is on Mount Washington, at 6262 ft (1090 m) in New Hampshire, USA. Regular observations started there on 13 November 1870 in an old engine house adapted for the purpose. It blew down in

Mt Washington Observatory, New Hampshire, USA, on a mid-winter day. (Courtesy Director, Mt Washington Observatory)

St Tropez, France, warming in the sunshine. (RG Holford)

Campbell-Stokes sunshine recorder and a normal incidence pyrheliometer. (P Defries; courtesy Kew Observatory, London)

Kew Observatory, London, built for George III in order to make observations of the transit of Venus on 3 June 1769. Meteorological observations started at the Observatory in 1773 and since 1842 the observatory has concentrated entirely upon meteorological and geophysical affairs. A Dines pressure tube anemometer can be seen on top of the dome and the grounds contain Stevenson screens, Marine screens housing electrical instruments, and experimental rains gauges. (P Defries; courtesy Kew Observatory)

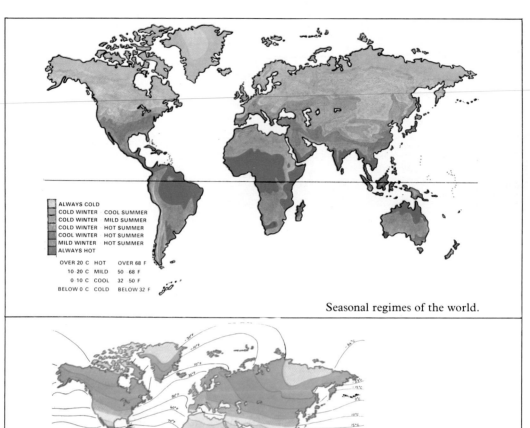

ALWAYS COLD
COLD WINTER · COOL SUMMER
COLD WINTER · MILD SUMMER
COLD WINTER · HOT SUMMER
COOL WINTER · HOT SUMMER
MILD WINTER · HOT SUMMER
ALWAYS HOT

OVER 20 C	HOT	OVER 68 F
10-20 C	MILD	50-68 F
0-10 C	COOL	32-50 F
BELOW 0 C	COLD	BELOW 32 F

Seasonal regimes of the world.

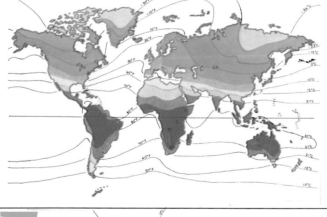

January isotherms.

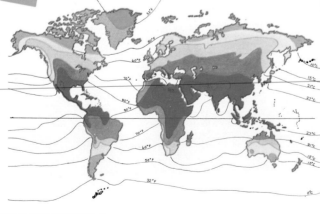

July isotherms.

Meteorograph in the Science Museum, London, designed by Teisserenc de Bort, used during the period 1898–1907. (P Defries)

January 1877 in gale winds of 186 mph (299 km/h), and no further observations were made there till better premises and more modern equipment were installed in October 1932. The observatory boasts the 'worst weather in the world' and certainly winter photographs are hardly suitable advertisement for a travel brochure!

Automatic instruments carried· by free travelling balloons, which burst on reaching a certain minimum pressure and descend to the ground by parachute, have generally superseded the need to go to such uncomfortable altitudes in order to observe.

A meteorograph registering pressure, humidity and temperature on charts attached to revolving drums, was first sent aloft attached to a balloon in France on 21 March 1893. The balloon weighed 40 lb (18 kg) and had a lifting capacity of 77 lb (35 kg). The instrument descended safely the next day after recording a highest flight point of 49 000 ft (15 000 m) where the temperature was −40°F (−40°C). This first balloon was made of gold-beater's skin (cattle gut, so named because of its use when beating gold into leaf thickness), but

later balloons were made of varnished paper. A famous balloon, named Cirrus after the highest type of cloud, was made of silk and

One of a variety of lightweight meteorographs designed by W H Dines, and used in the early part of the 20th century. (P Defries; courtesy Kew Observatory)

covered 700 miles (1126 km) from Berlin to Bosnia in July 1894. Mean velocity was 62 mph (100 km/h) and it reached a height of 54 000 ft (16 500 m) where temperature was −63°F (−52·8°C). It bettered its own record in April 1895 by reaching 72 000 ft (22 000 m) where the atmospheric pressure was 1·5 in (38·1 mm) of mercury.

William Henry Dines (1855–1927), English meteorologist, invented a lighter and more compact meteorograph which soon superseded the earlier instrument. It consisted of a large disc rotated by clockwork about its centre, on to which three styluses scratched traces recording temperature, pressue and humidity.

The International Meteorological Congress in Paris in 1896 made the first policy decision to send aloft several unmanned balloons, carrying meteorological instruments, from different places at the same time, so as to obtain a three dimensional picture of the atmospheric conditions over a large area. From then onwards balloon ascents were made regularly from certain observation stations all over the world. The Germans started upper air soundings from Samoa Island, Pacific Ocean in 1906. Berson made the first sounding from East Africa in 1908, and the Dutch from Batavia, Java in 1910. Griffith Taylor started upper air soundings from Australia after having accompanied the British Antarctic Expedition from 1910–13, where balloon ascents were made to 22 000 ft (6700 m).

Radio sonde upper air observations were first made in Britain in 1937. A small lightweight radio transmitter is incorporated in the meteorological instruments, and it sends back to the ground-receiving-station readings of pressure, temperature, humidity and wind data in the form of audio frequency notes which alter with varying conditions. This was a great stride forward, because the information could be received without delay, and was not dependent upon retrieval of the instrument.

Aircraft reports from commercial and meteorological flights supplement radio sonde upper air data in the impossible task of obtaining a complete picture of the atmosphere.

The first satellite to provide useful weather data was US Explorer VII, launched in October 1959. The first specialised weather satellite was Tiros I launched on 1 April 1960, and others followed at intervals. ESSA I was launched on 3 February 1966 and was the first to transmit cloud pictures.

Polar orbiting satellites now scan the Earth regularly each day, providing photographs of cloud cover in both the visible and infra-red wave lengths, as well as monitoring the temperature structure of the atmosphere with remote sensing techniques.

The troposphere is the lowest layer of our atmosphere, and the region in which weather occurs. Temperature within the troposphere generally decreases with height but usually at different rates at each level. Thus the temperature profile of the troposphere varies every day as the result of innumerable modifications, mixtures and confrontations of air masses which originate in one place and move on to another. James Glaisher discovered in his balloon flights that there are often quite abrupt discontinuities of temperature in the upper air, and on 12 January 1864 he noted that air was actually warmer between altitudes of 1300 ft and 6000 ft (400 m and 1800 m) than it was on the ground.

An inversion of temperature is an increase in temperature with height above ground, and is a frequent feature near the ground after a night of radiation cooling under a clear sky.

The tropopause is the boundary at the top of the troposphere where temperature ceases to fall with height. The tropopause varies from an average 10 miles (16 km) above ground near the equator to about 7 miles (11 km) near latitude 50° and reaches only about 6 miles (9 km) over the poles. The tropopause tends to be higher in summer than in winter.

Smoke (centre) trapped beneath a temperature inversion following a night frost in Dunedin, New Zealand, on 28 August 1965. Smoking chimneys on the ridge (upper right) are above the temperature inversion and therefore the smoke dissipates. (M J Hammersley)

Temperature at the tropopause is usually much lower over the equator than over the poles because air temperature can continue to decrease up to a higher tropopause than it can above the poles. A temperature at the tropopause of $-40°F$ to $-76°F$ ($-40°C$ to $-60°C$) is considered comparatively warm; $-76°F$ to $-112°F$ ($-60°C$ to $-80°C$) is comparatively cold.

During the nuclear tests in 1957 scientists took the opportunity of making meteorological soundings which recorded extremely low temperatures at the tropopause over the Christmas Isles and Maldive Isles. Mean monthly temperatures were between $-120°F$ and $-126°F$ ($-85°C$ and $-88°C$). Five successive readings on 19–22 February showed less than $-134°F$ ($-92°C$) with one extreme value of $-146°F$ ($-99°C$).

The stratosphere is the region above the tropopause which has very little change of temperature with height, sometimes even a slight increase of temperature with height. This region extends to an altitude of about 31

miles (50 km) above the Earth and its top boundary is called the stratopause. The stratosphere contains a relatively large amount of ozone; this absorbs much of the Sun's ultraviolet radiation which would be dangerous for plant and human life.

The mesosphere lies above the stratosphere between altitudes of 31 miles (50 km) and 50 miles (80 km). In this region temperature again decreases with height. The lowest temperature recorded so far was over Sweden between 27 July and 7 August 1963, when $-225°F$ ($-143°C$) was recorded at a height of 50 miles (80 km).

The thermosphere lies above the mesosphere, and there temperature increases with height all the way to our atmosphere's edge.

Atmospheric pressure is caused by the sum of all the layers of air which have a different temperature and density, and which exist above any particular place at any time. Pressure varies comparatively little throughout the world because of the regulating boundary of the tropopause. Surface air, which continually warms and rises over equatorial areas, has to cool over a greater height into the atmosphere than does air which is already cold and dense near the ground at the poles. The average weight of atmosphere which each area supports is not too dissimilar.

However, the sources of hot and cold surface air are not equally distributed between equator and poles but are an extremely complicated arrangement of adjacent land and sea areas. The balance of heat around the world is therefore achieved by means of an alternating sequence of relatively high and low pressure belts, which roughly follow parallels of latitude.

The equatorial low pressure belt lies 15–20° north and south of the equator and is partly determined by the constant high temperatures near the surface. Average surface pressure is about 1012 mb and the range above or below that level is small, particularly over islands well distant from large land masses.

Seasonal high pressure zones develop over large land masses in winter in high latitudes because of rapidly cooling air. The most pronounced winter high pressure occurs over central Asia, where average January pressure is between 1026 and 1036 mb.

Seasonal low pressure zones develop over large land masses in summer because of thermal heating. Since these areas are the same which have high pressure in winter, they also experience the greatest seasonal range in pressure. Average pressure over central Asia in July is about 960 mb.

Small areas of permanent high pressure exist over both poles where there is always a layer of very cold dense air.

Subtropical high pressure belts are centred around latitudes 30° north and south of the equator and **subpolar belts of low pressure** are centred around the arctic and antarctic circles. These belts fluctuate between the

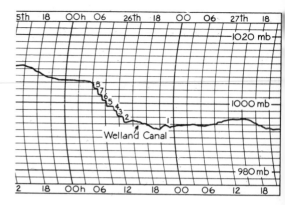

Barogram from a ship traversing the locks of the Welland Canal, during which a ship ascends 326 ft (99·4 m) as it goes from Lake Ontario to Lake Erie, North America. (Bristol City Lines)

permanent and seasonal pressure zones and experience quite a large range of normal pressures, between 950 mb and 1050 mb. Occasional vigorous cells of pressure, with much lower values than normal, travel the middle latitudes in a busy effort to balance the heat budget of the world.

The highest mean sea level pressure ever recorded was at Agata, north central Siberia, on 31 December 1968 when air temperature was −50°F (−46°C). The pressure was above 1070 mb for five days and culminated in 1083·8 mb. Five other stations in the region had similarly high pressure, discounting any probability of error.
Other exceptionally high pressures:

24 Jan 1897, Medicine Hat, Canada	1067·3 mb
9 Jan 1962, Helena, USA	1063·3 mb

Britain's highest pressure:

31 Jan 1902, Aberdeen	1054·7 mb

The lowest mean sea level pressure ever recorded was measured by US Air Force dropsonde in the eye of typhoon *June*, on 19 November 1975. This was 1 mb lower than the previous lowest recorded of 877 mb in the eye of hurricane *Ida* 600 miles (966 km) north west of Guam, Pacific Ocean on 24 September 1958.

Lowest recorded in Great Britain was 925·5 mb on 26 January 1884 at Ochtertyre, Perthshire.

The lowest actual atmospheric pressure at mean sea level may never be known, because it occurs in the centre of tornadoes. The chances of a barometer being in the right place at the right time are small, and the chances of the instrument surviving the tornado are even smaller.

Infra red picture of the world and its cloud systems on 21 April 1977. This was photographed by the geostationary satellite GOES-1, positioned above the equator at 75°W longitude and at an altitude of 22 300 miles (35 800 km). Pictures taken by GOES-1 are made by an 18-inch telescope scanning the Earth from west to east with each rotation (100 rpm) and stepping from north to south in about 18·4 minutes. (National Oceanic and Atmosphere Administration, Florida)

CHAPTER 5

THE NATURE OF WIND

Zephyrus, god of the west wind
Circulation of atmosphere

The Tower of the Winds, Athens, Greece, as shown on the emblem of the Royal Meteorological Society of Great Britain.

Surface wind blows below a height of 30 ft (10 m) above the ground, and is therefore the wind which affects all the normal activities of life. This wind must be the most keenly observed weather element of all time. Hunters have always watched it meticulously in order to avoid betraying themselves by scent when upwind of their quarry.

Personification of wind, ie naming winds after deities, was the natural outcome of lack of understanding about its cause. Aristotle used the allegory of human breath and called wind 'exhalation'. In Athens Andronicus of Cyrrhus (c 100 BC) Greek astronomer, built an octagonal marble tower, called the Tower of the Winds or Horologium. Each face was decorated with a frieze of figures, carved into the marble, to represent the eight principal winds; and each of those figures portrayed a deity appropriately dressed and equipped for the weather with which it was associated.

Boreas (from the north) and Notos (from the south) were primary and opposite winds which could not blow together. Winds from other directions, Zephyros from the west or Apeliotes from the east, were able to act in concert with the primary winds. The wind blowing from north east was called Kaikias, the south easterly wind was Euros, the south

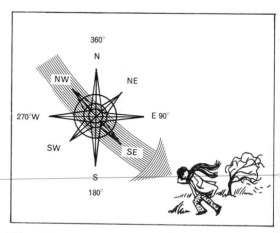

Wind is defined according to the compass point from which it is blowing, and in this case is a NW wind.

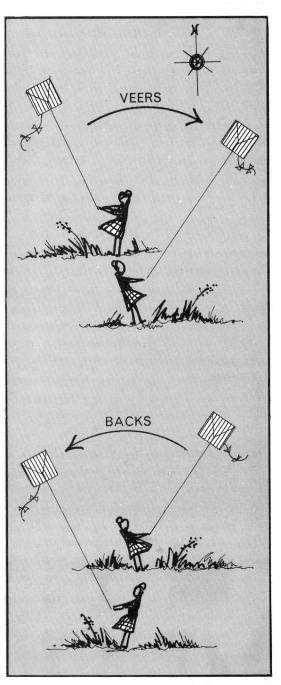

VEERS

BACKS

Wind *veers* when it changes in a clockwise sense and *backs* when it changes in an anticlockwise sense.

westerly was Lips and the north westerly was Skiros.

Below these figures, facing the Sun, were sundials indicating the time. Inside the building was a hydraulic clock which was used when the sky was overcast.

A statue of the sea god Triton, at the top of the horologium, turned with the wind and thus indicated its direction. This was the first use of weather vanes.

The magnetic compass was known to the Chinese possibly many centuries BC; but it was not introduced to Europe till the 12th century AD. Thereafter, wind came to be described either by the compass point, or by the number of degrees from north, *from* which the wind blows *towards* the observer. For instance a NW wind or a 315° wind blows from the north west towards the observer.

Wind *veers* if it changes direction in a clockwise sense, and **backs** if it changes in an anticlockwise sense.

A wind vane consists of a fin on the end of a horizontal arm which freely pivots on a vertical spindle in the wind. Wind pressure on the fin forces it away from the compass point from which the wind is blowing; the usual arrow on the other end of the horizontal arm therefore points to the direction from which the wind is blowing. Wind vanes have always been popular subjects for the skills of artists and craftsmen and evolved as 'house flags' bearing coats of arms or trade symbols.

The weather cock is a wind vane, adopted by the Christian church in the middle of the 9th century. The cock turns its head into the wind, and the choice of such a symbol was intended as a perpetual reminder of the cock which crowed at Peter's denial of Christ.

A remote reading wind vane permits wind direction to be read indoors; one of the first persons to make such an instrument for his own use was Erasmus Darwin (1731–1802). He simply pushed an extended spindle through the ceiling of his study, thus gaining continual surveillance of the wind. It enabled him to note that wind direction quite often changes suddenly, quite apart from the small fluctuations of direction which occur all the time. Modern wind vanes have changed little in principle but have improved in precision of construction. Remote vanes record electrically on to dial faces.

Wind names still persist all over the world, despite the more prosaic notation by compass point. Amongst well known winds are:–

Berg wind – (Afrikaans, meaning mountain) hot and dry wind coming from the interior of South Africa and blowing down the mountains and off-shore.

Brickfielder – very hot NE wind in south east Australia, blowing during the summer months and carrying dust and sand.

Buran – (Russian *Burán*, Turkish *Borán*) strong NE wind in Russia and central Asia. Most frequent in winter when it often carries snow and may then also be known as 'purga'.

Chinook – warm dry and often turbulent W wind that blows on eastern side of Rocky Mountains, North America.

Doldrums – region of calm or baffling wind near the equator where opposing trade winds converge.

Föhn – warm dry wind descending in the lee of the European Alps, principally in Switzerland. The wind acquired the name from the Latin *Favonius*, west wind, because the early Romans who campaigned in the region thought that such a warm wind must come from the west. However, the warmth of the Föhn wind is not due to origin of air but to compression when descending the mountain slopes (p. 119) and thus may blow from any direction. The term is now used generically to describe other winds which warm in the same manner.

Gregale (Latin *Graerus*: Greek) – strong NE wind blowing in the south Mediterranean mainly in the cooler months of the year.

Haboob (Arabic *habub*: blowing furiously) – any wind of a strength to raise sand into a sand storm, particularly in Sudan.

Harmattan – a dry and relatively cool NE or E wind which blows in north west Africa, average southern limit 5° N latitude in January and 18° N latitude in July. It is often dust laden and so dry as to wither vegetation and cause human skin to peel off, but it nevertheless gives welcome relief from the usual humid heat of the tropics.

Helm – strong and often violent cold NE wind blowing down western slopes of Cross Fell range, Cumbria, mainly in late winter and spring. Very gusty.

Karaburan (Turkish *kara*: black, *curan*: whirlwind) – hot dusty NE wind in central Asia.

Khamsin – oppressive hot, dry S wind over Egypt, most frequent between April and June, often laden with sand from the desert.

Levanter (from Levant: land at eastern end of Mediterranean) – moist E wind in region of Straits of Gibraltar, often strong and most frequent June–October.

Mistral (Latin *Magistral*: master wind) – dry cold NW or N wind blowing off shore along the Mediterranean coast of France and Spain. Particularly violent on the coast of Languedoc and Provence when it funnels down the Rhône Valley.

Calm conditions indicated by unruffled water.

Beaufort Force 2 – small wavelets with glassy crests which do not break. (*Yachting Monthly*)

Monsoon (Arabic *mausim:* time, season) – any markedly seasonal wind, particularly in east and south east Asia.

Pampero (Spanish *pampa:* great plain, prairie) – piercing cold SW wind which blows from the Andes across the S American pampas in Argentina and across Uruguay to the Atlantic.

Purga – strong NE winter wind in Russia and central Asia, often raising snow from the ground to cause blizzards.

Roaring Forties – region between latitudes 40° and 50° S where strong W winds, known as Brave West Winds, blow steadily. So named by sailors who first entered these latitudes.

Scirocco or *Sirocco* (Arabic *suruk:* rising of the sun) – an oppressive hot dry S wind on north coast of Africa blowing from Sahara. By the time this wind crosses the Mediterranean to Europe it has become slightly cooler but very moist. It produces languor and mental debility.

Seistan – strong N wind in summer in the Seistan region of eastern Iran and Afghanistan. It can attain velocities of over 100 miles (160 km) per hour and carries dust and sand.

Shamal – hot dry and dusty NW wind persistent in summer in Iraq and Persian Gulf area.

Southerly Buster – sudden cold S wind in south eastern Australia, usually strong and succeeding wind from some northerly point. The temperature can fall 36°F (20°C) or more in a very short time with the arrival of a Southerly Buster.

Trades – steady winds blowing between latitudes 10° and 30°, from the NE in the northern hemisphere, from the SE in the southern hemisphere. Of importance to sailing ships dependent upon wind power, hence called 'winds that blow trade' by navigators in the 18th century. Trade winds change in direction according to the seasonal shift in the high pressure belts.

Tramontana (Latin *trans:* across; *montem:* mountain; Ital. *tramontano:* between the mountains) – cool dry N wind blowing across the Spanish Mediterranean coast.

Wind speed cannot be evaluated by timing over a measured distance because wind is invisible. A good approximation can be made by timing light articles, such as balloons, blowing in the wind, or by timing the shadows of clouds over water. For practical purposes, the general public has to rely on seeing the effect wind has upon things which are visible.

The Beaufort Scale was originated by Commander (later Rear-Admiral Sir) Francis Beaufort, KCB, FRS (1774–1857), a contemporary of Lord Nelson. In 1805 he specified a scale of thirteen degrees of wind strength, as well as calm, which related to the amount of canvas which a sailing vessel could carry in those wind conditions. The next year he modified the scale by labelling both calm and light air Force 1 and combining the two upper wind strengths as Force 12 'a hurricane which no canvas can withstand'

The idea was good but the scale was dependent upon the subjective decisions of captains of different type vessels. Hence the scale was later adapted to relate to the visible effect of wind on sea, which was the same for every vessel afloat. The scale remains important for use at sea because a ship's own speed through

Beaufort Force 6 – large waves with white foam crests. (D C Clarke)

the water makes it difficult to isolate the speed of the wind alone.

Distance and speed at sea is measured differently from the way it is measured on land because the only visible points of reference are the planets and the time recorded by chronometer.

A nautical mile is the length of a minute of latitude and varies from 6046 ft (1843 m) on the equator to 6092 ft (1857 m) in latitude 60°. The international nautical mile is defined as 1852 metres. 1 knot = 1 nautical mile per hour, and obtained its name from the old method of measuring a ship's speed through the water. A float shaped to offer resistance to towage and attached to a long line knotted at equal intervals, was thrown into the water.

The number of knots passing freely through the hand over a period of time as the line spun out indicated ship speed.

An anemometer (Greek *anemos:* wind) is anything which measures wind speed. Washing blowing on a line is like a rudimentary anemometer, because the faster the wind, the stronger the force which it exerts and the more nearly is the tethered washing blown to the horizontal.

A wind sock is the simplest practical anemometer, and consists of a tube of cloth fixed to a metal ring which pivots on the top of a pole. It streams out at an angle from the pole according to wind strength, giving practised observers a very good visual indication of wind *speed.* The wind sock goes one stage further

THE BEAUFORT SCALE FOR USE AT SEA

Beaufort Force	Description	Sea state	Knots
0	Calm	Sea like a mirror	Less than 1
1	Light air	Ripples with appearance of scales, no foam crests	1–3
2	Light breeze	Wavelets, small but pronounced. Crests with glassy appearance, but do not break	4–6
3	Gentle breeze	Large wavelets, crests begin to break. Glassy looking foam, occasional white horses	7–10
4	Moderate breeze	Small waves becoming longer, frequent white horses	11–16
5	Fresh breeze	Moderate waves of pronounced long form. Many white horses, some spray	17–21
6	Strong breeze	Some large waves, extensive white foam crests, some spray	22–27
7	Near gale	Sea heaped up, white foam from breaking waves blowing in streaks with the wind	28–33
8	Gale	Moderately high and long waves. Crests break into spin drift, blowing foam in well marked streaks	34–40
9	Strong gale	High waves, dense foam streaks in wind, wave crests topple, tumble and roll over. Spray reduces visibility	41–47
10	Storm	Very high waves with long overhanging crests. Dense blowing foam, sea surface appears white. Heavy tumbling of sea, shock-like. Poor visibility	48–55
11	Violent storm	Exceptionally high waves, sometimes concealing small and medium sized ships. Sea completely covered with long white patches of foam. Edges of wave crests blown into froth. Poor visibility	56–63
12	Hurricane	Air filled with foam and spray, sea white with driving spray. Visibility bad	≥64

THE BEAUFORT SCALE, ADAPTED FOR USE ON LAND
and with the addition of speeds measured by modern instruments

Beaufort Force	Description	Specification on land	Speed mph	Speed km/h
0	Calm	Smoke rises vertically	Less than 1	
1	Light air	Direction of wind shown by smoke drift but not by wind vanes	1–3	1–5
2	Light breeze	Wind felt on face, leaves rustle, ordinary wind vane moved by wind	4–7	6–11
3	Gentle breeze	Leaves and small twigs in constant motion, wind extends light flag	8–12	12–19
4	Moderate breeze	Wind raises dust and loose paper, small branches move	13–18	20–29
5	Fresh breeze	Small trees in leaf start to sway, crested wavelets on inland waters	19–24	30–39
6	Strong breeze	Large branches in motion, whistling in telegraph wires, umbrellas used with difficulty	25–31	40–50
7	Near gale	Whole trees in motion, inconvenient to walk against wind	32–38	51–61
8	Gale	Twigs break from trees, difficult to walk	39–46	62–74
9	Strong gale	Slight structural damage occurs, chimney pots and slates removed	47–54	75–87
10	Storm	Trees uprooted, considerable structural damage occurs	55–63	88–101
11	Violent storm	Widespread damage	64–73	102–117
12	Hurricane	Widespread damage	≥74	≥119

A remote recording cup anemometer.
(C F Casella & Co Ltd)

The cup anemometer was invented by John Robinson in 1846, and is still the most widely used instrument for measuring wind speed. Three or four hemispherical cups pivot on a vertical spindle and rotate according to the force of the wind acting upon them. Each rotation makes an electrical contact and records the number of turns by counter or by pointer on a dial face which bears a scale.

The anemograph is an instrument which records the movement of an anemometer on a rotating chart. The instrument is often combined with a wind vane so as to record changes in wind direction on a different section of the

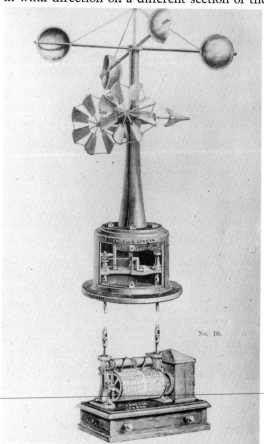

Anemograph invented by Robert Beckley, as shown in a 19th century catalogue of C F Casella & Co Ltd.

than washing-on-the-line, because it pivots to face into the wind and therefore indicates wind speed *and* direction, an invaluable aid to pilots of aircraft approaching a landing field.

A pressure plate anemometer was among the many ideas sketched in the note books of Leonardo da Vinci (1452–1519), the Italian painter, engineer and inventive genius, and was probably the first design for an instrument to measure the force of the wind. He visualised a metal plate, fixed at the top and free to swing alongside a curved graduated scale. The stronger the wind, the higher it forced the plate towards the horizontal. The idea was sound and was developed in later years as a standard anemometer.

It is interesting to note that at a wind speed of 100 mph (160 km/h) a person can lean forward on the wind with straight legs and touch the ground with his hand without falling. This makes him an upside-down-pressure plate anemometer, tethered to the ground!

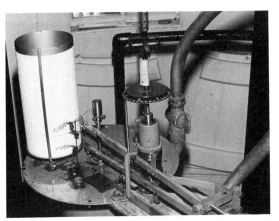

The internal arrangements of a Dine's pressure
tube anemometer, still working at Kew
Observatory, London. (P Defries)

chart. The anemogram is the resulting chart
which shows fluctuations in wind speed and
direction.

The exposure of anemometers was the
subject of research by W. H. Dines at the end
of the 19th century. He mounted several
anemometers on poles at the same level over
his house and found they did not read similarly
because of turbulence (p. 64). He then raised
them progressively higher till they all recorded
the same readings, which was about 15 ft
(4·5 m) above the roof top. Standard exposure
for an anemometer is 33 ft (10 m) on the top
of a pole well away from any building, or as
high as is practicable above the roof where
readings are required.

A wind rose is a diagram showing frequency
of wind at various speeds and from every
direction at a particular place over an extended
period of time.

Wind generally becomes stronger with height
above the surface, increasing rapidly in the
first 6 ft (2 m) and then at a more steady
slower rate. An experienced observer can get
some idea of speed and direction of winds at
different altitudes by watching the movement
of clouds. Very low cloud often appears to be
moving faster than it is, simply because it is
relatively near to the eye.

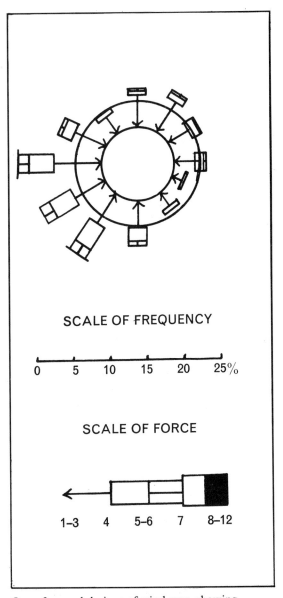

SCALE OF FREQUENCY

0   5   10   15   20   25%

SCALE OF FORCE

1–3   4   5–6   7   8–12

One of several designs of wind rose, showing
annual frequency of wind direction and force at
London Airport between 1949 and 1958. The
length of each symbol is proportional to wind
frequency of occurrence and the radius of the outer
circle is proportional to the frequency of calms,
which is also written within the circle.
(*Meteorological Glossary*; courtesy Director
Meteorological Office, Bracknell)

Tree in Guernsey, Channel Isles, shaped permanently by exposure to off-sea winds.

A nephoscope (Greek *nephos:* cloud) is a simple device for gauging high level wind speed and direction by 'tracking' a plume of ice crystal cloud of estimated height. A horizontal bar, with spikes at regular intervals (giving it the descriptive name 'comb' nephoscope) is turned so that the selected cloud appears to be travelling along the direction of the bar, giving the direction of wind at that level. Speed is estimated by timing the cloud

HIGHEST RECORDED GUSTS					
	Altitude		Gust Speed		
In the world	ft	m	mph	km/h	
Mt Washington, USA	6288	1916	231	371	12 Apr 1934
			220	354	frequently
In Great Britain					
Cairngorms, Scotland	3525	1074	144	232	6 Mar 1967
Kirkwall, Orkney			136	219	7 Feb 1969
HIGHEST MEAN HOURLY SPEEDS IN GREAT BRITAIN					
Great Dun Fell, Cumbria, England	2813	857	99	159	15 Jan 1968
Lowther Hill, Scotland	2415	736	99	159	20 Jan 1963
St Ann's Head, Dyfed, Wales			80	129	23 Nov 1938
HIGHEST MEAN 24 HOURS WIND SPEED					
Mt Washington, USA	6288	1916	129	208	11–12 Apr 1934

from one prong to another and referring to tables.

A pilot balloon is one which is filled with hydrogen to a predetermined pressure so that its vertical rate of ascent when released is known. The balloon can be tracked by a theodolite, and wind speed and direction can be calculated from the elevation and azimuth readings obtained. Balloon colour is chosen for optimum contrast against the background of grey or white cloud or blue sky into which the balloon is rising.

A modern refinement is to attach a radar reflector to the pilot balloon so that echo signals may be received at a station on the ground. This eliminates the need for visual theodolite sightings.

Wind statistics must be assessed in the context of altitude and time. Wind speed is normally greater at high altitudes than at low, and greater in gusts than averaged over a period of time. Even modest sounding wind speeds over a long averaging period may be extraordinary in the context of a low altitude station. Highest recorded wind speeds make no pretence of being the highest actual wind speeds, which may never be measured. All figures given are for surface wind unless otherwise stated.

The windiest place in Great Britain is the isle of Tiree, off the west coast of Scotland which has a mean annual wind speed of 17 mph (27 km/h).

The windiest place in the world is the coast of Eastern Adelie Land and West King George Land, on the edge of Antarctica. A French expedition maintained a station at Port Martin from February 1950 to January 1952, and made valuable discoveries about the inhospitable wind. It blows nearly always from ESE or SSE, which is from the ice cap towards the coast line, and it appears to be an exaggerated katabatic wind (p. 64). Intensely cold air over the high interior races downwards towards the coast over a 1-in-100 slope, slackening abruptly on reaching the warmer

sea. The wind is fairly steady while it blows but often starts and stops abruptly as if the supply of air suddenly had run out and had to accumulate again for its downhill run.

	mph	km/h
In 1951 there were 122 days with mean wind above	73	117
and 22 days only with mean wind below	31	50
the highest 24 hours mean wind, Mar 21–22 was	108	174
the highest monthly mean wind, March was	65	105
the annual mean wind was	40	64

Air is a fluid which behaves very much like visible liquids. A gradual appreciation of this fact enabled 17th century scientists to explain small scale winds in terms which were more realistic than a cherub puffing air in the corner of a map.

Wind is air in motion, obeying normal buoyancy rules. Dense cold air moves to replace warm lighter air which rises. The smallest winds are draughts through cracks in doors and windows, caused when cold outside air forces through to replace warmer air indoors. Outdoors, tiny movements of air occur because of differential heating of adjacent surfaces. A tarmac surface heats quickly in sunshine, air above it rises and colder air over adjacent grass moves in as replacement.

A thermal is a vertical wind created when air warms on contact with a heating surface, rises, and is replaced by colder air from above or alongside. A thermal may also develop when air travels over a sea surface which gets progressively warmer with latitude.

An anabatic wind is an up-slope wind created when air nearest the slope is heated quicker by sunshine than air at the same horizontal level but further from the ground. The warmed air rises and is replaced by cooler air from alongside. The anabatic wind is most pronounced in early morning, before sunshine has had time to stir up the air more generally.

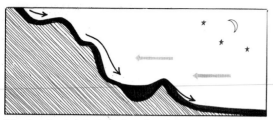

The katabatic wind during the night.

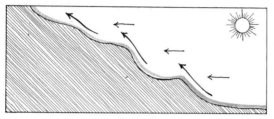

The anabatic wind during day-time.

A katabatic wind is a down-slope wind created on otherwise calm nights when air nearest the slope cools, becomes heavier and sinks as far as the slope permits. Sinking air is replaced by air from the same horizontal level alongside, which then cools in turn and sinks. Katabatic winds are most pronounced on cloudless nights when radiation cooling is greatest, and when there is no pressure gradient wind to stir up the air close to the ground.

Wind deviates in a horizontal plane in order to get round solid obstacles such as houses, hills, mountains, and it deviates in a vertical plane to surmount obstacles such as roofs or mountain tops.

Wind eddies backward into the relatively 'empty' space behind solid obstacles, which is called the leeward side. Therefore the immediate lee of a building or cliff does not always give shelter from the wind.

Wind is said to funnel when it has to squeeze through constrictions (between houses, cliffs or mountains) and increases in speed to do so. It is analogous to the increase in speed of water when forced through a constricting nozzle of a hose pipe.

A wave motion can be induced in an air stream forced over hills and mountains at high speed, and air may undulate in a vertical plane for a considerable distance on the leeward side, with pronounced crests and troughs similar to water waves. This is thought to contribute to the high speed of winds blowing down the leeward side of mountains in certain instances.

Turbulence is the irregularity of wind speed and direction caused by obstructions, the drag of surface friction or the superimposition of vertical winds on horizontal winds. There is no precise height at which the roughness of any terrain ceases to be effective on the movement of air, but for meteorological purposes it is considered to be 2000 ft (600 m) above the ground. Turbulence at higher levels often occurs when horizontal winds of different speeds or direction blow in adjacent layers of the atmosphere, and this is known as clear air turbulence (see also p. 73).

A gust is a momentary increase above the average wind speed and a **lull** is a momentary decrease below the average wind speed.

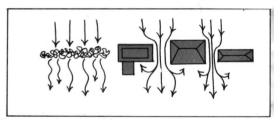

Wind filters through semipermeable obstructions, such as hedges, and its impact is lessened. Wind funnels through constrictions between solid obstructions and consequently increases in speed.

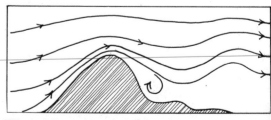

Wind eddies in the lee of solid obstructions and may undulate for some distance beyond.

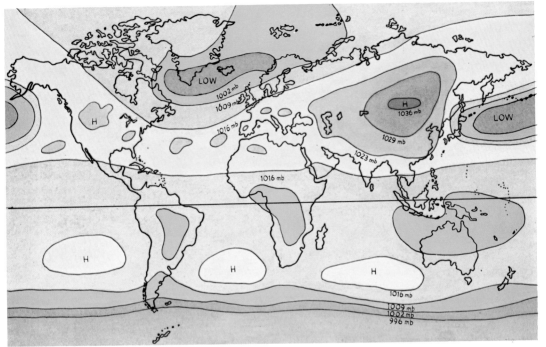

Average January isobars.

Average July isobars.

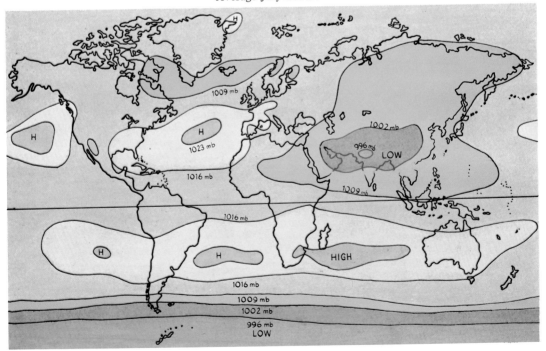

A dust storm approaching Phoenix, Arizona, USA, from the south east shortly after 1800 hours on 23 July 1972. (S B Idso)

Never believe a wind indicator which is too close to an obstruction! In this instance the wind was blowing directly on to the building from which the photograph was taken. Wind deviated in both directions to move around the obstacle in its way. (K F Style)

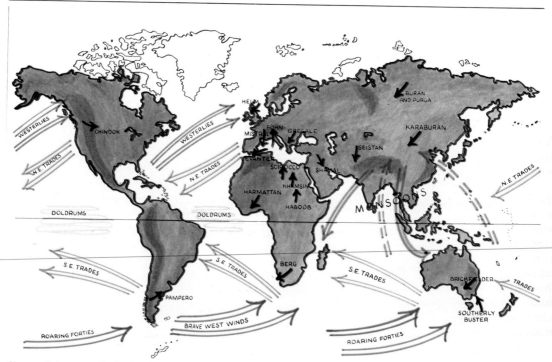

Some of the named winds of the world.

The sea breeze on a sunny day.

The land breeze on a clear night.

Wind exerts a pressure which is proportional to the square of the wind speed. A gust to *double* the average wind speed implies a *four-fold* increase in pressure.

The sea breeze blows on a sunny summer day from a cool sea surface on to land, where the air is warming and rising. By mid-afternoon a sea breeze can spread as much as 15–30 miles (24–48 km) inland.

The land breeze blows at night when clear skies cause rapid cooling over land so that the air over the sea is comparatively warmer. Cold air from the land flows out over the sea where the warmer air is displaced.

A monsoon wind changes direction markedly according to season, basically because of temperature differentials between adjacent large land and sea areas. Land is warmer than the sea in summer and therefore winds flow on-shore; but land is cooler than the sea in winter and wind blows off-shore. As early as 1686 Edmund Halley (1656–1742), English astronomer, likened monsoon winds to giant sea and land breezes and the comparison is apt, though not wholly correct. Monsoon conditions develop most dramatically in India, which experiences a change to the south west monsoon at the end of May, and a change

again to the north east monsoon at the end of October.

In the southern hemisphere, the summer monsoon winds come from the north near Mauritius and Madagascar, but on the north coast of Australia they blow from the north west. The Arabs had an extensive knowledge of monsoon changes at a very early date. A book, published in 1554 by Sidi Ali about navigation in the Indian Ocean, gave the commencing date of each monsoon at 50 different places.

Large scale winds circulating round the world were not so easily explained by early scientists in terms of cold air moving in to replace warm air. It was quite obvious that wind did not perpetually blow from the poles, where the air was cold at the surface, towards the equator where it was warm. For want of a *theory*, practical people began assembling observed *facts* in the hope that the correct explanations would then become apparent. It was no accident that many sailors became practical observers, because their lives depended upon the weather. Their keenest concern was often the vicious circular storms which, as the new sea routes of the world developed, they encountered in tropical latitudes.

Hurricane was a name probably derived from an Indian word used in the Caribbean meaning 'big wind'. It entered the Spanish vocabulary as 'Huracan' when the 15th century explorers first encountered these winds which were so much stronger than winds they had experienced in Europe. By meteorological definition the term hurricane is now reserved for winds of Force 12 Beaufort scale, ie more than 64 knots, 74 mph or 119 km/h.

Typhoon (Chinese *tai fung* – meaning 'wind which strikes'), was the name given to similar violent storms in the China seas. Some people think the word may have derived from the Greek mythological monster, Typhon or Typhoeus (meaning whirlwind) – the father of storm winds. The name persists today in the Pacific Ocean, and hurricane and typhoon are merely different names for the same phenomenon.

William Dampier (1652–1715), English sailor and buccaneer, published a most informative book about winds in 1697 called *A voyage around the world*. He accurately described a typhoon, and the data from his ocean journeys was an authoritative source of information for many years.

Edmund Halley (1656–1742), English astronomer, was the first to sense that wind was part of a general circulation of air all round the world caused by ascents of warm air in some places and descents of cold air elsewhere. In 1698 he published an account of trade winds and monsoons, with illustrative map, likening the monsoon to a giant sea breeze.

George Hadley (1685–1768), English scientist and younger brother of John Hadley who invented the sextant, was the first to mention that the rotation of the Earth might be a pertinent factor governing the movement of air, when he read a paper to the Royal Society in 1735. The idea did not make much impact until John Dalton took it up again 60 years later.

William Redfield (1789–1857), American saddler and transport manager, became interested in hurricanes after the September gale of 1821 in western Massachusetts. He wrote a treatise on West Indian hurricanes, published in 1833, in which he identified the hurricane paths as going first towards the west and then recurving towards the north or east.

Matthew Maury (1806–73) was an oceanographer and American naval officer, who was invalided out of the service in 1839. Thereafter he devoted nine years to the collection of wind and weather observations at sea, by distributing log books to ships' captains.

Heinrich Dove (1803–79), German scientist, described the essential difference between tropical storms of the two hemispheres of the world. Wind rotates in an anticlockwise manner (when imagined looking down on them) in the northern hemisphere, and in a clockwise direction in the southern hemisphere.

Colonel William Reid (1791–1858), Scottish soldier and later colonial governor, used the knowledge of circular motion of air to propound sailing rules for avoiding the worst perils of storms at sea. In 1838, he published *An attempt to develop the law of storms by means of facts*, and when he became governor of Barbados in 1847 he instituted the first system of hurricane warning signals at Carlisle Bay.

The Law of Storms was based on the assumption that a sailing vessel could not travel *against* wind of hurricane strength, but only *with* it. The *dangerous* semicircle of such a storm was that in which the circulating wind carried the ship along in the same general direction as that of the whole storm, thus prolonging the agony of being within the storm. The most hazardous quadrant of the dangerous semicircle was the forward quadrant, because then a ship running before the wind

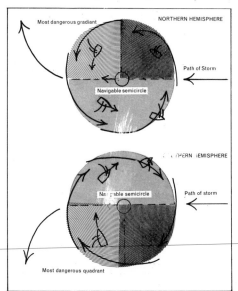

The Law of Storms, based on the assumption that a sailing vessel could not travel *against* hurricane winds but only *with* them.

was actually approaching the centre of the storm.

The *navigable* semicircle was that in which the wind was blowing in a general direction contrary to that of the storm centre, and the ship was therefore increasing the distance between itself and the storm.

The clockwise or anticlockwise manner in which wind in the ship's vicinity altered as the storm approached helped ascertain in which semicircle the ship lay relative to the storm.

Cyclone (Greek *kuklos*: cycle or circle) was a name first given to intense circular storms by Captain H. Piddington in 1848, who also recognised that the winds converged in towards the centre of the storms. The term cyclone is now usually confined to intense circular storms in tropical latitudes which do **not** attain the status of full hurricane. Circular storms in higher latitudes are called depressions.

Robert Fitzroy (1805–65) joined the navy as a boy, and spent a great deal of his life at sea. He was captain of the *Beagle* when it made its famous voyage round the world with Charles Darwin as naturalist. Of necessity, Fitzroy was a keen observer of the weather and of the barometer. He noted that falling or rising pressure, called 'tendency', was usually followed by certain types of weather, and he formulated forecasting 'Remarks' which became popular and were often nscribed on barometers, for example:

'A fall of half a tenth of an inch or more in half an hour is a sure sign of storm.'
'A fall when the thermometer is low indicates snow or rain.'
'A fall with a rising thermometer indicates wind and rain from the southward.'
'Steady rise shows that fine weather may be expected and in winter, frost.'

These were reasonably sound rules connecting pressure with weather, but did not recognise the relation between pressure and wind in general, as distinct from hurricane winds.

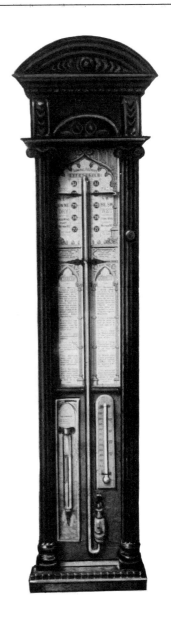

Fitzroy Barometer, inscribed with the Admiral's Remarks. (Courtesy D Allen)

Weather observers were being organised meanwhile on land. The Lunar Society of Birmingham, The Royal Society of London, The Société Royale de Médicine in France, amongst others, encouraged people to keep weather diaries and to make observations under standard conditions. The Societas Meteorologica Palatine in Mannheim, Germany, was in correspondence with 50 observers in 1778 and with 70 observers by 1784, including some in Baghdad, New York, Stockholm and St Petersburg. The Société de Médecine, France, had their work suppressed by revolutionary decree in 1793, but the observations collected before then were of a standard high enough to be of use to research workers today.

The electric telegraph, developed after 1836 by Samuel Morse (1791–1872), American artist and inventor, solved the critical problem of time lag in collecting weather observations.

James Pollard Espy (1785–1860), American meteorologist, was the first to organise for the US War Department a system of daily synchronous weather observations, transmitted by telegraph. He plotted observations on maps and recognised that wind blows inwards, towards the centre of cyclones.

Professor Joseph Henry (1797–1878), American physicist, had himself invented an earlier telegraphic device, and in 1849 inaugurated a service by which weather information was collected by the American telegraph companies and summaries of weather fed back to them.

The first government to collect data by telegraph was the Dutch government in 1855, the French government following the same year. Admiral Fitzroy, who became Chief Meteorologist to the Board of Trade after his retirement from the Navy, inaugurated the collection of daily weather observations in Great Britain on 3 September 1860. Countries all over the world soon followed suit.

Storm warnings were issued before countries developed proper weather forecasting services. Telegraph operators who were experiencing a storm in their area merely passed on the message to other telegraph stations who distributed the message to whomever they thought fit. The first government storm warning service was started in France in 1856, as a direct consequence of a weather disaster during the Crimean War. French and English warships were caught close to the coast near Balaclava, Crimea, Russia, in a violent storm on 14 November 1854; they suffered disastrous losses which might have been averted if news of the storm had been transmitted by telegraph, so that the ships could have sought more sea room. Admiral Fitzroy started a storm warning service in Great Britain in 1860, and telegraph messages were, and still are, conveyed by visual symbols at coastguard stations. A south cone, indicating gale winds from southward, hangs with the apex downwards; a north cone, indicating gale winds from northward, hangs with the apex upwards.

Pictorial representation of weather facts on maps had been talked about since the 18th century. Jean Baptiste Lamarck (1744–1829) French naturalist, and Antoine Lavoisier (1743–94) French chemist, were amongst those who maintained that weather maps could eventually lead to forecasting weather a few days ahead. The electric telegraph made the idea possible because observations were received before they became so out of date as to be useless for forecasting purposes.

The first weather maps published were sold to the public for one penny at the Great Exhibition of 1851 at the Crystal Palace, London by the Electric Telegraph Company.

Early weather maps differed from those made today in the minor matter of symbols representing various weather features. The major difficulty for a modern eye reading the old charts is that the presentation of pressure values makes no great visual impact. Heinrich Wilhelm Brandes (1777–1834), German meteorologist, used lines of equal deviation from normal, Admiral Fitzroy drew undulating lines across his maps giving barometer readings measured from the parallel of latitude above, and Buys Ballot (1818–90) Dutch meteorologist, at first used a system of vertical shading for areas which had pressure higher than normal, and horizontal shading for areas with lower pressure than normal. By concentrating on the undoubted fact that pressure *tendency* seemed a more important indication of weather than the *actual* pressure value, they missed the very simple connection between actual pressure and wind.

Buys Ballot made a vital discovery when he realised that wind, like other flowing liquids, tries to move from high‑pressure to low pressure. It is thwarted from achieving this direct route by the rotation of the Earth on its axis, which exerts a force deflecting wind by approximately 90° to the right in the northern

Weather map for 16 January 1861 as charted by Francis Galton, FRS, Honorary Secretary to the Royal Geographical Society. (*Meteorology in History* by Napier Shaw)

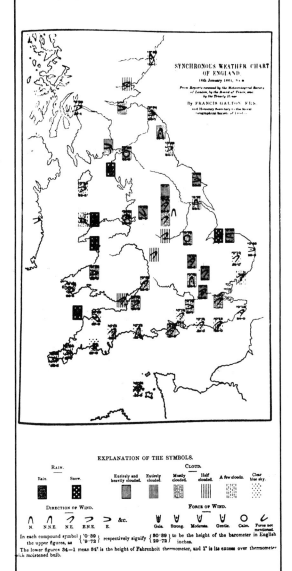

Weather map as issued with the prospectus of the Daily Weather Map Company, *c* 1863. (*Meteorology in History* by Napier Shaw)

hemisphere and 90° to the left in the southern
hemisphere. Friction keeps a better grip on
air near the surface and the deflection from the
high-to-low pressure direction is rather less,
about 70°–85° according to roughness of
terrain. This deflecting force is called the
Coriolis force, or Coriolis effect, after Gaspard
Gustave de Coriolis, a French mathematician
who first described it.

The geostrophic wind is the horizontal wind
caused by pressure differences and the deflecting Coriolis force. It blows according to Buys
Ballot's Law.

Buys Ballot's Law, enunciated in 1857,
states that when wind is blowing on an
observer's back, low pressure is always on the
left hand in the northern hemisphere, and
always on the right hand in the southern
hemisphere. Consequently, wind in the northern hemisphere blows in an anticlockwise
direction round a centre of low pressure and
in a clockwise direction round a centre of high
pressure. In the southern hemisphere, wind
blows in a clockwise direction round a centre
of low pressure and in an anticlockwise

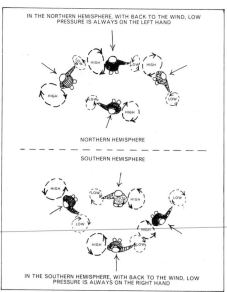

Buys Ballot's Law.

direction round a centre of high pressure.

Hurricanes, long known to sailors, are
merely special cases of low pressure circulations, all obeying similar wind rules.

An isobar is a line on a map joining places
having equal barometric pressure at a specified
height above ground. Isobars are drawn for
consecutive whole values of pressure, usually
at 2, 4 or 8 mb intervals either side of 1000 mb,
and are interpolated smoothly between actual
pressure readings received from observers.
The resulting map depicts pressure contours
and is analogous to a geographical contour
map.

The general public sees isobaric maps of
pressure at mean sea level, but the professional
forecaster also studies isobaric charts for higher
levels of the atmosphere.

Wind direction at 2000 ft (600 m) is considered to be above the influence of surface
friction. It blows parallel to the isobars according to Buys Ballot's Law. Winds at higher
altitudes also blow according to the same rules,
but parallel to the isobars at the specified level.

Surface wind direction is usually backed
from the direction of wind at 2000 ft (600 m) by
10°–30° in the northern hemisphere, and
veered from the direction of wind at 2000 ft
(600 m) in the southern hemisphere. In both
cases this implies a movement of surface air
inwards towards a centre of low pressure,
called **'convergence'**, and a movement of
surface air outwards from the centre of high
pressure, called **'divergence'**.

Wind speed is directly proportional to the
pressure gradient. The closer together the
isobars, the steeper the pressure gradient and
the stronger the wind. Wind generally increases with height above 2000 ft (600 m).

Surface wind speed over land is on average
$\frac{1}{3}$ the speed of wind at 2000 ft (600 m), and
over seas it is about $\frac{1}{2}$ the speed of that
measured at 2000 ft (600 m). Surface wind is
considerably less than average in lulls and may
be near the speed of wind at 2000 ft (600 m) in
gusts.

Coastal wind speed on a sunny day in summer is the resultant of the pressure wind and the sea breeze. Wind speed is stronger than that inland if the two act in the same direction, wind speed is less than it is inland if the two components act in opposite directions.

Wind chill is the dissipation of heat from bare skin by wind alone. Wind has greater power in this respect than very low air temperature. With a wind speed of 20 mph (32 km/h) and air temperature of 34°F (1°C), skin cools at the same rate as it would in calm wind with a temperature as low as −38°F (−30°C).

Americans have a 30-30-30 Rule of Survival for all those sojourning at bases in the Arctic and Antarctic. The grim message is that when exposed to a wind of 30 mph with a temperature of −30°F human flesh freezes solid in 30 seconds.

The effect of wind upon sea became an important branch of meteorology and has resulted in a feed-back of information to the nautical fraternity, which made such valuable contributions in earlier days.

Sea waves are defined in three dimensions. *Height* is the distance between wave crest and wave trough. Wave *length* is the distance between the crest of one wave and the crest of the next, and wave *period* is the time taken by two consecutive wave crests to pass a fixed point.

Fetch is the uninterrupted distance which the wind has been blowing across the sea before arriving at the place of observation.

Average wave height is a function of wind strength and duration, as well as the fetch. The stronger the wind and the longer the duration and fetch, the worse is the state of the sea.

WIND-CHILL CHART

Estimated Wind Speed mph	Actual Thermometer Reading °F.											
	50	40	30	20	10	0	−10	−20	−30	−40	−50	−60
	EQUIVALENT TEMPERATURE °F.											
Calm	50	40	30	20	10	0	−10	−20	−30	−40	−50	−60
5	48	37	27	16	6	−5	−15	−26	−36	−47	−57	−68
10	40	28	16	4	−9	−21	−33	−46	−58	−70	−83	−95
15	36	22	9	−5	−18	−36	−45	−58	−72	−85	−99	−112
20	32	18	4	−10	−25	−39	−53	−67	−82	−96	−110	−124
25	50	16	0	−15	−29	−44	−59	−74	−88	−104	−118	−133
30	28	13	−2	−18	−33	−48	−63	−79	−94	−109	−125	−140
35	27	11	−4	−20	−35	−49	−67	−82	−98	−113	−129	−145
40	26	10	−6	−21	−37	−53	−69	−85	−100	−116	−132	−148
Wind speeds greater than 40 mph have little additional effect	LITTLE DANGER FOR PROPERLY CLOTHED PERSON			INCREASING DANGER			GREAT DANGER					
				DANGER FROM FREEZING OF EXPOSED FLESH								

To use the chart, find the estimated or actual wind speed in the left-hand column and the actual temperature in degrees F. in the top row. The equivalent temperature is found where these two intersect. For example, with a wind speed of 10 mph and a temperature of −10°F., the equivalent temperature is −33°F. This lies within the zone of increasing danger of frostbite, and protective measures should be taken. (National Science Foundation, Washington DC.)

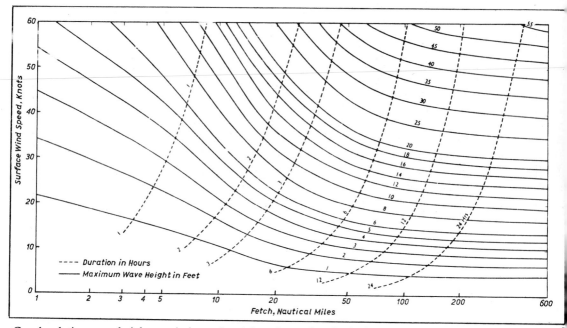

Graph relating wave height to wind speed and duration and to fetch, for coastal waters. (Institute of Oceanographic Sciences)

However, wind is never constant and each individual wave varies from the average, both in height and period. The sea is alive with waves travelling at different speeds and when one catches up another it creates a much larger wave which lasts only momentarily in the combined state.

Statistical calculations agree remarkably well with the practical experience of seamen about how often these large waves occur.

● One wave in 23 is twice the average wave height.

● One wave in 1175 is three times the average wave height.

● One wave in 300 000 (which is the normal number that a ship encounters during one month at sea), is four times the average height.

The *Daunt* light vessel off Cork, Eire, recorded a wave 4·1 times the average height, on 12 January 1969. The height of the wave was 42 ft (13 m).

The maximum wave height is the height of the highest wave observed, usually during a typical ten-minute period.

In the southern North Sea, the maximum wave height in an average year is likely to be 30 ft (10 m).

In the south western coastal waters of the British Isles the maximum wave height is likely to be 50 ft (15 m).

In the northern North Sea and the open North Atlantic the maximum wave height in an average year is likely to be 70 ft (21 m).

A working estimate of maximum wave heights can be obtained from diagram (below), by utilising the values of wind speed, fetch and duration of wind at that speed.

The significant wave height is the practical 'average worst' which interests seamen. It is taken to be the average height of the highest one third of all waves observed in a ten minute period. The average wave height is about 0·63 of the significant wave height.

The measurement of waves by eye when at sea is very difficult because the observer's ship pitches with the waves. It requires nerves of iron to study a huge wave dispassionately enough to give a reliable result. These qualities certainly applied to Admiral Fitzroy: during a gale in the Bay of Biscay he 'measured' the crests of waves against the centre of his main mast when the ship was upright in a trough. He deemed several waves to be higher than 60 ft (20 m) so an extreme wave would have been bigger still.

Waves are sometimes measured around oil rig platforms by wave staffs which are clamped to the legs of the platform. Waves complete the circuit between electrical contacts at various heights up the staffs. The method is not very satisfactory because the waves are distorted by the presence of the rig itself.

A wave rider buoy floats on the surface of the sea and measures wave height by means of an accelerometer. It gives reliable measurement providing it is moored at least half a mile (800 m) from an obstruction such as an oil rig, but it does sometimes tear loose in rough weather.

A ship-borne wave recorder measures height of waves by a combination of accelerometer and atmospheric pressure sensor which is welded to the bottom of the ship below the water line. It gives best results on deep seas when the waves are high and long.

Extreme wave heights have been recorded for only a fraction of all the large waves which must form. The evidence, however, is enough to indicate that sailors' tales of monstrous waves are not as ridiculous as have been thought in the past.

The highest reliably observed wave was 112 ft (34 m), experienced by the USS Ramapo in the North Pacific on the night of 6–7 February 1933. Average wind speed was 78 mph (126 km/h).

The Weather Ship *Famita*, 160 miles (260 km) east of Peterhead, Scotland, during the

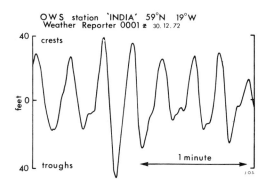

The highest wave ever measured by instrument was recorded on 30 December 1972 by the Ocean Weather Ship *Weather Reporter* and was 86 ft (26 m) from crest to trough. (Institute of Oceanographic Studies)

winter 1969–70 recorded a 61 ft (20 m) wave on a Shipborne Wave Recorder, and estimated the maximum wave to be 76 ft (23 m). In the same area a Dutch Wave Rider Buoy recorded a wave of 72 ft (22 m) on 21 October 1970.

The highest instrumentally measured wave was 86 ft (26 m) recorded on the Ocean Weather Ship *Weather Reporter* in the Atlantic at 59°N 19°W on 30 December 1972.

It has been estimated that Edward Heath's yacht *Morning Cloud*, which foundered off the south coast of England on 2 September 1974, could have encountered a wave of 26 ft (8 m) within the three hours of the gale, and that there was a 1 per cent chance of a wave of 30 ft (10 m) or more.

Swell is wave motion in the sea resulting from wind-generated waves many miles away. Swell may persist long after the original disturbance has died away, particularly in the Southern Atlantic Ocean and the Southern Indian Ocean where there are few interrupting land masses. Huge swell waves in these areas are called South Atlantic Rollers.

Swell has been detected off Cornwall, England as a result of storms off the Falkland Islands, latitude 52° S in the South Atlantic Ocean.

A tsunami is a wave generated by an earthquake and not by the wind or tide. It is incorrect, therefore, to call a tsunami a 'tidal wave'.

The highest recorded tsunami was one of 220 ft (67 m) which appeared off Valdez, south west Alaska, after the great Prince William Sound earthquake of 28 March 1964. Tsunami (a Japanese word which is singular and plural) have been observed to travel at 490 mph (790 km/h). Between 479 BC and 1967 there were 286 instances of devastating tsunami.

Pilots of all kinds of aircraft have contributed considerably to our knowledge of horizontal and vertical winds.

A jet stream is a narrow belt of high speed wind near the tropopause, whose existence was suspected in the 1920's and confirmed during the Second World War when pilots started flying at very high altitudes. USA bombers, capable of a ground speed of 350 mph (560 km/h) and flying over the Pacific Ocean towards Japan found their speed in the air reduced to about 200 mph (320 km/h). Subsequent research showed that there are usually two westerly jet streams, subtropical and polar in each hemisphere, blowing with speeds of between 100 and 200 mph (160 km/h and 320 km/h). They become stronger in the winter when there is greatest contrast between polar and equatorial temperatures and 350 mph (560 km/h) has been recorded.

Clear air turbulence occurs when there is rapid change with height of horizontal wind speed, causing dry air to turn over vigorously without any 'tell-tale' cloud indicators. This turbulence often happens above or below the jet stream, especially when that is accentuated by passing over mountains, and aircraft can encounter extremely rough conditions without warning. A research flight over Sierra Nevada, USA, in February 1967 encountered such violent turbulence at a height of 50 000 ft (15 240 m) that it lost control and fell a few thousand feet before being able to recover.

Thermal currents are the main power source for gliders, and they rise as follows:
    a weak thermal $1\frac{1}{2}$–3 ft/s ($\frac{1}{2}$–1 m/s)
    a moderate thermal 3–9 ft/s (1–3 m/s)
    a strong thermal more than 9 ft/s (3 m/s)

A glider requires an air current which is rising faster than the craft is sinking, which means about $2\frac{1}{2}$–3 ft/s (nearly 1 m/s). In Great Britain thermals are usually only strong enough for gliding between approximately 11 am and 7 pm during summer.

The strongest thermals occur in deep shower clouds (p. 123), and aircraft of the USA army co-operated with the US Weather Bureau in daring investigations of these clouds during the 1950's. Pilots deliberately flew into the clouds at various levels and allowed the thermals to take control of the aircraft. Updraughts as strong as 3000 ft/min (1000 m/min) were usual and 5000 ft/min

Icarus falls to his death while Daedalus, in the background, demonstrates mastery of the soaring technique.

(1500 m/min) were encountered occasionally in clouds whose tops reached 60 000 ft (18 000 m).

Strong thermal upcurrents delay considerably the fall by parachute from an aircraft. On 26 July 1959 an American pilot ejected from his plane at 47 000 ft (14 400 m) and took 40 minutes to fall through a thunder cloud instead of the expected 11 minutes.

The greatest wind-powered flights are achieved on a combination of thermal currents, horizontal pressure wind and uplift in wave motion over mountains. The flight of the mythological Daedalus (from whom Socrates was reputed to be descended) some 750 miles (1200 km) from Knossos in Crete to Cumae in southern Italy is considered to have been possible. There was adequate fabric and woodworking skill available at the time to build a sail-plane and there was suitable topography along the route to give enough lift in suitable conditions to achieve that journey. It would have needed a high standard of wind detection, which the ill-fated Icarus presumably did not have, so that he fell into the sea and was drowned.

Among modern record distances achieved by wind power are:

Gliders:
908 miles (1461 km), Lubeck to Biarritz, 25 April 1972, by Hans-Werner Grosse.
1004 miles (1616 km), Lock Haven, Penn, USA to Tennessee and return, 19 May 1976, by Karl H. Striedieck.

Hang gliders:
Vertical descent 15 324 ft (4671 m), horizontal distance 13·6 miles (22 km) by Rudy Kishazy from Mount Damavand, Iran, 29 August 1975.

Even a heavy aircraft designed for powered flight can find air currents in which to glide. The pilot of a Lockheed F5 aeroplane, with engines dead and propellers feathered, soared for more than one hour between heights of 13 000 ft and 31 000 ft (4000 m and 9000 m) over the Sierra Nevada Mountains, USA, on 5 March 1950.

A modern hang glider, controlled by moveable cross bar, soaring in the wind blowing on to a mountain face. (J Taylor)

Leeward downdraughts can be hazardous in mountainous areas and could account for hitherto unexplained aircraft accidents. Several instances have been reported, by pilots of powered aircraft, of downdraughts greater than 30 ft/s (10 m/s) to the lee of the Little Carpathian Ridge, Czechoslovakia. These caused forced altitude drops between 900–1400 ft (300–500 m).

Free-fall parachuting requires minimum thermal currents and is best accomplished in high pressure situations.

A 60 seconds free fall in a mean pressure wind of 45 ft/s (15 m/s) gives the parachutist a drift in the direction of the mean wind of 3000 ft (900 m). Experienced parachutists can control direction and forward speed when the mean wind speed is as high as 15 ft/s (5 m/s) by day and as high as 13 ft/s (4 m/s) at night. Safe landings can be made in surface winds up to 30 ft/s (10 m/s).

CHAPTER 6

PRESSURE PATTERNS AND STORMY WINDS

Poseidon, sea god and a Normad storm detector.

Pressure patterns vary infinitely around a few basic types which govern the circulation of air around the world. Their modern meteorological descriptions derive from earlier traditional names.

An anticyclone is a circulation of air round a centre of high pressure. Wind speed is generally light near the centre but can be strong on the outer fringe where it blends in towards a low pressure circulation. Anticyclones are often persistent, air in the system has time to stagnate and modify, and the systems drift rather than travel with measurable speed. Pressure rises steadily when an anticyclone is developing, and falls when it is receding.

A ridge of high pressure is an elongated extension of isobars from an anticyclone. Wind is often, but not necessarily, light, and there is pronounced divergence of surface air when the isobars curve markedly.

A depression is a circulation of air round a centre of low pressure, usually between 950 mb and 1020 mb. A depression is 'deep' if it has a strong pressure gradient and the centre is encircled with many isobars, indicating strong wind. A depression is 'shallow' if there is little pressure gradient, few isobars and light wind. An embryo depression may deepen to maturity and travel towards the east with a measurable speed, before filling up, slowing down and eventually losing identity. At other times an embryo depression may disappear without having made much impact. Pressure falls at places towards which a depression is advancing and rises again when the depression moves away. Gales in middle latitudes nearly always occur round depressions.

A trough of low pressure is an elongated extension of isobars from a depression. Wind is often light in a trough, but there is marked convergence of surface air where the isobars have a pronounced curvature. Any particularly elongated trough is a likely breeding place for a new depression, called a secondary depression.

A col is the calm area between diametrically opposite depressions or anticyclones.

A tropical cyclone is a low-pressure circulation in tropical latitudes, having wind speeds more than Beaufort Force 8, but less than Force 12, which denotes a full hurricane.

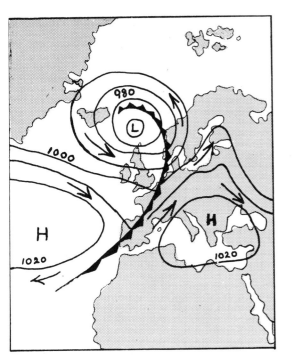

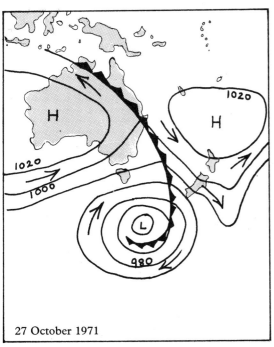

27 October 1971

Left: The isobaric pattern over Australia and New Zealand on 27 October 1971 was on the weather map issued by the New Zealand Meteorological Service. The pattern has been 'peeled' up from the bottom of the southern hemisphere map and laid down upon the European map to demonstrate how wind circulation differs in the two hemispheres.

A hurricane or typhoon is an intense tropical cyclone having average surface wind speed of 74 mph (119 km/h) or more. Hurricanes form and travel over the oceans and once they reach land they usually degenerate to depressions.

Upper air pressure patterns are similar to the patterns which feature the surface weather maps, but they are usually less pronounced.

Tornadoes, whirlwinds, dust devils, water spouts and **water devils** are low pressure circulations of such a small cross section that they are not discernible on normal weather charts. They have winds of great strength and are dealt with separately in chapter 15.

A storm surge is caused by a deep and fast moving low pressure system travelling across the sea, and is additional to the turmoil stirred up on the sea surface by the changing directions of the air circulation. Pressure falls ahead of any travelling depression and rises behind it, thereby allowing the sea level to rise or fall a matter of 4 in (100 mm) during the passage of the system. When this occurs slowly it is hardly noticeable, but when it occurs rapidly it has a plunger effect upon the sea and creates a large scale undulation. This may be noticeable as swell in the open sea many miles away from the place it originated. If such a storm surge is driven into the closed confines of land, it forms inflated waves and floods over the land. This is often called a tidal wave, erroneously because it has nothing to do with the tides caused by the pull of the moon. However, the worst storm surges are those which occur at the same time as a predicted high tide.

The power of storm surges can be gauged from a few notable examples from the past: 1737, Calcutta, India: 300 000 lives lost.

The Royal Victualling Yard, Grove Street, London, after the storm surge in the Thames on 6 January 1928. (Greater London Council)

1876, Backergunge, India: 100 000 lives lost.

1899 (5 March), Bathurst, Queensland, Australia: centre of cyclone 914 mb passed over pearling fleet and caused 300 deaths. Combined tide and surge 40 ft (12 m).

1900 (9 September), Galveston Bay, Texas, USA: 5–6000 lives lost.

1970 Coast of East Pakistan: more than 200 000 lives lost.

Storm surges also occur in Europe: on 6 January 1928 a depression moved rapidly down the North Sea, generating a storm surge which travelled up the Thames estuary to London. The river topped the embankments, which collapsed in several places, roads were torn up and the Tate Gallery was flooded almost to the tops of the ground floor doors. Fourteen people drowned in basements because of the rapidity of the inundation, and 4000 people were left homeless.

1953 (1 February): a storm surge was generated by deep depression travelling south east down the North Sea. In England there was extensive flooding and breach of sea walls all round the east coast. A total of 307 lives were lost, of which 58 were drowned on Canvey Isle and 35 at Jaywick, both in Essex; 30 000 were made homeless, $\frac{1}{4}$ million acres of land was contaminated by sea water.

Holland received direct impact from water piling down the North Sea and innumerable dykes protecting reclaimed land collapsed: 1800 people drowned, over 50 000 people were evacuated from low lying areas, and it was nine months before sea walls were finally repaired.

Canvey Isle, Essex, and the breaches in sea walls in the Tewkes Creek area, after the storm surge down the east coast of England on 1 February 1953. (Popperfoto)

Areas most susceptible to hurricanes, typhoons and tropical cyclones, are those between latitudes 10° and 30° north and south of the equator, in the Indian Ocean, in the Caribbean Sea and Gulf of Mexico, in the south China Sea, and off the east and north west coast of Australia.

General portrait of a hurricane: The most likely seasons for hurricanes are summer and autumn, when the sea is at its warmest. The average life span of hurricanes is nine days, the average forward speed is 12 mph (20 km/h) and the general track is towards the west and then recurving again towards the east.

Few hurricane winds can be measured because the anemometers collapse, but sustained speeds of 100 mph (160 km/h) gusting to 150 mph (240 km/h) probably occur often. Sustained speeds of 150 mph (240 km/h) gusting to 225 mph (360 km/h) probably occur occasionally. Wind speed increases steadily to within 20–30 miles (32–48 km) of the centre, which is called the 'eye', and then remains at maximum speed within a belt 15–25 miles (24–40 km) wide around the eye. The eye has an average radius of 7 miles (11 km) and within the area wind speed falls to about 15 mph (24 km/h) which seems calm in comparison with that which preceded. The calm of the eye is followed by hurricane wind speeds from the opposite direction as the system progresses.

Rotating winds may extend to a height of 6 miles (10 km), but speed decreases with height. Deep banks of cloud spiral inward around the centre, but the eye is cloudless.

Hurricanes are given names for easy identification, and the custom was started first in Australia by Clement L. Wragge of the Queensland Weather Bureau between 1887 and 1902. The story is told by A J Shields, Regional Director, and R G Gourlay, both of the Bureau of Meteorology, Brisbane, Australia, in *Science News*, 4 May 1975.

'Wragge's charts indicated the daily migration of weather systems over Australia and the surrounding oceans. Each identifiable system of highs, lows, monsoons, etc., was named by Wragge who used what he considered appropriate appellations. On one series of charts he named the systems *Razis* (a Persian), *Ram, Rakem, Sacar, Talmon, Ramath, Uphaz* (all biblical), *Vaubon* (a French engineer), and *Eline*, reminiscent of "dusky maidens with liquid eyes and bewitching manners", to quote Wragge who had sojourned in Polynesia. On other occasions he offered his public *Xerxes, Hannibal, Blucher, Nachon, Machina, Leonata,* and the politicians *Drake, Barton,* and *Deakin.*'

Wragge was inclined to engage in heated public controversy on all kinds of scientific matters, and politicians who incurred his wrath were liable to find their initials attached to particularly pernicious meteorological disturbances on the weather maps. His adversaries were not averse to referring to Clement Wragge as 'inclement Wragge' or 'wet Wragge'.

The naming of cyclones fell into disuse in Australia after Wragge's time, and was revived again by the Americans during World War II. One story attributes the initiative to a radio operator who issued a hurricane warning and then started to sing a few bars of 'Every little breeze seems to whisper Louise', and the hurricane was thereafter referred to as *Louise*. Whether or not this was the exact way the christening custom was revived, it was a thoroughly practical idea for accurate transmission of weather information. There are

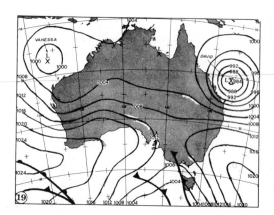

Both *David* and *Vanessa* are marked on the Australian weather map for 19 January 1976, demonstrating impartiality between feminine and masculine names for cyclones! (Bureau of Meteorology, Brisbane)

often several low pressure systems over a large area at once, and it was particularly important for long range aircraft missions that they could be easily identifiable in radio or published weather forecasts. Feminine names have been universally allocated until recently. Atlantic names start afresh at the beginning of the alphabet each year and the names rarely get to M (13 hurricanes) in a year. In the eastern Pacific, however, names frequently reach initial letter P (16 storms). In the western North Pacific names continue to the end of the alphabet regardless of date, and often have more storms during a single year than names available in one list. In Australia, however, the opponents of sex discrimination protested at the hurtful practice of always naming such devious, destructive and demoniacal phenomena after the ladies. From 1975 the aspersions have been cast equally between male and female, so that weather charts, such as that for 19 January, 1976 which indicates both a dying *Vanessa* and a vigorous *David*, have become a symbolic sign of the times.

Notable hurricanes in the North Atlantic in recent years show that the early treatises of the 19th century were basically correct in stating that hurricanes move first towards the

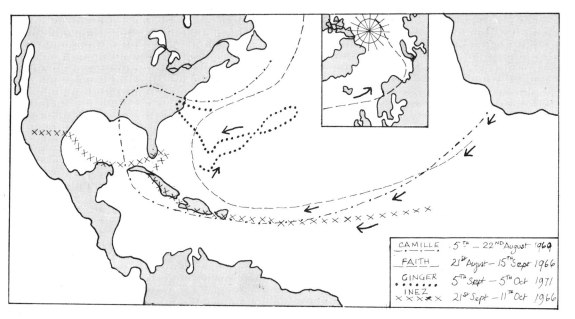

CAMILLE	5TH – 22ND August 1969
FAITH	21st August – 15th Sept 1966
GINGER	5th Sept – 5th Oct 1971
INEZ	21st Sept – 11th Oct 1966

Four very different hurricane tracks in the North Atlantic. (From information supplied by National Hurricane Center, Florida)

west and then recurve later to the north and east. However, tracks plotted by satellite pictures and measurements of pressure and wind by modern instruments indicate that there is much temperamental variation from the normal by individual hurricanes.

Audrey 27 June 1957, exceptional intensity for that time of year. Estimated depth 945 mb, estimated surface wind speed 135 mph (217 km/h).

Arlene 2 August 1963, passed within few miles Kindley Air Force Base, Bermuda, so that her 'portrait' was taken by barograph and radar. Eye was about 28 miles (45 km) in diameter, calm lasted only 3 minutes. Peak gusts 97 mph (156 km/h).

Camille 17–18 August 1969, one of most destructive hurricanes to affect the eastern states of USA. Relatively small but very intense, depth 901 mb, wind approximately 172 mph (276 km/h).

Beulah
Chloe } 14–16 September 1967, triplets in North Atlantic occurring at the same
Doria } time.

Connie
Diane } 12–19 August 1955, two in a week in North Atlantic.

Faith 21 August–15 September 1966, long distance roamer, originating west of Africa and finishing up near the North Pole; 26 day journey.

Ginger Longest lived hurricane in North Atlantic: 4 September–5 October 1971. Of these 31 days, Ginger had 20 days of hurricane status, a very large assymetrical eye 80 miles (129 km) across, and a double-back track.

Inez 24 September 1966, highest recorded gust of 197 mph (317 km/h) read at 8000 ft (2438 m) from an aircraft. Sudden change of track on 3 October to enter Gulf of Mexico.

Inga 20 September–14 October 1969 performed a drunken loop in mid-Atlantic during her 25 days as a named system.

In the Arabian Sea, 'portraits' of two recent intense cyclones indicate the characteristics of all intense low pressure storms.

Cambay Cyclone: on 29 May 1976 at 70° E 12° N a depression started to move northwards and developed into a tropical cyclone by 31 May. It intensified further to a severe cyclonic storm on 2 June, attaining brief hurricane status in the early morning. The cyclone dodged closely between three oil rigs, stationed in the same latitude as Bombay, before entering the Gulf of Cambay and crossing the coast of India near Port Cambay on 4 June. The cyclone was tracked by satellite and radar, augmented by reports from ships, oil rigs and land based weather stations. The accompanying charts indicate the wave heights (recorded by reference to markings on the legs of the oil rigs) and wind speeds experienced by the rig operators. Very high storm surges were expected in the Gulf of Cambay, and because of an efficient storm-warning system the whole coastal area was evacuated before the storm arrived. At Gogha Port waves, probably augmented by storm surge, reached the roof of two buildings of approximately the same 40 ft (13 m) height. A total of 2500 villages in nine districts of Gujarat State were affected, 70 persons lost their lives, 4500 head of cattle perished and about Rs 30 million worth of damage occurred. Nevertheless, damage was not very great in the light of the intensity of the storm. There were even benefits accruing because the heavy rainfall which accompanied the storm filled the irrigation tanks. Moreover, the discharge of rainwater at Bhavnagar through the Kansa river was so great that it flushed away silt and sand which had accumulated in the harbour. Routine dredging ceased and may not be required again for another eight to ten years.

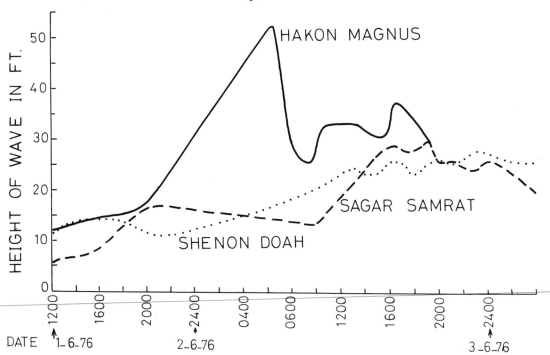

Height of waves recorded on oil rigs in the Arabian sea during the passage of Cambay cyclone. June 1976.

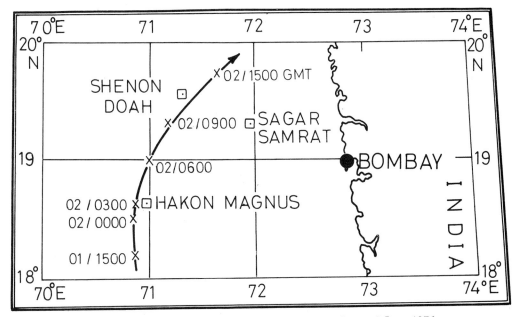

Cambay cyclone, tracked by Radar fixes, in the vicinity of oil drilling rigs. 1–2 June 1976.

102 Km (approx)

scale

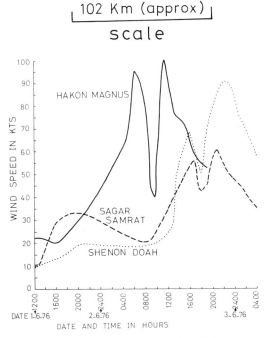

Wind speeds recorded on the oil rigs during the passage of the Cambay cyclone. June 1976.

Porbandar Cyclone: in October 1975, a depression in the Bay of Bengal moved west across the south of India into the east central Arabian Sea. It intensified within three days to a severe cyclonic storm on 21 October and developed a core of hurricane winds soon afterwards. The storm crossed the Gujarat coast near Porbandar on 22 October, the first time the area has experienced such a storm so late in the season. Jamnagar experienced winds exceeding 100 mph (160 km/h) between 1930 and 2000 h, Indian time, on 22 October, four hours after the storm reached the coast.

Satellite pictures taken of the storm show typical 'comma' pattern circular banding of clouds around the centre. The infra-red picture shows clearly the ice crystal cirrus cloud flowing out from the top of the storm in the western and northern sectors. The picture taken on the visible waveband shows clouds in the eastern and southern sectors — views which are suppressed in the infra-red picture.

Meteorologists can deduce wind speed in cyclonic storms by the definition of cloud patterns shown in satellite pictures. The more pronounced the dark spot in the eye and the more distinct the spiralling bands of cloud the stronger is the wind speed. Maximum wind speed in the Porbandar cyclone was estimated to be 132 mph (212 km/h).

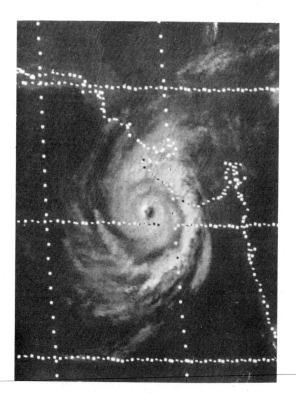

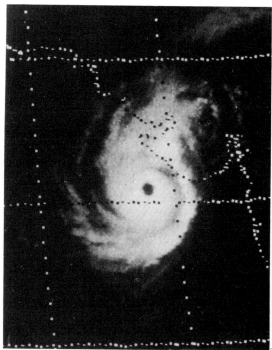

Porbandar cyclone, 22 October 1975, photographed at 0935 Indian Summer Time on visible wave length by NOAA-4 satellite. The spiralling nature of the cloud system is clearly visible. (Meteorological Office, New Delhi)

The same Porbandar cyclone as left but photographed on infra red wave length. This emphasises the cold ice crystal cloud flowing outward from the centre of the storm, but diminishes the view of the thicker but warmer water drop cloud below the cirrus canopy. (Meteorological Office, New Delhi)

In the Pacific Ocean, two particular hurricanes developed at extremely inconvenient times.

On 17 September 1945, a typhoon travelled towards Japan and centred over the Island of Kyushu, with a lowest pressure of 916·6 mb. It was just 42 days after Hiroshima had been devastated by atom bomb and communications were still disrupted. No advance warning could be relayed to Hiroshima, nor was that city in any condition to cope with the new hazard of hurricane. Over 2000 people died in the hurricane and 2500 were wounded.

On 25 December 1974, the inhabitants of Darwin, Northern Territory, Australia, found themselves pummelled by hurricane *Tracy* instead of relaxing with Christmas festivities. The storm had been plotted accurately for four days and plenty of warnings had been given to the public of its approach. By the time it reached Darwin wind speed was gusting up to 100 mph (160 km/h), not abnormally strong for a hurricane. However, the majority of homes were of light frame construction and no match for *Tracy*. The town was almost flattened, 48 people were killed and 90 per cent of the population left homeless. Trees were stripped of foliage and 26 000 people had to be evacuated by aircraft within the next few days.

In the Indian Ocean, south of the equator, tropical cyclones are not unusual, but *Monique,* 25–31 March 1968, was amongst the worst. She was detected by satellite when still in embryo stage at 82° E, 11° S and was traced over a classical track towards west-south-west until she passed close to Rodriguez island, 300 miles (480 km) due east of Mauritius, before curving round again towards the south east. *Monique* reached maturity on 29 March when Rodriguez reported the lowest pressure ever recorded in the Indian Ocean, 934 mb. The maximum known wind gust in the Indian Ocean, 173 mph (278 km/h), was recorded at Rodriguez at 1700 hours on the same day. *Monique* destroyed all standing crops and much of the recently planted forest.

The most disastrous depression to affect southern England, giving sustained winds of hurricane speed occurred on 26–27 November 1703 (old calendar style). It can be reconstructed from a detailed account written by Daniel Defoe (1659–1731) English author, who lived in London at the time.

A depression approached south west England and moved north eastward across Wales to south Yorkshire. SSW gale winds blew across southern England on the afternoon of 26 November, causing great damage and disastrous flooding in the Severn Valley. The Eddystone lighthouse disappeared without trace with all its occupants including the designer, Winstanley, who was visiting at the time.

The storm increased in intensity and reached a peak in the eastern English Channel between 0200 h and 0500 h on 27 November. The average wind speed at the peak of the storm was probably over 100 mph (161 km/h). About 8000 lives were lost, mainly at sea. Many ships were collected in harbours or at anchor in the English Channel awaiting favourable winds after a succession of gales in the previous fortnight. Warships and supply vessels were waiting to sail for Spain or just returned from the summer campaign in the Mediterranean. Twelve men-o'-war were wrecked on the Goodwins alone, and hundreds of ships were tumbled together in harbour, in the Thames, and along the south coast. Roofs were damaged everywhere, 100 churches were stripped of lead, 400 windmills overturned, about 800 houses destroyed. Countless trees were uprooted, even really large specimens which are usually able to stand their ground. Defoe counted 17 000 trees down in Kent alone before he tired of the task; he estimated 450 parks lost between 200 and 1000 trees each, and the New Forest about 4000. Average wind of hurricane strength must have persisted for more than two hours on this occasion, an experience which has not happened since.

THURSDAY   FRIDAY   SATURDAY

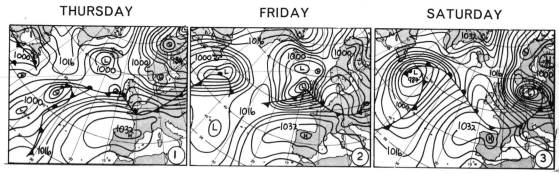

Weather maps for 1–3 January 1976. (*Weather*)

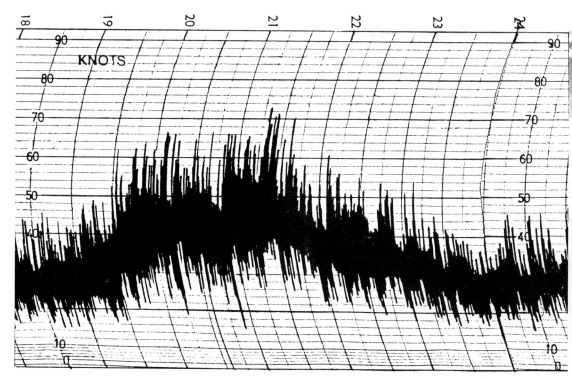

Section of an anemogram recorded on 2 January 1976 from 1800 hours until midnight at Elmdon airport, near Birmingham, Warwickshire. (*Journal of Meteorology*)

An example of an extremely vicious depression, as experienced in middle latitudes, occurred on 2–3 January 1976 in north west Europe. A depression travelled eastward across southern Scotland to Denmark and Germany on 2 and 3 January 1976. The centre deepened to a lowest value of 968 mb when half way across the North Sea. Wind speed was highest in the southern part of the circulation, and Ireland, the Midlands and Northern England suffered the most damage in Great Britain.

Material consequences were 28 deaths in Great Britain, 36 deaths in the rest of Europe. Tens of thousands of trees were blown down, 650 in Norwich City alone. Innumerable roofs were damaged, including that of Worcester Cathedral. Railway services were disrupted by fallen trees and collapsed power lines. Worst damage was done on land, but six fishing boats were destroyed in Denmark, and one trawler sunk off the Dutch coast. Flooding on west coast of England and Wales, and inundation of Severn Beach in Avon County due to coincidence of high tide and driving westerly gale. Sea walls breached at Walcott, Norfolk and Cleethorpes, Humberside. There was considerable flooding and damage in low lying coastal areas of Holland, Denmark, and West Germany, caused by driving NW wind behind depression on 3 and 4 January.

	mph	km/h
Birmingham, Warwickshire, 2 January 1976		
3½ hours, 1930–2300 hrs, continuous gale, mean speed	44	71
2 hours, 1945–2145 hrs, gusts of hurricane speed	74	119
1 hour, 2100–2200 hrs, mean speed	51	83
Berlin, Germany, 3 January 1976: maximum intensity mid-morning		
24 hours continuous gale, mean speed	44	71
17 hours frequent gusts to storm speed	66	106
Notable gusts		
Cardington, Bedfordshire	95	153
N Ireland	100	161
Island of Sylt, Germany	101	163
Norwich, Norfolk, England	102	164
Cromer, Norfolk, England	104	167
Wittering, W Sussex, England	105	169
Zugspitz, Black Forest, Germany (high altitude)	116	187

The most unusual intensification of gale winds by a physical obstruction was associated with a depression which travelled north of Scotland on 16 February 1962. Some places in Scotland had a mean hourly wind speed of 65 mph (105 km/h). In the Midlands average wind speed was 45 mph (72 km/h) and the isobars on the weather map were spaced accordingly. At Sheffield, however, mean wind speed increased to 75 mph (120 km/h) during the early hours of the morning and gusts reached 96 mph (154 km/h). A few miles away from Sheffield, mean wind speed was considerably *less* than 45 mph (72 km/h), sometimes as low as 18 mph (29 km/h).

Subsequent investigation by the Meteorological Office indicated the cause to have been exaggerated wave motion through about 2 miles (3 km) depth of the atmosphere induced by the lift of air over the Pennine Range. Air flow was compressed into the bottom of the wave-trough just over Sheffield, giving exceptionally high wind speed; air flow was stretched out over considerable depth at the wave crest and surface wind elsewhere was abnormally reduced.

Low pitch aluminium roofs, which were inadequately anchored to house walls at Hatfield, Herts, and were ripped off during a gale on 4 November 1957. (Building Research Station)

Scotland has the greatest frequency of gales in the British Isles. Glasgow suffered two specially disastrous gales this century:

On 28 January 1927, there was a deep depression west of Scotland. Peak winds occurred in the afternoon, gusting frequently 70–80 mph (113–129 km/h) with one peak gust at Paisley 102 mph (164 km/h). Eleven were killed in Glasgow alone and much material damage was done especially from flying chimney pots.

On 15 January 1968, the depression moved eastward across central Scotland. Average wind speed between 0200 and 0300 hours was 61 mph (98 km/h) with one gust to 102 mph (164 km/h). A dredger in Clyde capsized,

drowning two people. Nine people were killed in Glasgow, again mainly from flying debris and collapsed buildings.

Scotland generally suffered badly on 31 January 1953, when a depression passing north of Scotland made a capricious change of course to travel south eastwards down the North Sea causing storm surge on the east coast on 1 February (see p. 78).

	mph	km/h
Orkney Isles, Scotland:		
mean 1 hour wind speed	90	155
Maximum gust	125	201
Central Scotland:		
mean 1 hour speed at 2000 ft		
(600 m)	175	282

A strong following wind drives this dinghy 'on to a plane', which means that it skims *over* the water instead of sailing through it.

More trees were blown down than are normally felled in a year, and much structural damage was done. The ferry *Princess Victoria* bound from Stranraer to Larne, Ireland, sank in the Irish Sea with loss of 133 lives, after suffering damage from a high sea. Rescue work was hampered by bad visibility caused by flying spray and snow showers.

Sand storms occur regularly wherever there are large stretches of sand. They are not usually disastrous, because people have adapted their buildings accordingly, but they are thoroughly unpleasant.

The most violent sand storms are called 'haboobs', and are frequent in the Sudan and in the Arizona Desert, USA. They occur in advance of large convection clouds or cold fronts when strong horizontal pressure winds combine with the vertical winds causing the cloud to create particularly turbulent conditions. Cold down-draughts of air from within the cloud spread out over hot dusty ground, and then convect upwards into a dense turbulent roll of air carrying sand which often reduces visibility to nil.

The most frequent duststorms in the USA occurred during the prolonged years of drought in the 1930's which created the Dust Bowl of the central plains. Dust not only obscured visibility locally, but was often carried aloft and transported at high altitudes. It was carried to the ground in very distant areas with rain or snow falls, creating curious colouring effects. The Great Duststorm of 12–13 November 1933, carried dust from as far as Montana State all the way to the Atlantic seaboard. 'Black rain' fell in New York State, 'brown snow' in Vermont. In 1934 there were four major dust storms, the most widespread on 9–12 May and christened 'Black Blizzards'.

The most renowned fall of dust in Europe occurred over Switzerland on 14 October 1755. 'Blood red rain' fell at Locarno and 'red snow' at higher altitudes in the Alps, and the coloured dust probably originated in North Africa. It was estimated that of 9 in (228 mm) rain which fell during the night, 1 in (25 mm) was dust and affected an area of 360 sq miles (930 km^2).

The most recent fall of dust in Great Britain occurred on 1 July 1968, after a slow southerly air flow from the Sahara reached the country, laden with dust, at altitudes between 10 000 ft and 17 000 ft (3000–5000 m). Heavy rain and thunderstorms broke out over England and Wales during the night, washing the dust to ground. An estimated total of 5000 tons of dust fell, mainly sand with a little clay, and technicolour dust covered all parked cars next morning, south east of a line Plymouth–Edinburgh.

One of the most dramatic sand storms in non-desert regions occurred in Scotland at the end of the 17th century.

Culbin used to be a rich estate on the shores of Moray Firth, Scotland, but sand banks and dunes had started to shift by the 1690's, because the coarse binding grass was depleted for use in thatching. In the autumn of 1694 a deep depression caused a yellow sand blizzard which lasted all night and drifted high against all the houses. The inhabitants had to dig themselves out and fled inland with as many cattle as they could gather together, but after a short lull there was a renewal of the storm which finally submerged the whole village in sand. An arid desert of sand 8 square miles (21 km²) was left, with rolling billows and some sand mountains 100 ft (30 m) high. Storms in subsequent centuries remoulded the sand into different shapes, and in the 19th century the tips of some of the houses were temporarily uncovered.

The last sandstorm in the area occurred in May 1920 when huge billows of sand rolled inland to submerge a wood. Since then the Forestry Commission has planted grass, brush wood and young trees as a successful three-line defence against the wind and sand.

CHAPTER 7

WATER IN ITS THREE DISGUISES

Balloon with radar reflector attached.

Water is the raw material from which all visible weather is made. Both the liquid and solid states of water are so familiar that they need no introduction, but the advent of thermometers permitted many interesting and hitherto unknown facts about water behaviour to be discovered.

Water is a compound of one volume of oxygen and two volumes of hydrogen, chemical formula H_2O. Although water is colourless when clean it is a versatile solvent and therefore easily gets dirty. Rainwater accumulates organic matter, salts, minerals and other soluble ingredients during its run over land to the sea but is still considered comparatively 'fresh' when it reaches the sea.

The density of water is greatest at a temperature of 4°C and then equals 0·99997 grams per cubic centimetre. It is sufficient to remember the density as 1 gram per cubic centimetre,

which it was thought to be when originally decided upon as an international standard by which to measure densities of other substances.

The density of fresh water increases with fall in temperature till the maximum is reached at 39·2°F (4°C) and thereafter density decreases until water solidifies, forming ice.

Fresh water starts to freeze at a temperature of 32°F (0°C) when in bulk rather than in the form of drops.

Calm fresh water freezes on the surface soon after sustained cooling has reduced the water temperature throughout to 39·2°F (4°C). Upside down convection (p. 17) then ceases because of the density anomaly and any further

Fresh water is most dense at a temperature of 4°C, and any water which is colder is less dense and lies above. Sea water increases in density all the time it cools towards freezing level, and is therefore subject to upside-down convection.

cooling remains concentrated in the upper layer of less dense water.

River ice forms most readily on inner curves where the flow is slowest, and least readily wherever the stream is increased along an outer bend or round an island.

Individual water drops can remain liquid when 'supercooled', that is, when they have temperatures below the normal freezing level of 32°F. (0°C). Supercooled drops can exist in clouds at temperatures as low as −40°F (−40°C), but the whole state of supercooling is precarious. Droplets freeze instantly on contact with ice crystals or other particles having sub-zero temperature.

Sea water contains approximately 3 per cent salt as well as other minerals, but the proportion varies considerably according to the ground over or through which the sea has been fed. The most saline sea, and therefore the most dense, is the Dead Sea, which is a large inland lake 1296 ft (395 m) below the level of the Mediterranean, and is the lowest body of water on the Earth's surface. Dead Sea water contains about 25 per cent salts, of which 7 per cent is common salt (about 12 650 million tons). There is no life possible and normal salt water fishes die at once when put into this lake.

The density of sea water increases continuously with falling temperature until it freezes.

Sea water freezes at a lower temperature than fresh water, between 29°F and 28°F (−1·5°C and −2°C) according to salinity. Sea water precipitates its salts on freezing and becomes a mixture of fresh water ice, brine and air. The brine gradually gravitates out, so that water just below sea ice may be more salty than the rest.

Deep oceans do not freeze because surface sea water becomes more dense as it gets colder, and therefore continually sinks to be replaced by warmer less dense water from below (upside-down convection). Sea ice forms in shallow water which has a chance to

cool to freezing temperature throughout its depth. Sea ice breaks loose from shallow water because of mechanical pressures or driving wind and then travels into deep water as ice floes.

Estuary water is a mixture of sea water and fresh river water, and is therefore less saline than the sea. Consequently, estuaries freeze more readily than the sea but stay open to shipping for longer than rivers during cold winters, a useful factor for inland ports such as Quebec in the St Lawrence River estuary in Canada.

Slippery water is a shallow surface layer of warm water which slides *en masse* with very little friction over denser cold water below. Under such circumstances the wind easily drives the top layer over the bottom, a feature first used to good advantage by the British Yachting team at the Olympic Games at Acapulco, Mexico, in 1968.

The oceans and seas cover 139 670 000 sq miles (361 740 000 km²), which is 7/10th of the total Earth's surface. The half world centred around Tahiti in the Pacific Ocean consists almost entirely of water, and the other half, centred over eastern Europe contains the remaining $\frac{1}{5}$ of all the water surface and almost all the world's land surface. Early cartographers did not believe such inequality of distribution possible, and because they lacked factual evidence often added imaginary land in the southern hemisphere to 'balance' the world.

Ocean currents are permanent movements of water driven by wind and deflected by land masses till they arrive in regions where their temperature is higher or lower than that normal for the latitude. Currents were first discovered by Matthew Maury (p. 66) who aptly described them as 'rivers in the ocean'.

Ice is the solid state of water. It appears white when broken or frozen unevenly because of the refraction and scattering of light by the many faces of the ice pieces

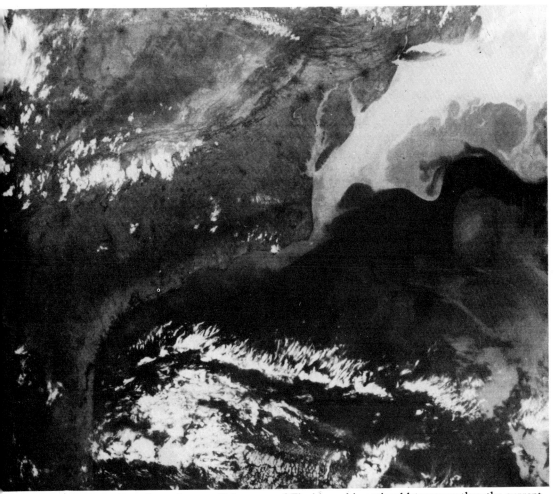

The Gulf Stream (black) curls north east off the coast of Florida and is noticeably warmer than the current moving towards the south (light grey) from Labrador. Picture taken by high resolution infra-red sensor on the polar orbiting satellite NOAA-5, flying at an altitude of about 900 miles (1450 km) on 14 April 1977. (NOAA, National Environmental Satellite Service)

Black ice is not really black, but a transparent frozen film of water which takes the colour of the material on which it forms. 'Black' probably originated from the dark colour of roads which appear normal even though slippery with ice.

The density of ice is 0·92 grams per cubic centimetre. This low density is achieved abruptly when water solidifies, and is accompanied by an equally abrupt increase in volume of about $\frac{1}{10}$. This gives ice its terrific power when formed in confined surroundings: bottles, metal pipes, and cleft rocks can all burst with the expansion of freezing water. Ice is as hard as metal at about $-40°F$ ($-40°C$).

Frazil ice (French-Canadian *frasil*: cinder) consists of small pieces of ice forming in the sea or rivers which are flowing too fast to permit formation of a solid ice sheet.

Black and white ice on an uneven terrace. Thin films of water froze to black ice, deeper puddles iced on top first and then cracked when the water below froze later.

Ice floes are slabs of ice broken free from the area where they form. They travel along rivers or with ocean currents.

The largest extent of sea ice in the northern hemisphere occurs north of latitude 60° N during winter. It persists all the year in the Arctic Ocean, which is centred around the North Pole and consists of a restless circulating mass of ice floes of an average thickness of 10 ft (3 m). For this reason, discovery of the North Pole was not just a question of sticking a flag into the ice as proof of arrival. The ice travels the whole time, and any discovery flag with it.

The first to claim arrival at the North Pole were Dr Frederick Albert Cook (1865–1940), USA, on 21 April 1908, and Commander Robert Edwin Peary (1856–1920), USA, on 6 April 1909. The first indisputable claim which was independently checked by US Air Force weather aircraft was that of Ralph Plaisted, USA, and three companions on 1 April 1968, after a 42-day trek in four Skidoo (snow-mobiles). The Arctic Ocean is a perpetual challenge to explorers because of it commercial possibilities in linking the in habited continents by the shortest routes The first surface ship to reach the North Pole was the Russian nuclear-powered ice breaker *Arktika*, 18 172 tons, in August 1977.

The first vessels to cross the Arctic Ocean beneath the ice were the USA nuclear submarines *Nautilus* and *Skate* in 1958.

The first trans-Arctic crossing by sledge and dogs over the ice was made by a team led by Wally Herbert between 21 February 1968 and 29 May 1969. The distance covered as the crow flies was 1662 miles (2674 km) but drifting ice increased that distance by a further 700 miles (1126 km), quite apart from diversions on the ice due to open leads of water. Temperature fell to −47°F (−44°C) during the trek.

Shallow seas which are confined by land and do not benefit from stirring by strong tides and currents, freeze more readily than open sea. The Hudson Bay, Canada, the Bering Sea between Alaska, USA and USSR and the northern Baltic Sea between Sweden and Finland are all ice covered during winter even though much of the Atlantic in the same latitude remains ice free because of the North Atlantic Drift current.

Invasion across the ice by Polar bears is an annual problem in the Hudson Bay for the town of Churchill. Bears wander into the surroundings of the town during winter when the frozen Bay provides them with secure trails When the Hudson Bay thaws again in spring bears which have failed to get away in time have to remain in the neighbourhood until the ice forms again in the winter before being able to move northwards to their breeding grounds. They adapt to urban life and become expert thieves of food stores, which necessitates constant patrols by vigilant inhabitants.

In the southern Baltic Sea, adjacent countries tend to judge the severity of their winters according to whether or not they become ice bound.

Denmark is separated from Sweden by two sea channels: the Kattegat, between 30–80 miles wide (48–128 km), and the Sound, which is only a few miles wide. The two countries are usually bound together by ice several times each century, thus providing temporary thoroughfare for sociable visits by sledge. In the past, however, when the two countries were at war, the disappearance of the defensive barrier of water was not always welcomed, as is apparent from the many historical events recorded:

In 1307 the Danish peninsula of Jutland was completely ice bound; the ice measured 30·8 in (782 mm) in thickness near Humblebaek on the Sound.

In 1658 Carl Gustav, King of Sweden, carried out manoeuvres with his army on the iced-up Sound, and the Danes were very apprehensive of invasion.

In 1716 King Carl XII of Sweden assembled his soldiers to cross the ice to the Danish island of Zealand, where the coastal area was evacuated as a precaution. The thaw came on

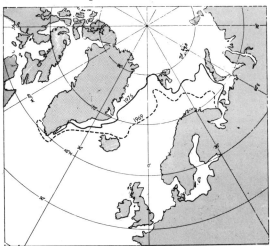

The edge of Arctic ice in March 1969 compared with the edge in March 1976. (Meteorological Office, Bracknell)

5 February before the invasion could take place.

In 1799 people were still driving by sledge between Denmark and Sweden on 26 March, and there was ice on the Sound until 11 May.

In 1830 there was a big New Year's party in the middle of the Sound with restaurant facilities provided by a Swedish entrepreneur. It was not entirely convivial, as fights broke out because of 'exaggerated patriotism, wine or alcohol which had been taken in too big a quantity'.

On 18 March 1834 Prince Christian, later Christian IX of Denmark, drove with a party across the ice from Copenhagen, Denmark to Malmö, Sweden and back again. The Kattegat (Denmark–Sweden) was also covered with ice during the whole winter.

The most southerly limit of North Atlantic sea ice in recent years occurred during spring 1968, when a bridge of ice between Iceland and Greenland provided uncomfortably easy access for Polar bears to renew acquaintance with Iceland after 50 years absence. Consequent gloomy predictions about the likelihood of an immediate new Ice Age were confounded by the spring of 1976 when the Arctic ice edge had retreated almost to the coast of Greenland and up to the west coast of Spitzbergen.

Summer sea ice in the northern hemisphere generally retreats towards the 78th parallel of latitude, but Canada and USSR have difficulty in keeping any sea routes open along their northern boundaries – even in summer.

Sea ice in the southern hemisphere surrounds the continent of Antarctica, and in winter ice may extend well north of the 60° S latitude. Some of the ice is sea ice, formed in shallow coastal waters, but much is compacted snow which has gradually crept off the continent and broken into icebergs which travel the sea.

Measuring the thickness of sea ice by lowering an iron bar vertically and bringing it up below ice in a horizontal position. (N A C Croft; courtesy Scott Polar Research Institute)

The most dangerous form of sea ice occurs in regions where warm sea currents enable ships to remain afloat during winter, but where air temperature occasionally falls well below freezing level when wind blows off frost-bound continents. Ships sailing in such conditions at sub-freezing temperatures are in danger of capsizing as the waves spraying their superstructures continuously freezes.

Colour photographs were taken on the tanker *British Trust*, while on passage from the Isle of Grain in Kent, England, to Sundsvall in the Baltic Sea, north of Stockholm, Sweden, during January 1968. Ice formed during a north easterly gale, mainly on the fore deck, while the vessel was moving into a head sea. No ice formed on the decks because steam coils in the cargo tanks kept the oil at a temperature of approximately 100°–120°F (38°–49°C), which in turn warmed the decks. Ice on the hand rails was well over 1 ft (30 cm) thick and the entire bridge front was coated in ice except for a clear view screen kept free of ice by means of boiling water. Much ice was knocked off with sledge hammers in order to enable the crew to work the ship in port, the decks were safe to walk on because of the heated cargo and the danger of casualties from

ice blocks falling from the rigging fortunately did not materialise.

Other ships have not been so lucky because ice can accumulate at the rate of 40 tons per hour, which dangerously alters the stability of a ship. On 4 February 1968, trawlers from Hull, England, were fishing west of Iceland when a deep depression travelled south of Iceland and caused wind in the fishing grounds to become easterly and of hurricane strength. Spray from mountainous seas filled the air whose temperature was 12°F (−11°C), and ice accumulated on the trawlers making them increasingly difficult to handle. The *Ross Cleveland* eventually capsized and sank in a few seconds, only one of the crew surviving.

Rivers in the centre of large land masses north of latitude 50°N are liable to freeze most winters. Exceptionally hard winters result in polar scenes considerably further south than 50°N. North America had its coldest winter ever recorded in January and February 1977, and by the beginning of February the normally busy Hudson River was thick with ice floes near New York (41°N).

Rivers in Great Britain freeze only in exceptionally cold winters when the wind predominates from the continent of Europe.

The most recent occasion on which the Thames was frozen, so that people could walk across at places above Kingston-upon-Thames, was February 1963. Below Kingston, river water remained at a temperature about 45°F (7°C) the whole winter because of waste heat from the power station.

Most winters in Great Britain yield ice on puddles and many winters bring ice to ponds. Occasionally sea ice forms along the east coast, which happened most recently in December 1976.

Domestic ice was a precious commodity in Great Britain before the days of refrigerators. Even a thickness of half an inch (12 mm) was gathered and hoarded when a mild winter

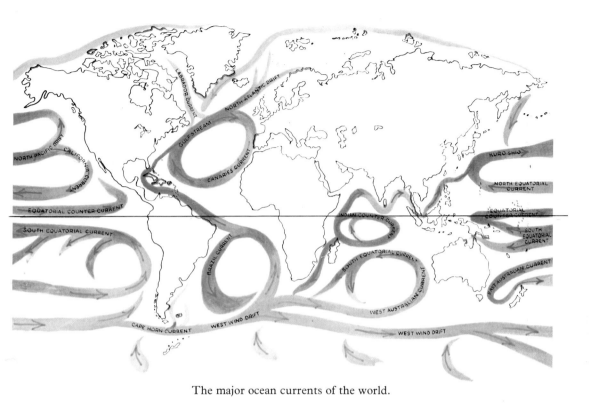

The major ocean currents of the world.

Water covers 7/10ths of the Earth's surface, and the half world centred around Tahiti in the Pacific Ocean is almost entirely covered in water.

The North Pole is situated in the Arctic Ocean which is covered by a restless circulation of ice floes.

The South Pole is situated on the continent of Antarctica which is covered in sheet ice – the compressed snowfalls of many centuries.

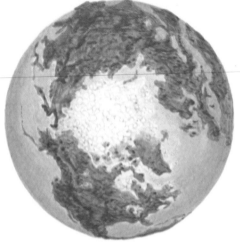

Left:
Ice accumulated on the lifeboat aboard *British Trust* in January 1968 while on passage from the Isle of Grain, Kent, to Sundsvall in the Baltic Sea. (T R Hughes)

Below left:
A cup of boiling water, thrown into the air during an Antarctic winter when air temperature was – 60°F (–51°C), explodes into ice crystals. (W Herbert)

Below right:
Water vapour, exhaled into the very cold air in Antarctica, is immediately deposited as frost over the face. Dark glasses are essential against glare from the snow during summer in Antarcica. (W Herbert)

Building an igloo. (Dr I D Calder; courtesy Scott Polar Research Institute)

could produce no more. It was stored in ice houses usually built into the sides of hills. An entry was made at a central level of the house, the ice was stored in the lower pit where the coldest air remained, and any warmer air which penetrated via the entrance rose to the upper part of the chamber. The pit was often layered with straw on top of a chalk or stony soil base giving natural drainage. Ice usually lasted till the following October. Modern top-opening freezers can be left open without undue loss of cold air for the same reason. It is so dense that it settles as low as possible.

An ice house built for human shelter uses the density characteristics of air in the opposite way to that used in an ice storage house. The shelter incorporates an upper ledge so that people can sit in the warmest air while cold air settles into the lower pit below body level. Mountaineers and explorers have learnt the skill of building protective shelters from hard compacted snow from the Eskimos whose traditional home is the igloo. An initial small trench is cut into the snow and blocks then carved from the walls of the trench. The blocks are laid around the pit in a circle, spiralling inwards until a dome forms with only one small hole left at the top, into which a wedge-like block is dropped to keep the whole structure stable. The entrance is at a low level.

In order to melt ice, heat is required – a fact which comes as no surprise to anyone who has seen the Sun do the job outdoors or who has melted ice in a pan over a flame. However, the advent of thermometers enabled scientists to quantify the heat required and to discover some rather extraordinary features of the melting and freezing processes.

Ice always starts to melt at 32°F (0°C). It takes as much heat to melt one gram of pure ice at a temperature of 0°C as it takes to raise the temperature of one gram of liquid water through 80°C, which is 80 calories. Yet all that heat is used entirely for melting the ice and not for raising the temperature of the mixture of ice and the resulting melt-water, which remains at a constant 0°C till all melting is completed. Such a mixture is therefore useful for calibrating thermometers.

The reverse process of freezing causes a similar amount of heat to be released, 80 calories per gram of water. This is why bulk water solidifies slowly. Every time a little freezes, it releases heat to delay the solidification of the rest. Even at air temperatures as low as −40°F (−40°C), which is frequently experienced in polar regions, a cup of water taken outside and poured to the ground will take some moments to freeze. If the water is first thrown into the air to split it into smaller amounts, however, it explodes into a dazzling shower of ice crystals, which also emit an audible hiss at temperatures as low as −60°F (−°51C).

Latent heat is the name given to the heat which is released during a change of state of a substance without causing any change in temperature.

Latent heat of fusion of water into ice can be put to practical use for frost protection. If blossom is sprayed with a fine jet of water when air temperature reaches 32°F (0°C) it becomes encapsulated in a sheath of ice at 32°F (0°C). Providing the water spray continues to maintain a mixture of ice and water over the blossom, its temperature will remain at 32°F (0°C), however low the air temperature may

Sea ice off the coast of Antarctica during January 1915. (Frank Hurley; courtesy Scott Polar Institute)

fall. Apart from practical and financial problems of this method, an obvious hazard is that the blossom may break off under the weight of accumulated ice, even if it does not die of cold!

The melting point of ice is reduced by the application of pressure.

This means that if ice is already near the normal melting temperature of 32°F (0°C), any pressure applied to it may tip the balance and cause it to melt. Therefore, skating is easier on comparatively warm ice than on ice at very low temperatures because the melt water created by the pressure of the skate blades acts as a lubricant.

Regelation is the refreezing of melt water once temporary pressure is withdrawn. A weighted piece of wire will go right through a block of ice without apparently cutting it, due

to regelation. Pieces of ice which previously have separate identities but become coated with a film of melt water when under pressure bond together in the refreezing process. Ice floes may rise out of the water under initial impact with others and then bond together under the continual release and application of pressure which exists in moving water. The resulting pack ice therefore has a humpy appearance.

The last Frost Fair on the river Thames in 1814 was possible due to regelation. During the very cold month of January in 1814, ice floes drifted down to London from the upper reaches of the river. Old London Bridge was still standing and its small archways were unable to provide through passage for the ice. The pressure of one floe behind the other and

The last frost fair on the Thames, 1814. (Radio Times Hulton Picture Library)

the jostling for position near the bridge caused the whole lot to bond together. It was humpy ice like that experienced in polar regions. On 31 January the first people ventured on to the ice and for five days a Frost Fair, with entertainments and stalls was the talking point of Londoners. On 5 February the wind shifted to the south, it then rained in the evening and the thinner bonding ice was the first to melt. The river became a mass of crashing ice floes released from bondage; several lives were lost, and an enormous amount of damage was done to moored vessels.

Water vapour, the invisible state of water, was not really understood until the 18th century. The word 'vapour' had been used right back to the days of the Greek philosophers, but it described mist and moisture which was *visible*, really tiny drops of liquid water. People also talked about 'exhalation', implying that the Earth breathes moisture like human beings. Everyone knew that water disappeared when boiled too long, and they noted that water often disappeared at ordinary air temperature, but they did not know how.

Robert Boyle (1627–91), Irish chemist and physicist, was the pioneer in the study of gases. He had been to Italy and studied the works of Galileo, and by 1662 he had proved that gas is compressible. Boyle's Law states that when temperature remains constant, the volume of a given mass of gas is inversely proportional to the pressure acting upon it. He used this principle to invent an air gun.

Jacques Alexandre César Charles (1746–1823), French physicist, formulated Charles' Law, which states that when pressure is constant, the volume of a gas is proportional to the temperature. Gases at constant pressure lose 1/273 part of their volume at 0°C for each 1°C that their temperature falls. Hence at −273°C the volume of a gas should in theory be reduced to zero which is called absolute zero.

New gases were meanwhile discovered: *Oxygen* was independently discovered between the years 1771-4 by Carl Wilhelm Scheele (Swedish chemist) and Joseph Priestley (English chemist). Priestley named the gas 'dephlogisticated air', because he found it to be the inflammatory constituent of air. It was named oxygen a few years later by the French chemist Antoine Lavoisier (1743–94).

Hydrogen was discovered by Henry Cavendish (1731–1810), English chemist and physi-

Robert Boyle, 1627–91.

cist, who described it to the Royal Society in 1776. It was named hydrogen 20 years later by Lavoisier. Hydrogen is the lightest gas, and its discovery opened the ballooning era. However, hydrogen is highly explosive, and therefore helium, after its discovery in 1895 by Sir William Ramsey, was used instead.

Nitrogen was discovered in 1772 by Daniel Rutherford (1749–1819), Scottish chemist.

Dry air proved to be a composition of 78 per cent nitrogen and 21 per cent oxygen, together with small proportions of other gases.

Atmospheric air was discovered to consist of dry air together with water vapour, which exists as an independent gas in variable quan-

tities. Each of the constituent gases contributes its own independent pressure to the total exerted by the atmosphere. Nitrogen exerts a pressure of about 750 mb, oxygen about 230 mb and vapour anything between 5 mb and 30 mb.

James Hutton (1726–97), Scottish geologist, who was researching the subject of rain, made important experiments in 1792 which showed that evaporation necessitates the use of heat. He mounted two thermometers side by side and moistened the bulb of one with water. As the water evaporated, the level of mercury in the wet bulb thermometer fell below that in the dry bulb thermometer, and remained lower so long as its bulb was kept moist. Hutton concluded that heat had been filched from the bulb itself, and thereby provided an explanation to a phenomenon which had been known for years. A porous container holding water permits evaporation from the outer surface during hot, dry weather and keeps the inner contents cool.

John Dalton (1776–1844), English chemist, was keenly interested in the weather. He kept careful records of weather for 46 years, often using home-made instruments, and accumulated something like 200 000 weather observations. He applied his own theories of the atomic properties of matter to the new laws of gases and thereby laid down the fundamental meteorological principles governing water vapour in the atmosphere.

Evaporation is the escape of water molecules from the surface of water into gaseous disguise. Evaporation can only take place until a certain maximum vapour pressure, called **saturated vapour pressure**, has built up over the surface of the water, and this amount is different for every air temperature. Warm air is more hospitable to vapour than cold air. Whereas vapour pressure can build up to a maximum of 42·43 mb when air temperature is 86°F (30°C), air which is as cold as −40°F (−40°C) has a maximum vapour pressure of only 0·19 mb.

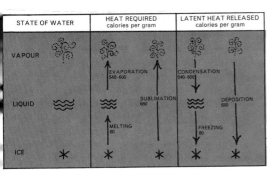

STATE OF WATER	HEAT REQUIRED calories per gram	LATENT HEAT RELEASED calories per gram

The quantities of heat involved when water changes its disguise.

Condensation is the return of vapour to liquid water. It occurs when air, which already has attained saturated vapour pressure, cools still further so that its vapour content is more than the maximum possible for the lower temperature. Air at a temperature of 86°F (30°C) can hold 27·69 grams of vapour per kilogram of air, approximately 0·03 per cent of its mass, for potential use in the production of visible wet weather, and this is nearly 240 times as much vapour as air at −40°F (−40°C) can hold. (0·12 grams of vapour per kilogram of air.) The temperature at which condensation occurs is called **Dewpoint**.

Sublimation is the escape of water molecules direct from a surface of ice into gaseous form. The molecules are more rigidly structured in ice than in liquid water, and the saturated vapour pressure possible over ice is slightly less than over water. If air contains both ice crystals and supercooled water drops, there can be saturation vapour pressure with respect to ice, but not with respect to the water drops.

Deposition is the return of vapour direct to ice form. It occurs when air already has saturated vapour pressure and a temperature below 32°F (0°C) and then cools further.

Latent heat is released during condensation and amounts to 540–600 calories per gram, which is the same as the amount of heat required to change one gram of water to vapour.

Latent heat is released during deposition and amounts to 680 calories per gram, − the same amount of heat as is required to change ice direct to vapour.

Air is said to be moist or dry according to whether its vapour pressure is near saturated level or well below. The more moist it is, the more readily a given amount of cooling produces condensation.

The relative humidity of air (abbreviated RH) is the actual vapour pressure expressed as a percentage of the saturated vapour pressure which would be possible at that air temperature. It is a necessary concept for gauging the readiness with which vapour will condense from the atmosphere, because there are always two variables concerned, actual vapour content and the capacity of air to hold it, determined by temperature. To use a domestic comparison, a trickle of water poured into a thimble may fill that small container to 100 per cent capacity, and the slightest upset to its equilibrium will cause the contents to spill out. The same trickle of water in a jug may only fill it to one per cent capacity, and there is little danger of it spilling out.

Relative humidity usually increases during the night, because temperature falls even though the amount of water vapour may remain constant.

A hygrometer is an instrument for measuring the humidity of air, and the earliest instru-

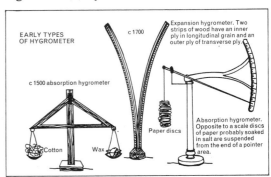

Early hygrometers, as exhibited in the Science Museum, London.

ments merely weighed the amount of water which dry fibrous material absorbed.

An absorption hygrometer was sketched by Leonardo da Vinci in one of his notebooks. It consisted of a pair of sensitive scales holding a piece of cotton fibre in one pan, and an equal weight of wax in the other. In moist air, the cotton became heavier while the wax did not, so that the depression of the balance arm from the horizontal indicated the moisture in the air.

A paper hygrometer in the Science Museum, London, dating from about 1790, consists of a series of paper discs, probably impregnated with salt to attract moisture, suspended at one end of a pivoting arm. The other end of the arm moves against a graduated scale and indicates the weight of water absorbed by the papers.

Expansion hygrometers utilise the known property of fibrous materials to swell when wet. A very simple hygrometer in the Science

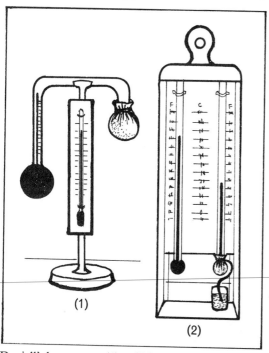

(1)

(2)

Daniell's hygrometer (1) and Mason's hygrometer (2).

Museum, London, dating from about 1700 consists of two strips of wood secured together in a common base. Each strip is two ply having the longitudinal grain on the inside and the cross grain on the outside, the strips having been assembled when thoroughly moist. Wood shrinks more across the grain than with the grain, so that the drying out process causes the strips to splay apart according to the dryness of the air.

The first hair hygrometer was made in 1783 by Horace-Bénédict de Saussure (1740–99), Swiss physicist. A hair, fixed at one end to a brass frame, passed over a wheel carrying a long arm which moved over a graduated scale. Humidity was indicated by the position of the pointer between two fixed points, determined when the hair was saturated with water and therefore fully expanded, and when it was absolutely dry and therefore at its shortest.

A dew point hygrometer measures the temperature at which condensation from air occurs. The first instrument was made in 1820 by John Frederic Daniell (1790–1845), English physicist. He used ether, which evaporates quickly, as his cooling medium. The instrument consisted of a glass tube bent at right angles in two places to form an inverted U shape and with a bulb at each end. One bulb was blackened and contained ether in which a thermometer was mounted; the other bulb was covered in muslin and soaked in ether. As the ether evaporated from the muslin, the bulb cooled, and vapour condensed inside. In consequence, ether inside the blackened bulb evaporated, and cooled that bulb in turn. When the bulb was so cold that condensation from the air appeared on the blackened bulb, the thermometer was read and gave dew point. The greater the difference between dew point and air temperature, the drier the air. When air was saturated, dew point and air temperature were the same. The method was effective, but cumbersome.

James Glaisher (1809–1903), English meteorologist, owned a Daniell dew point hygro-

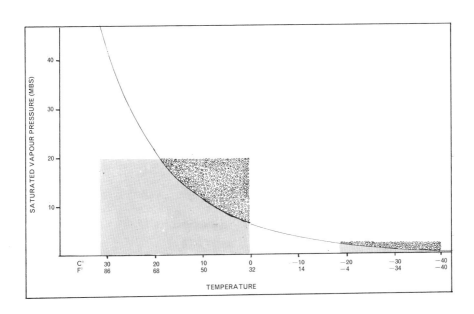

Graph illustrating saturated vapour pressure for different temperatures. Air with a temperature of 86°F (30°C) and having a vapour content exerting a pressure of 20 mb can cool approximately as far as 66°F (19°C) before becoming saturated. Thereafter, further cooling causes condensation. Very little vapour can exist in the atmosphere at low temperatures.

meter as well as two ordinary thermometers with wet and dry bulbs such as Hutton had used. He made thousands of observations over a period of years, comparing dew point, wet and dry bulb temperatures, and eventually compiled mathematical tables specifying the relationships between the three temperatures and relative humidity. The dew point of unsaturated air is always below the wet bulb temperature, because the miniature environment over the wet bulb is always saturated. When the general environment is saturated the wet bulb, the dry bulb and the dew point temperatures are all the same.

Mason's hygrometer was a commercial development of Hutton's wet and dry bulb thermometers by Sir John Leslie of Edinburgh and Mason of London, and it remains the standard popular hygrometer. The wet bulb is covered with muslin and ties with a wick which dips into a container of distilled water.

A whirling psychrometer consists of a wet and dry bulb thermometer packed into a wooden frame which pivots on a handle and looks remarkably similar to a football match rattle! It is operated in the same enthusiastic manner, by whirling, in order to ensure a steady maximum flow of air across the two thermometer bulbs.

A hygrograph is a self-recording hygrometer which provides a continuous trace of humidity, usually by pen on a clockwork rotating drum.

The human body is like a wet bulb instrument, which regulates excessive body tem-

Bottle garden at Syon House, Brentford, Middlesex, which is self watering. The initial water supply in the soil is absorbed by the roots, transpired by the leaves as vapour, condensed again on the sides of the bottle and used again after running down into the soil. It is a microcosm of the way water is recycled on Earth and in the atmosphere.

perature by means of evaporation of moisture.

Insensible perspiration moistens the surface of the skin all the time, and its evaporation is adequate for an unclothed body at rest to remain in thermal equilibrium with air having a temperature of about 86°F (30°C). At higher air temperatures, or when the body generates heat by exercise, sweat glands start operating and provide more moisture for evaporation. The process works most efficiently when the air is dry. When air is very humid, evaporation may not take place fast enough for comfortable dissipation of heat. Air which has a temperature of 90°F (32°C) and a relative humidity of 75 per cent taxes the body to the limit, and sweat pours in order to maintain core body temperature. A higher air temperature of 100°F (38°C) with a lower relative humidity of 50 per cent is equally uncomfortable. The victim who was coated in impermeable gold paint in the James Bond film *Goldfinger* died because no evaporation could take place from the body at all!

Heat stroke is the breakdown in efficient thermal control of excessive body temperature, and it can be fatal.

In the British Isles, very hot summers are rare, but when they do occur they are inclined to be moist. Most heat waves result in some deaths, which are mainly or partly attributable to the heat, and often these could be avoided, if people appreciated the need to drink enough liquid to replace sweat evaporated.

During an average summer in the United States of America there are about 175 deaths caused by heat strokes. During the heat waves of the 1930's which created the drought areas of the Dust Bowl, USA, it is estimated that nearly 15 000 people died of heat stroke between 1930 and 1936, 4768 of these being during 1936.

Relative humidity in the British Isles varies between 60 per cent and 95 per cent most days with frequent occasions between 95 per cent and 100 per cent; 40 per cent RH is rare even in summer; 10 per cent occurs so seldom that the lowest record is still 24 May 1901, when Parkstone, Dorset recorded 9·5 per cent RH at 1600 h GMT.

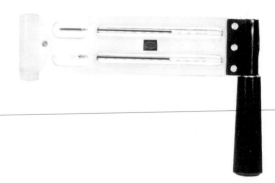

A whirling hygrometer. (C F Casella & Co Ltd)

Relative humidity in low latitudes falls well below 40 per cent during the day in regions removed from the sea and hardly ever rises to 100 per cent. In coastal areas, for instance Bahrein in the Persian Gulf, day temperature of 100°F (38°C) may be accompanied by 50 per cent RH, which is very uncomfortable. At night relative humidity never approaches 100 per cent till air temperature has fallen to about 80°F (27°C). The evolution of the human body has been achieved with these limits in mind. Supposing normal body core temperature had been as low as 75°F (24°C), then inhaled air of 80°F (27°C) with a 100 per cent RH would cause vapour to condense in the lungs and cause drowning!

Relative humidity in high latitudes in winter is nearly always above 80 per cent. The water vapour content at very low temperatures can only be small and the additional vapour breathed out by human beings is enough to cause condensation in the immediate environment of the face.

Indoor relative humidity is materially affected by artificial heating systems. A person sitting indoors, normally clothed, is usually comfortable in an air temperature of 75°F (24°C) and relative humidity of 50 per cent.

Outdoor air, even with 100 per cent RH, which is brought indoors and heated artificially suffers a marked fall in relative humidity. Extreme examples occur in places like Whitehorse, Alaska, USA, where outdoor temperature sometimes falls as low as −50°F (−45°C) with relative humidity near 100 per cent. When such air is warmed indoors to 75°F (24°C) it suffers a fall in relative humidity to 5 per cent. The air is then so dry that it evaporates too much moisture from the skin and makes people feel colder than the temperature alone warrants. Even humidifiers have difficulty in raising the vapour content of air to a comfortable 50 per cent RH in those conditions.

CHAPTER 8

DEW, FROST AND FOG

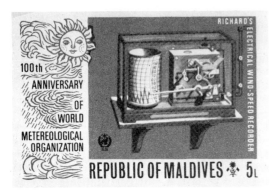

Richards electrical wind-speed recorder.

By the beginning of the 19th century a great deal was known from laboratory experiments about the transformation processes of ice, water and vapour, and people started thinking more seriously about the natural cooling methods by which wet weather is produced.

Radiation heat loss from the ground on occasions when there is no blanket of cloud in the sky to reflect back that heat, provided an explanation for some of the simpler weather phenomena, and was first brought to public attention not by a physicist, but by a physician.

An Essay on Dew was written in 1814 by Doctor Charles Wells, who was born in Charleston, USA, in 1757, and later became physician at St Thomas' Hospital, London. He maintained that dew is caused by condensation direct from air which is in contact with a surface cooling by radiation. Air becomes progressively colder as the temperature of the surface falls, until eventually air near the surface reaches dew point. The vapour content is then the maximum possible for that low temperature, and further cooling produces condensation as dew. Dew forms most readily in calm air when there is no turbulence to stir up the cooling air.

The concept of moisture being breathed from the ground was not entirely dead, because grass and plants do transpire vapour, making a particularly moist micro environment for themselves. The ready formation of dew on grass occurs partly because of the high humidity in the vicinity of grass blades, and partly because the air spaces between the blades insulate against any heat conducted up from the subsoil which might counteract radiation cooling. Metal radiates heat rapidly, which is why parked cars quickly induce condensation.

Guttation is transpired water which is unable to evaporate into the air because saturation vapour pressure has already been reached. It hangs as single large drops at the tips of grass blades, whereas dew which is condensed from the air consists of much smaller drops all along the flat surface of the blades.

Measurement of dew can be made by weighing the amount deposited on a known surface or by photographing drops and comparing size and quantity with known deposits. However, it is not a very meaningful measurement because dew varies considerably with the cooling properties of the material on which it forms. The amount produced at any one place in the British Isles is thought to be less than 0·4 in (10 mm) per annum.

Dew drops on spider's web. (Heather Angel)

Dew ponds were built in England by the Romans, often on high ground like the Sussex Downs. One which was recently repaired had four layers, an upper layer of chalk rubble, then one of reeds, the next a thin layer of charcoal and finally an impervious layer of clay. The rubble served as a condensation surface and the air space within rubble and reeds permitted water to run down to the impervious base. The same air spaces hindered conduction of heat from the subsoil which might warm the cooling rubble and hinder condensation. Sloping sides facilitated the collection of dew fall. Dew ponds are of course replenished by rain water and by dripping fog, so that the term dew pond is something of a misnomer in the British Isles.

Dew traps in Lanzarotte, a small volcanic island in the Canary Isles, North Atlantic, are extremely efficient. The craters are approximately 10 ft (3 m) in diameter, and 6 ft (2 m) deep in the centre, and are clustered together to give the impression of a lunar landscape. They contain a top layer of glass-like volcanic ash, called 'picon' or 'lapilli', for a thickness of 2–4 in (50–100 mm). This insulates soil below from the heat of the Sun during the day, and also presents an admirable cooling surface for condensation at night. Frequent warm and moist winds from the south west provide ample vapour for condensation as dew, invaluable for an island whose annual rainfall is normally less than 8 in (200 mm). Each crater has a vine growing in the centre, and semicircular low walls protect these from the east winds, which are the driest and therefore most greedy to evaporate water. The years 1975 and 1976 had practically no rainfall at all, but the vines generally struggled through on dew alone. There is no artificial irrigation possible on the island at the moment.

Advection dew forms when moist warm air moves over surfaces which are already very cold. It happens after a cold spell when the wind suddenly changes to a warmer direction, and vapour condenses over all surfaces until they gradually acquire the higher temperature of the new air stream. House walls run with condensation, furniture in unheated rooms 'blooms' with minute droplets of condensation, and the windows of cars taken out of cold garages continually mist over till they warm to the outside air temperature.

Supercooled dew sometimes forms in very cold weather, but this liquid state is very unstable. Any attempt to rub a window clean merely provokes rapid freezing of the droplets and a much more opaque glass in consequence.

Dew drops freeze when air temperature falls below 32°F (0°C) after condensation has already occurred at a higher temperature. Frozen dew drops are usually mixed with hoar frost which forms *after* air temperature has fallen below freezing level.

Hoar frost is deposition of vapour directly from air whose dew point is lower than 32°F (0°C). It consists of ice crystals, usually needle-shaped, which appear white *en masse* because of the reflection and refraction of light through them. Hoar frost occurs under the same conditions as dew: most frequently through radiation heat loss on calm cloudless nights, and, in the first instance, on surfaces near the

Hoar frost on leaves.

ground where cold air has settled. Hoar frost can whiten the ground beneath trees while their tops remain in air with a temperature above freezing level, a fact which many fruit growers have blessed at blossom time.

Hoar frost is a visible symptom that air temperature in the immediate environment has fallen to 32°F (0°C) or below. It is not, however, a *necessary* symptom of air frost because air temperature can be below 32°F (0°C) and still not be saturated. It is air frost which is the enemy of plant tissue, not hoar frost crystals themselves, and in certain circumstances hoar frost may even protect against air frost. Thickly encrusted over a glass cold frame, hoar frost may prevent radiation heat loss from the surface below the glass and provide an extra 4°F (2°C) protection beyond that given by clear glass alone.

Fern frost often occurs inside windows during severe weather. Condensation occurs first as dew which remains supercooled for some time after its temperature falls below 32°F (0°C). The first ice crystals which form trigger off a chain reaction throughout all the supercooled drops, which freeze one by one to form beautiful patterns like ferns, Christmas trees or curled feathers. If water drops are large they freeze more slowly because of the

Fern frost on window pane.

release of latent heat from the initial crystallisation. Patches of sheet ice then appear on the glass instead of a spontaneous crystalline pattern.

Radiation mist or fog occurs when the air is moist, when the ground cools by radiation under clear skies and when a wind speed of about 5 mph (8 km/h) ensures the stirring of cooled air above the ground.

It occurs *most often in winter*, because of long hours of night cooling, and *most often inland* where the moderating influence of the sea is non-operative. Fog forms *quickest over open country* where vegetation, rivers and lakes provide extra moisture, and *most frequently in hollows and valleys* into which cooling air drains. Fog is *thickest in industrial areas*, because dirt particles in the air facilitate condensation, and is *most persistent in winter* when the altitude of the Sun during the day cannot counteract the cooling effects of long nights. Fog is *least persistent in summer* when the Sun can easily undo the efforts of a short night of cooling.

Fog droplets are very small and therefore are more conveniently measured in small units, called microns or micrometres.

1 micron = 0·001 mm = 0·000039 inches.

Fog consists of droplets whose radius is between 1 and 10 microns.

Mist consists of droplets whose size is less than 1 micron.

Visibility in fog is less than 1 km (1 100 yd), according to international definition. However, for practical purposes a lower classification is needed which more closely relates to traffic disruption. The word *fog* is often reserved for a visibility of 600 ft (180 m) or less, and *mist* used to define any greater visibility up to 1 km.

Radiation fog forms patchily because the moisture content and cooling properties of the many materials which constitute a ground surface vary. Clear visibility can alternate with dense fog patches over a short distance, until prolonged cooling reduces air temperature everywhere to below dew point and creates uniform thick fog. Fog clears patchily as well because the same surfaces which cool most rapidly at night heat up quicker than others the next morning.

Multiple road crashes are the frequent consequences of this intractable problem of alternating good and negligible visibility. One of the worst motorway accidents in Great Britain occurred on 29 November 1971 when belated fog patches stirred up from moist fields alongside the M1 long after the rest of the fog had cleared. Cars were travelling at

Mist forms most readily over damp fields bordering streams.

normal speeds in bright sunshine when the first car plunged into a fog patch, braked, and the rest piled up behind. Fifty vehicles were smashed, seven people died, and 45 were injured in those few nightmare moments.

On 4 January 1977, there was a traffic pile-up in dense fog on the motorway between Naples and Rome, in Italy, in which eleven people died and twenty-six were injured.

Similar accidents have been repeated in all countries where heavy traffic moves at speed along good roads, and they are likely to happen again because of the difficulty of devising a realistic warning system which people can rely upon. A fog forecast can only specify general area and approximate time of formation, and it cannot pinpoint exactly where the first patches will form. Warning lights may therefore be justifiably lit, but become discredited if fog is not seen on a particular journey. Next time the lights are showing, they may be ignored, yet fog patches will be encountered.

The most significant increases in radiation fog took place during the years of the industrial revolution, when pollution from chimneys provided many more dirt particles on which condensation could take place. In Great Britain the 'pea-soupers' of the Victorian era were so named because the fogs were coloured by chemical pollutants.

The foggiest year in London in the last century was 1873, which had 74 days with thick fog. The worst month was December 1879, having 17 days with periods of fog.

In the 20th century London has twice suffered 114 hours continuous fog, from 26 November–1 December 1948 and from 5–9 December 1952.

Smog combines the two words 'smoke' and 'fog', and is the 20th century equivalent of the 'pea-souper'. The most lethal smog occurred in the London area between 5–9 December 1952. It formed in an easterly drift of air, and brought a maximum concentration of dirt from industrial areas; some estimates put the amount as high as 1000 tons of dirt particles.

The colour of the smog became steadily more evil, and sulphur dioxide combined with water drops and oxygen to form sulphuric acid as a health hazard. Deaths during this period were seven times greater than usual for that time of the year. Probably 4000 people, mainly the aged and ill, died in the London area because of the smog, though the certified causes of death were usually bronchitis or pneumonia.

The Clean Air Act of 1956 was the chosen weapon in the battle against smog. Great Britain is gradually converting to smokeless fuels, and fogs have gradually become less frequent, and noticeably cleaner.

Supercooled fog exists when air temperature is below 32°F (0°C). Droplets remain liquid when in suspension in the air, but freeze at once on contact with cold objects. Supercooled fogs with temperature below 14°F (−10°C) have been known in Great Britain, but usually air is moist enough to condense to fog long before temperature has fallen that far.

Rime is the crust of ice which builds up on twigs, branches, fences etc., when in a supercooled fog. The first frozen droplets freeze the

Rime on a bush of broom.

Ice accretion on the windward side of the trig point on Herbert Peak, Banks Peninsula, nr Christchurch, New Zealand, after a southerly storm. (M J Hammersley)

next supercooled drop which touches them, and if there is no wind, rime builds up evenly all round the exposed objects. If there is a slight wind, rime accumulates on the windward side which is obstructing the supercooled droplets. Rime is white like hoar frost and has the same loosely packed appearance, but it is granular rather than crystalline. It tends to whiten the whole landscape and not only ground surfaces. In countries like Great Britain, where supercooled fogs are not often experienced on the ground, rime is most frequent on mountain tops, which are enveloped in supercooled cloud.

Ice fog consists of minute ice crystals deposited directly from air at temperatures lower than −22°F (−30°C). These fogs scintillate in filtered sunlight and have therefore earned the name of 'diamond dust'.

The town of Fairbanks, Alaska, USA, frequently suffers ice fog. The air temperature is often below −40°F (−40°C) in winter, and little vapour can exist naturally in the atmosphere. However, power plants and factories discharge water vapour from their chimneys and the inhabitants exhale moisture, so that between them they create their own ice fog. The situation is made worse by the fact that the town lies in a shallow basin, and cold air stagnates very close to the ground. Even katabatic winds blowing down the Tanana valley slither *above* the cold pool of air instead of sweeping it away. One of the more dangerous aspects of being out of doors in an ice fog is that ice crystals may accumulate around one's nose when inhaling and cause suffocation. Great Britain does not expect to have ice fogs, but occasionally supercooled fogs may crystallise to ice over favourable nuclei. Ice fog was observed near Bracknell, Berkshire, on 15 December 1975 when air temperature was between 21°F and 26°F (-6°C and -3°C), and wind was drifting from a nearby industrial estate, probably carrying suitable seeding particles.

Advection fog occurs when the wind brings warm air across a cool surface. In Great Britain this usually happens after a cold winter with easterly winds has left the ground snow covered or frozen hard, and then wind changes suddenly to the south west. Advection fog is usually short-lived because the enveloping warm air stream soon raises the temperature of the ground.

Sea fog is basically just an advection fog which forms when warm air cools to dew point over a cold sea. *It tends to persist* because the sea surface temperature does not change appreciably in the short period, but *it may be patchy* because of slight local variations in sea surface temperature due to upside-down-convection (p. 17). Fog drifting from the sea across the land may clear during the daytime because of the warming effect of the Sun on land. Sea fog can exist in wind speeds up to 15 mph (24 km/h) because turbulence merely

Sea fog (background) rolling over the seaward area of San Francisco, USA. It has cleared inland but smog remains trapped below a temperature inversion. (R Cotter)

Arctic sea smoke. (W Herbert)

Dew drops and guttation on blades of grass.

Winter morning fog in the Porter River
valley, New Zealand. It formed just before
dawn in the cold air draining from the snow
covered mountains on either side, and
dispersed again about an hour after sunrise.
(M J Hammersley)

brings more moist air into contact with the cooling surface. Any wind stronger than that usually lifts fog off the surface to give very low cloud.

Sea fog is a regular occurrence over the cold California Current, which flows down the Pacific coast of the United States of America. On a sunny morning which generates a sea breeze, the sea fog rolls on-shore with the breeze like a kind of tide, dispersing gradually as it spreads over the warming land. The cool air stream, even when cleared of fog, still traps the pollution of cities below an inversion of temperature, as seen in the accompanying photograph from San Francisco.

Sea fog along the shores of Great Britain occurs most frequently on the west coast during spring when the sea is at its lowest temperature but south westerly winds bring warm air. On the east coast, sea fog occurs most often in summer when warm continental air cools in passage across the North Sea. (In winter the North Sea is usually a *warming* agent for cold continental air rather than a *cooling* agent.)

One of the worst sea fog disasters in recent years occurred on 25 July 1956. The Italian luxury liner *Andrea Dorea* (29 000 tons) was approaching the American coast in the vicinity of the Nantucket Lightship, Massachussets, in thick fog. The Swedish liner *Stockholm* (12 644 tons), was moving east at 18 knots in clear moonlight. Suddenly the *Andrea Dorea* came out of the fog across the bows of the *Stockholm* which rammed her, so that she slowly sank and disappeared under the sea 12 hours later; 52 people were killed by the impact or were drowned.

Mixture fog occurs when ocean currents of widely different temperature meet, and the air streams above the currents mix. The most notorious fog banks of this nature occur near Newfoundland, off the coast of north east Canada. There the cold Labrador current from the north meets with the warm moisture laden Gulf Stream from the south west. The temperature difference between the air streams may be as much as 30°F (17°C), and the temperature of the mixed airs often cannot contain the vapour content of the mixture. Fog forms and may persist for weeks at a time. The Grand Banks off Newfoundland suffer more than 120 days of fog per annum.

Steam fog occurs when very cold air passes over water which is at least 18°F (10°C) warmer than the air. Evaporation from the warmer water condenses again at once in the colder air above, and forms a shallow layer of swirling fog.

In Great Britain steam fog occasionally forms over rivers or lakes on very cold nights and in cold winters. However, it is more frequently encountered in unheated bathrooms when hot baths are drawn!

Arctic sea smoke is steam fog in polar regions, and occurs when intensely cold air from above pack ice or snow blows over open stretches of comparatively warm water.

A photochemical fog is caused by the reaction of sunlight on hydrocarbons in the atmosphere. Visibility may be reduced to fog level even though no water droplets are present. Photochemical fogs are a special problem for large cities which have considerable motor traffic, and which experience temperature conditions that keep pollution near the ground. The most notorious photochemical fogs occur in Los Angeles, USA, when air off the cold California sea current blows on shore at surface level, but remains trapped beneath warmer air aloft from the Mojave Desert in the interior. When such meteorological conditions exist, power stations sometimes have to run at reduced capacity in order to decrease the danger from stagnant poisonous fumes. The authorities are also investigating methods to control car exhaust emission.

Fog dispersal has been a major challenge since the development of aviation. Aircraft must land before their fuel runs out, and if pilots cannot see, it is impossible to land. Electronic systems of 'talking-down' are not the whole answer. FIDO was the affectionate name for the Fog Investigation and Dispersal Operation in the early 1940s. Fuel burners along runways raised air temperature enough to improve visibility materially in the immediate vicinity, despite adding pollutants from the burning fuel. The method was expensive and it was nerve-racking for pilots to land between flames.

The Cornell Aeronautical Laboratory, USA, has seeded fog with salt in order to provide extra nuclei on which vapour could condense. They have managed to improve visibility eight-fold by changing a fog of small droplets into a thinner fog of larger droplets; but the resultant salt fog is too corrosive to be a practical proposition.

The New Jersey State Highway Department, USA, has given consideration to a device used by engineers above a valley in Antofagasta Province, Chile, where there is a shortage of water. Fog brooms made of closely spaced nylon threads on wooden frames are placed on the mountain tops which are frequently in cloud. As the wind blows droplets against the lattice of threads, the water runs down to collect in pipes. The question is whether droplets could be drawn off in a similar manner, and in enough quantity to ease the fog problem on susceptible stretches of highway. There is a long way to go before such an idea proves practical. Dense barriers of trees or shrubs always trap some water drops when fog drifts through, but such fog drip is not sufficient to materially improve visibility. However, dense barriers of vegetation can divert draining cold air from one area to another where it causes less trouble. This is a method used successfully by gardeners to escape frost in sloping gardens, but on the larger scale, necessary for fog diversion, suitable natural topography would be required before any vegetation barrier could ameliorate the situation.

Fog drip is the sole source of water for the living creatures inhabiting the Namib desert which abuts the Skeleton Coast of South West Africa. Sea fog which forms over the very cold Benguela Current rolls on-shore with the sea breeze, usually clearing over the hot sand during the day, but often persisting during the night when the sand cools rapidly. Lizards, snakes and the sand burrowing blind mole come out from hiding in the sand and lick the fog which falls upon themselves. One species of beetle has adapted to foggy conditions with particular efficiency. It stands on its front legs so that its shiny back, turned into the wind, collects fog drip which runs down into its eagerly waiting open mouth.

Fog creation is as big a research project in horticulture as fog dispersal is in aviation. Since whole orchards cannot be covered in opaque materials to prevent radiation cooling to frost level, many attempts have been made to make fog do the job instead. Smoke alone has proved to be too difficult to control and an inadequate barrier against heat loss. Water fog has the best ability to absorb and reflect heat. In California, some fruit growers have installed overhead pipes carrying water which is forced through a series of fine nozzles along the pipes. This produces droplets small enough to remain suspended in mid air for a considerable time, and the method has been having success.

CHAPTER 9

CLOUDS

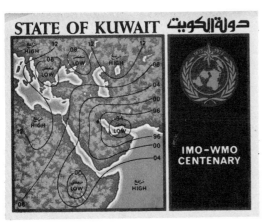

Isobaric chart for the Middle East.

The only clouds which can be explained by radiation or contact cooling are very low cloud sheets which are really lifted fog.

The 18th century scientists were still groping for explanations of the other higher and more shapely clouds, but their lack of causative theory did not deter them from attempting cloud classification according to appearance.

Jean Baptiste Lamarck (1744–1829), French naturalist and pioneer of the theory of evolution, was one of the first to propose a classification of clouds into three levels and five types which was published in the *Annuaire Météorologique* in 1802. He emphasized that cloud forms were not the result of chance, but some combination of conditions which it would be useful to recognise. He did not press his ideas, and in the same year a similar suggestion was made in England with greater impact.

Luke Howard (1772–1864) was an English manufacturing chemist, who attained enough success in his business ventures to be able to concentrate on his other interests, of which meteorology was the foremost. He was a member of the Askesian Society of London intellectuals, who took it in turn to read papers to each other on scientific matters. In 1802 Howard read to them an *Essay on the Modification of Clouds*, which was published with sketches in a limited edition in 1804. It remains the basic classification of clouds today, even though Howard admitted at the time that he did not understand why such clouds formed.

Three main types of cloud were named by Howard, who used Latin words in his classification so they could be used internationally.

Cirrus (curl of hair)	parallel, flexous or diverging fibres, extending in any or all directions.
Cumulus (heap)	convex or conical heaps increasing upwards from a horizontal base.
Stratus (prostrate)	widely extended continuous horizontal sheet increasing from below upwards

The above basic cloud classification was amended over the years as the theory of cloud-formation evolved.

1840 Ludwig Kaemtz (Russia), suggested strato cumulus as a name for flat sheet cloud, breaking into rounded patches due to convection within the layer.

1855 E J Renon (France) suggested using height of cloud as a basis of classification, incorporating a medium level as well as high and low levels.

1886 Ralph Abercromby (Scotland), and H. Hildebrand Hildebrandsson (Sweden), met at Upsala, Sweden, and jointly published a classification of clouds in ten main types, illustrated for the first time by photography.

1890 Hildebrandsson, Neumayer and Köp-pen published an atlas of cloud illustrations with full text in four languages.

1891 The International Meteorological Congress at Munich agreed to compile the first International Cloud Atlas which was published in 1895.

1894 Rev. W Clement Ley published a book called *Cloudland* in which he attempted to classify clouds by their method of formation. It was not a practical classification because

WMO   CLOUD

Genus (with abbreviation)	Ht of base (ft)	(m)	Temp at base level (°C)	Official description
Cirrus (Ci)	16 500 to 45 000	*5000 to 13 700*	−20 to −60	Detached clouds in the form of white, delicate filaments, or white or mostly white patches or narrow bands. They have a fibrous (hair-like) appearance or a silky sheen, or both.
Cirrocumulus (Cc)	16 500 to 45 000	*5000 to 13 700*	−20 to −60	Thin, white patch, sheet or layer of cloud without shading, composed of very small elements in the form of grains, ripples, etc., merged or separate, and more or less regularly arranged.
Cirrostratus (Cs)	16 500 to 45 000	*5000 to 13 700*	−20 to −60	Transparent, whitish cloud veil of fibrous or smooth appearance, totally or partly covering the sky, and generally producing halo phenomena.
Altocumulus (Ac)	6500 to 23 000	*2000 to 7000*	+10 to −30	White or grey, or both white and grey, patch, sheet or layer of cloud, generally with shading, composed of laminae, rounded masses, rolls, etc. which are sometimes partly fibrous or diffuse, and which may or may not be merged.
Altostratus (As)	6500 to 23 000	*2000 to 7000*	+10 to −30	Greyish or bluish cloud sheet or layer of striated, fibrous or uniform appearance, totally or partly covering the sky, and having parts thin enough to reveal the Sun at least vaguely.
Nimbostratus (Ns)	3000 to 10 000	*900 to 3000*	+10 to −15	Grey cloud layer, often dark, the appearance of which is rendered diffuse by more or less continually falling rain or snow which in most cases reaches the ground. It is thick enough throughout to blot out the Sun. Low, ragged clouds frequently occur below the layer with which they may or may not merge.

clouds often have several causes, and because the system could not be used by anyone who was ignorant of theory. However, two of Ley's terms have found a place in modern classification: 'Anvil' and 'Mammatus'.

1956 The World Meteorological Organisation published an International Cloud Atlas dividing cloud into ten genera, with further detailed subdivisions.

Erasmus Darwin (1731–1802), English physician, was the first to suggest that the lifting of air into heights above the ground was an important natural cooling mechanism. His essay published in the *Philosophical Transactions* of the Royal Society in 1788 was called *Frigorific Experiments on the Mechanical Expansion of Air.* His experimental equipment was simple but effective, and his conclusions were vital.

CLASSIFICATION

Stratocumulus (Sc)	1500 to 6500	*460 to 2000*	+15 to −5	Grey or whitish, or both grey and whitish, patch, sheet or layer of cloud which almost always has dark parts, composed of tessellations, rounded masses, rolls, etc., which are non-fibrous (except for virga) and which may or may not be merged.
Stratus (St)	surface to 1500	*surface to 460*	+20 to −5	Generally grey cloud layer with a fairly uniform base, which may give drizzle, ice prisms or snow grains. When the Sun is visible through the cloud its outline is clearly discernible. Stratus does not produce halo phenomena (except possibly at very low temperatures). Sometimes stratus appears in the form of ragged patches.
Cumulus (Cu)	1500 to 6500	*460 to 2000*	+15 to −5	Detached clouds, generally dense and with sharp outlines, developing verically in the form of rising mounds, domes or towers, of which the bulging upper part often resembles a cauliflower. The sunlit parts of these clouds are mostly brilliant white; their bases are relatively dark and nearly horizontal.
Cumulonimbus (Cb)	15 to 6500	*460 to 2000*	+15 to −5	Heavy and dense cloud, with a considerable vertical extent, in the form of a mountain or huge towers. At least part of its upper portion is usually smooth, or fibrous or striated, and nearly always flattened; this part often spreads out in the shape of an anvil or vast plume. Under the base of this cloud, which is often very dark, there are frequently low ragged clouds either merged with it or not, and precipitation, sometimes in the form of virga.

Darwin charged an air gun (without using any pellets) and then allowed it to rest for a while until it acquired the temperature of the room. He then discharged the gun on to the bulb of a thermometer, and its temperature fell. He reasoned that the sole cooling agent must have been the sudden expansion of the air as it was released from compression in the gun, and that a similar reduction in pressure imposed on air which is forced to lift over mountains could account for cloud frequently seen over heights.

John Dalton was aware of Darwin's experiments which may have nudged him towards his own famous work on the behaviour of gases (p.100).

Christian Leopold von Buch (1774–1853), German geologist, expressed the opinion in 1816 that rising currents of one sort or another could probably explain all weather phenomena.

Heinrich Brandes (1777–1834), German mathematician and meteorologist, concentrated his attention on thermal upcurrents as a lift mechanism. He propounded the theory of convection and also realised that convergent air masses with different temperature and humidity characteristics must maintain identifiable boundaries until they have had time to mix together.

James Espy (1785–1860), American meteorologist, focused attention in 1830 on the importance of latent heat of condensation in clouds as a factor prolonging the upward rise of thermal currents.

Jacob Aall Bonnerie Bjerknes, born 1897, Norwegian-American meteorologist, and his father Vilhelm Bjerknes, Norwegian physicist, organised a network of weather observing stations all over Norway during the 1914–18 World War. From the extensive observations which accrued, they developed the 'air mass' principle to account for extensive sheets of

cloud associated with low pressure systems. Air stagnates over the semi-permanent high pressure areas of the world acquiring the characteristic temperature and humidity of the area. When widely different air masses are brought together they form an important convergence zone, in which the warmer air must rise over the colder. They called the boundaries between such air masses 'fronts' and in the 1920s and 1930s analysed the method by which weather battles were fought at these fronts.

Adiabatic is a word that was coined from the Greek language during the years following the major discoveries about the behaviour of gases. *A* means not and *diabaino* pass; so that adiabatic means impassable to heat, occurring without heat entering or leaving the system.

Adiabatic changes of temperature occur without any external sources of heat or cooling when a gas is either compressed or expanded. The temperature of air in a bicycle pump rises because of its compression when the pump is being used. The temperature of gas in a cartridge falls when it is released from compression into a soda syphon. In the atmosphere, lift of air into regions of lower atmospheric pressure causes expansion and fall in temperature, irrespective of the surrounding atmosphere and its temperature. Air which sinks into regions of higher pressure warms because of compression alone.

The dry adiabatic lapse rate is the rate at which dry air cools with height, when forced to rise into regions of lower pressure. It is always the same: 5·4°F fall per 1000 feet rise in height, 1°C fall per 100 metres rise in height. Dry sinking air warms at the same rate.

The saturated adiabatic lapse rate is the rate at which air cools when forced to rise *after* it has cooled to dew point. Condensation releases latent heat to counteract cooling by the adiabatic process and the saturated lapse rate is therefore less than the dry lapse rate by an amount which varies with temperature and the amount of vapour available for condensation. The saturated lapse rate is very small at high air temperatures but increases to approximately the same as the dry lapse rate when air temperature is as low as −40°F (−40°C). The saturated lapse rate throughout the depth of the troposphere averages 3·5°F per 1000 ft (0·6°C per 100 m).

Air in the troposphere also cools with height at an average rate of 3·5°F per 1000 ft (0·6°C per 100 m), but the temperature does not decrease smoothly with height as do temperatures which cool because of forced lift into the atmosphere. The vertical temperature profile of the environment on any day is a result of its past history, sometimes lower than usual sometimes higher than usual.

Buoyant air is air which, when forced to rise from the surface, continues rising within the environment because it is warmer (even after cooling at the adiabatic lapse rates) than its surroundings.

Non buoyant air is air which, after being forced to rise from the surface, stops rising because it becomes colder (after cooling at adiabatic lapse rates) than its surroundings.

An environment is said to be unstable if rising air can remain buoyant to great heights. Air masses which originate in polar regions and are particularly cold aloft, but which have warmed in the lower levels by travelling into lower latitudes, are usually unstable environments.

An environment is said to be stable if rising air quickly becomes non-buoyant. Air masses which originate from tropical regions and are warm aloft but have cooled in the lower levels by travelling into higher latitudes, are usually stable environments.

The most stable air is that beneath an inversion of temperature such as occurs near the ground after a night of intense radiation cooling.

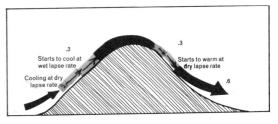

Stable air may be forced upwards over hills or mountains, but it will then descend with equal vigour on the far side in order to comply with the non-buoyancy conditions of the environment. Air lifting on the windward side cools at the dry adiabatic lapse rate till cloud forms, and thereafter cools at the lesser saturated lapse rate. If condensation is jettisoned as water drip on vegetation, drizzle or rain, the water content of the air stream is less when starting descent on the leeward side than when it started ascent on the windward side. Therefore, during descent to leeward, cloud evaporates at a height above the ground which is greater than that at which it formed to windward, assuming the same ground level either side of the mountain. Descending air therefore cools for longer at the higher dry lapse rate and reaches the ground appreciably warmer than when it started ascent to windward.

The föhn effect is the phenomenon of temperature rise in valleys when adiabatic processes act upon stable air forced over high mountains.

The Föhn itself is a warm down-slope wind experienced in the European Alps, but the name has been adopted as a generic description for *all* downslope winds which are warmed by compression. The extent of temperature rise depends upon the amount of condensation jettisoned on windward slopes and on the summit, and also by the height of the mountain slope down which air descends. In the European Alps, deep valleys may experience a sudden temperature rise of between 18° and 27°F (10°–15°C) when a Föhn wind blows, and similar rises occur down mountain barriers in Greenland and in Antarctica. Grytviken, South Georgia, Antarctica, experiences temperature rises of between 18° and 22°F (10°–12°C) in half an hour, or less when the wind is 15–20 mph (24–32 km/h) and from a direction between WSW and SE. The record

January temperature of 65°F (18·3°C) at Aber, Gwynedd, Wales, on 10 January 1971 was probably partly due to föhn effect.

Temperature rise caused by adiabatic compression in föhn situations is not as great a problem as the inevitable accompaniment of falling relative humidity. When the Föhn wind blows in Switzerland, relative humidity may fall to 30 per cent or less, and remain at that low level for perhaps three or four days. This sudden dryness has an aggravating effect upon the human constitution, affecting both the blood circulation and the nervous system. Mental stability suffers and the Föhn wind results in an increased tendency to suicide. Fire risk also increases greatly during these conditions, as the exceptionally dry air sucks moisture greedily from wooden buildings and vegetation. Swiss history is peppered with tales of fire disasters, which have reduced villages to ashes, and householders now have a statutory obligation to fire-watch during Föhn conditions, just as the British had to fire-watch during the war.

Water drop cloud consists of both warm and supercooled drops whose size varies between 1 and 50 microns. Supercooled water drops can exist at temperatures as low as −40°F (−40°C), but an increasing number of ice crystals occur in cloud at temperatures below −4°F (−20°C). There is no visible difference between a warm cloud and a supercooled water drop cloud.

Glaciation is the sudden change from supercooled water drop cloud to ice crystal cloud, and it is accompanied by a more intense white appearance of the cloud. Glaciation occurs when cloud temperature falls to about −22°F (−30°C) or below and the process can be facilitated by seeding, ie introducing cold nuclei into the cloud. Glaciation is an important factor in the production of rain.

Entrainment is the mixing of cloudy air with the clear environment at the edges of a cloud. Some evaporation of water drops occurs, using heat from the boundary air in the process. Consequently, boundary air becomes colder and starts to sink, causing some blurring of the outline of cloud.

There are four major lift mechanisms which explain cloud formation: turbulence, orographic lift, convection and convergence, either separately or together.

Turbulence alone may be sufficient to cause lift and condensation to cloud when the air stream is moist.

Stratus, often called 'scud', is formed in this manner either over the sea, or beneath thicker cloud from which rain or drizzle is falling, or even lifted from wet forests after rain. Radiation fog lifts to cloud in turbulent wind with a speed of more than 10 mph (16 km/h).

Orographic cloud forms when air is forced to lift over hills or mountains, and the cloud may be any of several types:

Hill fog is very moist air which cools to dew point before reaching the top of the hill. Cloud clings to the windward slopes and to the summit, and resembles fog to anyone out on the hill. Hill fog often acquires a local name in places where it occurs frequently. For example, Scotch Mist (in Scotland), Mizzle (in Devon and Cornwall), and the Table Cloth (over Table Mountain, Cape Town, S Africa).

The Table Cloth hanging over Table Mountain, Cape Town, South Africa. (*The Argus*)

Stratocumulus. (D Davies)

Cirrus.

Altocumulus and altostratus.

Cirrostratus. (P Defries)

Cumulonimbus.

Cumulus.

Nacreous cloud, photographed from Inverkeithing, Scotland, on 22 February 1974. (J Imrie)

Orographic cloud formed temporarily in an anabatic (up-slope) wind during early morning on the island of Capri, Italy.

Cumulus formed in the thermals rising from a power station. (N Bibby)

Breaking billow clouds, formed at an altitude where wind direction changes abruptly. (J Cooley)

Scud rising from the top of forest on Frasers Hill, Malaya, after rain. (J C Stone)

A contrail from an aircraft is shadowed upon the top of the cloud sheet below. (P Defries)

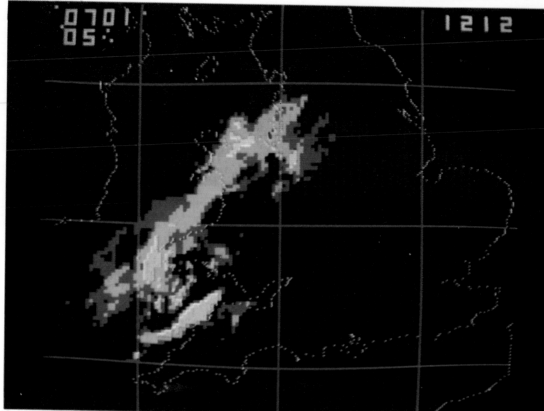

Cold front rainfall on 12 December 1975 at 0701 GMT, as 'seen' by radar signals from two sites, Llandegla near Wrexham, North Wales and Castle Martin, Pembroke, South Wales. The signals have been subjected to digital processing and transmission techniques, and a colour code has been superimposed. Yellow for heavy rain, light blue for moderate rain and dark blue for light rain. (Meteorological Research Unit, Royal Signals and Radar Establishment)

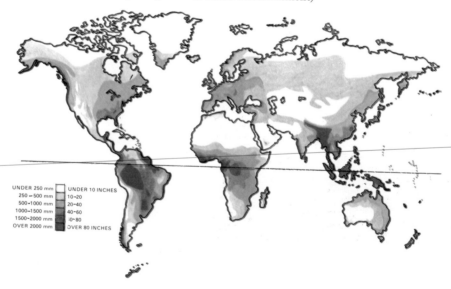

UNDER 250 mm	UNDER 10 INCHES
250 – 500 mm	10–20
500–1000 mm	20–40
1000–1500 mm	40–60
1500–2000 mm	60–80
OVER 2000 mm	OVER 80 INCHES

Average annual rainfall.

Banner cloud on the lee side of the Matterhorn, Switzerland. (Swiss National Tourist Office)

Cap cloud forms when air is comparatively dry and cools to dew point only after being lifted clear of the hill top. A cap cloud remains above the summit, apparently stationary despite the wind, but it is not really the same cloud the whole time. It continually forms on the windward side and disperses on the leeward side within the blowing air stream.

A typical cap cloud is the Helm which sits above Crossfell, Cumbria, in NE winds.

Banner cloud can be seen on the leeward side of high mountain peaks which do not present a large enough surface area to the wind to necessitate air lifting over the top; instead the wind divides either side of the peak. This causes eddying on the leeward side and sufficient turbulent lift to produce cloud in moist air streams. After forming behind the peak it blows with the wind and gradually evaporates, so that it appears like a tapering flag hoisted at the peak.

Well known banner clouds include those which often stream from the Matterhorn (Switzerland), Mount Everest (Nepal), Mount Teide (Tenerife, Canary Islands), and Mount Fujiyama (Japan).

Lenticular wave clouds appear in the crests of an air stream which undulates after being forced over a mountain when the environment air is stable. The cloud tops have a smooth lens shape indicating lack of buoyancy, and the clouds get smaller in each progressive crest as the wave motion dampens down

Rotor cloud is produced in the turbulent eddy to leeward of mountains. The clouds may form a long cylinder of cloud having a horizontal axis parallel to a range of mountains.

The Helm Bar forms to leeward of Crossfell, Cumbria, at a distance up to 4 miles (6 km) away, on occasions when the Helm sits over the top of the range.

Convection clouds, called cumulus, are formed by lift in thermal upcurrents. Rising air cools as it is carried up into the atmosphere, it condenses when dew point is reached and forms a cloud base. Cloud continues building upward so long as the rising air current remains buoyant within its environment. Down

Lenticular clouds piled above each other, looking east towards Los Angeles, California, USA, from Santa Monica. Note the resemblance to some descriptions of 'flying saucers from outer space'! (G Uveges)

currents, in which air warms by compression, balance the rising thermals and this accounts for the clear air between individual clouds.

Cumulonimbus are cumulus clouds which are large enough to produce showers.

Cumulus clouds are diurnal over land; they form when the Sun stimulates thermal activity during the day, and they disperse in the evening when the Sun sets and thermal activity dies out.

The appearance of cumulus varies with each stage of their development. Bases are low and uneven when thermals first start in the morning, because there is unevenness of moisture near the ground, and dew point is reached in the rising air at different levels. Once the lower layers of air have been well stirred up, cloud bases tend to rise and often appear quite level, indicating a homogeneous environment where dew point is reached at the same height above ground everywhere.

Cumulus tops are crisp and billowing so long as vigorous thermals continue to be buoyant, but they become blurred when they reach the limits of buoyancy, and cloud edges start to mix with the environment air and evaporate.

The whole outline of cumulus clouds becomes blurred when thermals cease and the cloud is about to disperse. This happens regularly in the evenings, but also occurs when an upper cloud sheet, such as cirrostratus or altostratus, spreads across the sky and cuts off heat from the Sun before the normal sunset time. Premature disappearance of cumulus, which cannot be explained by either of these two facts, probably indicates increasing stability of the atmosphere and development of a high pressure system.

Dispersing cumulus.

No cumulus clouds occur on a sunny day, when the environment is very stable and thermals reach the limit of buoyancy before the rising air has had time to cool to dew point.

Cumulus clouds which form over the sea are not diurnal because the thermal trigger is not the Sun, but a sea surface which gets progressively warmer with latitude. The clouds have the same appearance as those over land, but they change according to distance rather than time of day. Cold air which is only starting to travel towards the equator only experiences sufficient convection to produce small cumulus with low blurred bases; but these grow to towering clouds by the time the air stream has travelled towards the equator through 20–30° of latitude over warming sea. Cumulus clouds over the sea do not die out at night except when they cross over a land surface which is colder than the sea. However, they do not disperse immediately the thermal source is cut off, and therefore coastal areas often have convection cloud at night when the wind blows off the sea even though inland areas are cloud free.

A street of cumulus is a procession of clouds down-wind of a pronounced thermal source, and a cluster of clouds in an otherwise clear sky over the sea indicates an island or peninsula which is acting as a thermal source.

The size of cumulus clouds varies according to their vertical development. On days when rising air manages to cool to dew point and form cloud, but a stable environment limits vertical development, the sky becomes full of small-based shallow clouds, looking like tufts of cotton wool. When the air in the surrounding environment is moderately unstable, cloud tops develop higher and bases broaden out until only a few clouds, looking more like large cauliflowers, manage to fill the whole sky within view. On days with very unstable air streams, cumulus tops may grow to several miles high, and the base of one cloud may be broad enough to fill the overhead sky for perhaps 15 minutes or half an hour while it travels past. When a cumulus develops to such a large size it is ready to produce a shower and is called a **cumulonimbus**.

Anvil cloud is the glaciated top of a cumulonimbus which has flattened out at the limit of buoyancy, usually near the tropopause. There the winds are stronger than at lower levels, and the ice crystal cloud gets drawn out into the projecting shape of an anvil.

The life of an individual cumulus is short. A small cumulus may have an identifiable life of 5–15 minutes before being superseded by another. A cumulonimbus may have a life span of 45 minutes or one hour before losing separ-

Developing cumulonimbus and formation of anvil top, taken at three minute intervals.

ate identity. The water droplet part of the cloud then disperses or merges with another cloud developing in an adjacent active thermal, while the glaciated top of ice crystals often persists for much longer.

The tallest cumulus occur in summer in equatorial latitudes because there the Sun is most powerful and the tropopause is highest. Therefore there is a very large difference between surface air temperature and the temperature of air near the tropopause, and consequently great instability of the atmosphere. An abundance of vapour in rising air provides much latent heat of condensation to prolong buoyancy. Cumulus frequently develop to 9 miles (15 km) and heights of 11 miles (18 km) have been known.

The most modest maximum cumulus tops occur in very low latitudes where the tropopause is low and the cold air contains little water vapour available for condensation and the release of latent heat. Thermals over land are mainly confined to areas with bare rock surface, and most cumulus activity occurs when particularly cold air blows over ice-free water, especially over warm currents. Cumulus clouds cannot remain buoyant to the tropopause and rarely attain heights of more than 2–4 miles (3–6 km).

In Antarctica cumulus tops have not been noted higher than 1·5 miles (2·5 km).

The tallest cumulus in temperate latitudes usually occur over land in spring, when the Sun is high enough to heat the land rapidly but air streams of polar origin are still very cold aloft. Cumulus may then reach heights up to 8 miles (13 km). When air is particularly moist because of a long track over the sea, cumulus may be so frequent and large that the bases merge, with only fleeting glimpses of blue sky between one cumulus and another. Over the sea, cumulus in temperate latitudes attain maximum heights in autumn when sea temperature is at its highest and the vapour content of air abundant.

Convergence cloud occurs when air streams with different characteristics meet, causing the warmer air to lift over the colder and cool to dew point.

A sea breeze front exists when a light pressure wind blows off-shore, but the sea breeze is strong enough to maintain its separate identity in the opposite direction. The incoming cold air from the sea undercuts the warm air over the land, which rises and cools to form a line of shallow cloud. If the sea breeze is much stronger than the pressure wind, the frontal cloud may be driven inland, giving visible indication of impending change in surface wind. Glider pilots look for a sea breeze front to guide them to rising air currents.

Convergence cloud can occur in valleys running across mountain barriers which separate airs of different characteristics. A well-known example occurs between the Sierra Nevada Mountains and the Tehachapi Mountains in California, USA. Cool breezes blowing up the mountain sides from the west meet with warm air from the Mojave Desert at the eastern end of a pass to form a horizontal cylindrical roll of turbulent cloud called the 'Tehachapi Roll Cloud'.

Convergence of airs along a trough of low pressure or towards the centre of a depression results in cloud which has considerable vertical depth.

The Inter Tropical Convergence Zone occurs where the north east trade winds of the northern hemisphere converge near the equator with the south east trade winds of the southern hemisphere. Both trade winds blow round semi-permanent high pressure belts which move fitfully between latitudes 20° and 50°. Convergence results in considerable cloud even though the characteristics of the two air streams on the equatorial side of these pressure belts are not very different.

The polar fronts are caused by convergence of warm air from the non-equatorial side of

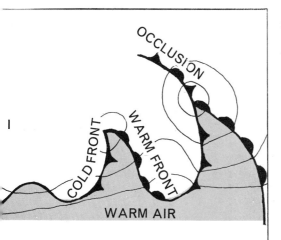

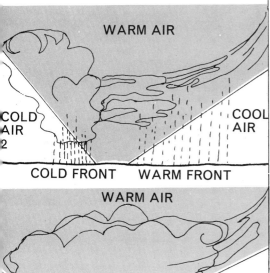

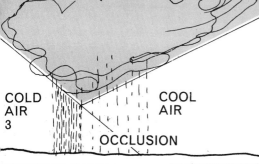

Plan view (1) and vertical cross sections (2) and (3) of typical frontal systems.

the subtropical high pressure belts with very much colder air from polar regions. The air masses have very different temperatures and extensive cloud results from the lift and undercutting which ensues.

Wave motion along the polar fronts results in travelling depressions. These carry along with them warm air which becomes caught in a pincers' squeeze between cold air behind, and cool air ahead. The warm air makes the only escape possible, by slithering forwards over the cool air ahead, and by lifting vigorously when undercut by the cold air at the rear.

A warm front is the surface boundary between warm air and cool air ahead. It is drawn on weather charts either as a red line or as a black line with semicircles on the side towards which the front is advancing.

A cold front is the surface boundary between warm air and pursuing cold air. On charts it is drawn as a blue line or as a black line with teeth on the side towards which the front is advancing.

The warm sector is the fold of warm air between the cold and warm fronts.

A cold front travels faster than a warm front, eventually overtaking it. The warm sector is then lifted off the surface and the fronts are said to be occluded. An active cold front may travel at 30 mph (50 km/h), but a trailing occlusion in a trough may remain stationary.

An occlusion is the surface boundary between new cold air and modified cool air ahead. It is drawn on weather charts as a purple line, or as a black line with alternating semicircles and teeth on the side towards which the occlusion is advancing.

Cloud sequence ahead of a surface warm front:
Wispy cirrus at 400–600 miles (650–950 km) distance, consolidating to a continuous film of cirrus which dims the Sun or Moon, and sometimes encircles them with haloes.

Cloud at a cold front advancing on Christchurch, New Zealand, from the south on 12 November 1975. Within minutes of this picture being taken torrential rain fell with hail and lightning. (M J Hammersley)

Continuous alto stratus at 250–300 miles (400–500 km) distance obscuring and then hiding the Sun or Moon, and giving rain or snow.

Nimbostratus with very low patches near the surface warm front.

Cloud in the warm sector:
Little high or medium level cloud.
Small cumulus in spring or summer in the stable warm environment.
Low stratus in autumn or winter caused by turbulence in moist air cooling over cold ground

Cloud in vicinity of cold front:
Towering cumulonimbus causing heavy showers.

All fronts are empirical descriptions of what actually happens. The reasons *why* they happen lies in complex behaviour of the atmosphere at all levels and is not entirely under-
stood. Fronts, like photographs of human beings, are useful guides for recognition purposes, but cannot be relied upon to indicate unvarying and consistent behaviour. Fronts and the depressions with which they are often associated may speed up, intensify, or apparently die for no known reason.

Other cloud variations on one or more of the lift and descent themes:

Stratocumulus forms when cumulus clouds reach a stable layer and then spread sideways into a continuous sheet.

Cellular clouds occur because of convection within a shallow cloud sheet. The top of the layer cools because of radiation from the top surface, the lower surface warms because it absorbs long wave radiation from the ground. This is why stratocumulus often breaks up into irregular pancake shapes prior to dispersal.

ileus cloud. (M J Hammersley)

Mackerel cloud consists of small cells of cirrocumulus or altocumulus caused by convection within a thin sheet of cloud, and arranged symmetrically often by wave motion into regular patterns resembling mackerel skin.

Billow clouds are high or medium level rolls of cloud arranged across the direction of the wind. They form in wave motion or turbulence between adjacent air streams moving at different speeds or in different directions.

Pileus cloud is a smooth cap cloud which forms in a stable layer above a cumulus when air is temporarily forced upwards by the vigorous thermal below.

Contrails (abbreviation for condensation trails) are high clouds which form in straight lines behind aircraft because of water vapour ejected from the engines. When the environment is very dry, contrails disperse quickly, but when air already has a high humidity the cloud can persist for long periods. A succession of persistent contrails may merge together to form a large sheet of cloud obscuring the Sun.

Distrails (abbreviation for dissipation trails) are paths of clear air evaporated from cloud by the passage of aircraft when the heat from the engines is a more important factor than the emission of water vapour.

Virga.

A fallstreak hole is formed in cloud when the passage of an aircraft induces freezing of some of the super-cooled drops which then fall from the cloud. The circular shape of such a distrail is caused by the chain reaction of freezing amongst other super-cooled drops radially outwards from the initial crystallisation.

Virga are streaks of ice crystal cloud or water drops which trail below the main base of a cloud, but evaporate before reaching the surface.

Hurricane clouds are very deep cumulonimbus formed in the spiralling winds towards the centre of a hurricane. Near the centre, winds rotate in almost circular fashion at all levels without convergence at surface level towards the centre. Balancing downcurrents from the top of the cumulonimbus are therefore able to spill downwards into the centre, causing air to warm by subsidence and cloud to evaporate in the eye.

A funnel cloud forms round the core of a tornado or water spout, the wide part of the funnel merging into the base of a cumulonimbus and the thinner part tapering downwards, and sometimes reaching the surface.

Castellanus (Latin *castellum:* castle) are cumulus clouds which develop rapidly in an unstable layer of air above a lower stable level.

Castellanus cloud developing upwards over mountains. (R G Holford)

It requires excessive build up of heat in the lower layer or the additional forced lift over mountains to break down the barrier between the two layers. Castellanus get their name from their turreted appearance. Their high bases are often obscured by the accumulated haze of a heat wave.

Nacreous clouds, often called 'mother of pearl' clouds because of their irridescence, form in the stratosphere and are visible at night when illuminated against a dark sky by the Sun from below the horizon. They have a lenticular shape, and result from wave motion over mountains which is transmitted throughout the troposphere and into the stratosphere. This occurs when the wind is consistent with height throughout the troposphere.

Nacreous clouds are frequently sighted in Antarctica where there is often deep cold air of consistent direction at all heights and plenty of mountains to induce wave motion. These clouds were first described in 1911 by Sir George Simpson, when he was a meteorologist with Scott's last expedition. He drew attention to the fact that the clouds did not produce halo phenomena and they were therefore unlikely to consist of ice crystals. Subsequent observations have confirmed that

Right:
9 October 1976: depressions with associated cloud systems affected western Europe while south eastern Europe was dominated by an anticyclone. The situation at 1200 GMT, indicated by the inset chart, developed into that photographed at 2001 GMT on infra red wavelength by satellite NOAA 5. Frontal cloud had just cleared Iceland (top centre) and Lisbon, Portugal (left of lower centre); cumulus clouds were streaming southwards over the Atlantic east of Greenland (top left), while northern England and southern Scotland (right of centre) were the only cloudless areas of the British Isles. The lower right portion of the picture indicates clearly the typical temperature pattern of a cloudless anticyclonic night in early autumn. The Mediterranean (dark tone) was warmer than the land, the mountain heights (lightest tones) were colder than the plains. The rivers draining from the European Alps into the Swiss lakes are as clearly visible as if etched in ink. (Satellite picture received at Dundee University)

nacreous clouds probably consist of super-cooled water droplets, despite the fact that air temperatures at the altitudes 11–18 miles (18–30 km) are usually as low as $-112°F$ ($-80°C$). It is not known why the drops can remain liquid at such low temperatures; possibly it is because of lack of nuclei to induce freezing, or because the droplets only exist for a very brief period in the crest of the wave motion.

Nacreous clouds have been seen on several occasions over Scotland, usually in consistent deep cold air streams at the rear of a depression, and were photographed successfully from Inverkeithing, Fife, on 22 February 1974, by Mrs Imrie. The clouds formed in the crests of wave motion to the lee of the Scottish Highlands.

Noctilucent clouds are seen in latitudes higher than 50°, usually about midnight, and they look rather like cirrostratus clouds with a blue or yellow tinge. They appear to form at altitudes of about 50 miles (80 km) and travel north eastwards at 100–300 mph (160–480 km/h), but it is not yet known if they consist of ice crystals or dust. A network of observers in Western Europe and the Atlantic, between areas approximately 50–60° N, report sightings of noctilucent clouds to the Department of Meteorology at Edinburgh University, Scotland. Positive sightings in each year 1964–76 numbered 23, 21, 24, 34, 32, 21, 15, 18, 22, 28, 41, 38 and 36. In the Shetland Islands, sightings are only one or two a year, because the long hours of daylight prevent the clouds being recognised at the peak of the observing season.

Smoke from a factory drifts almost horizontally downwind, indicating stable air with little vertical air movement.

CHAPTER 10

RAIN

Selene, moon goddess and map of world rainfall.

Precipitation is the collective name given to drizzle, rain, snow, sleet or hail which falls out of clouds. By 1815 precipitation was recognised as merely one phase in the continual re-cycling of the world's fixed supply of water. Vapour in the air condenses as dew, fog or cloud; then falls from the clouds as precipitation, and goes into temporary storage upon or under the ground, in streams, rivers and seas until evaporated once again into air as pure water, leaving its salts and impurities behind. There remained the question of how cloud droplets which were suspended in the air managed to acquire a large enough size to fall to the ground.

James Hutton, Scottish geologist (p. 100), thought that rain resulted from the mixture of air streams with different temperature and humidity – but this only produces water drops in suspension. Even the lift mechanisms producing deep clouds are not sufficient to explain rain, and the theories which have evolved in the 20th century are still not entirely adequate.

One important clue resulted from some careful study of cloud behaviour. Individual cumulus clouds which are well separated from their neighbours can often be observed to their full vertical extent. Their tops gleam particularly white in the sunshine when they become glaciated, and in the 1920s it was noted that glaciation was frequently followed by rain.

Tor Harold Percival Bergeron, Swedish meteorologist, born 1891, suggested in 1933 that the presence of ice crystals in cloud was a necessary precondition for rain; and the idea was further developed by Walter Findeisen (1909–45), a German physicist.

The Bergeron-Findeisen theory of rain concentrated on the fact that the saturated vapour pressure over ice is less than the saturated vapour pressure over water:

A large cloud contains supercooled water drops, therefore saturation vapour pressure exists with regard to water.

Ice crystals introduced into such a cloud experience *super*saturated vapour pressure with regard to ice, and therefore grow because of deposition from the immediate environment.

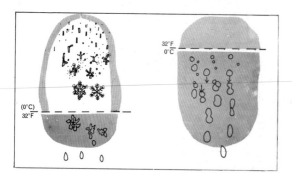

Left: The Bergeron Theory, that ice crystals grow at the expense of super cooled water drops.
Right: The Langmuir Theory, that large water drops overtake smaller drops and coalesce.

The deposition of crystals releases latent heat which lowers the relative humidity with respect to water, and permits evaporation from adjacent supercooled drops.

Ice crystals grow at the expense of supercooled drops till the cloud becomes glaciated and crystals coalesce because of collisions within the cloud.

When they are large enough they fall as snow against the rising air currents within the cloud.

Snow melts to rain soon after the descending flakes reach surroundings which have a higher temperature than 32°F (0°C). Hence the only condition that precipitation should reach ground as rain, is that the air temperature near ground level should be above freezing.

The Bergeron theory was not entirely confirmed by empirical observations because rain sometimes falls from warm clouds containing no ice crystals; so the following theory gained credence:

Irving Langmuir (1881–1957), American physicist and Nobel Prize winner, drew attention to the variety of size drops which can exist in a water cloud because of different sizes of nuclei present. Water drops accelerate under the force of gravity until a certain **terminal velocity** is achieved, when the weight of the drop is counterbalanced by the upthrust of rising air and frictional drag. Terminal velocity is greater for large drops than for small drops, which may hardly achieve any speed at all.

The Langmuir Chain-Reaction theory suggests that large water drops overtake slower small drops and coalesce on collision, rather like motor traffic would collide if there were no controlling division into fast and slow lanes. The resultant large drops acquire higher terminal velocity and gather up more drops in the process until they fall as rain.

Drizzle drops have radius 0·002–0·02 in (0·05–0·5 mm), reach a terminal velocity 2·3–6·6 ft/s (0·7–2·0 m/s) and are just heavy enough to fall out of cloud.

Rain drops have radius 0·02–0·1 in (0·5–2·5 mm) and reach terminal velocity 12·8–30 ft/s (3·9–9·1 m/s). Drops with radius larger than 0·1 in (2·5 mm) usually break up under aerodynamical forces.

Rain is measured in linear units, and gives the depth of rain which would cover absolutely flat impermeable ground in a specified period. Such natural surfaces do not exist, so sample rainfalls are collected in graduated vessels. (The results include melted hail or snow.)

42 rain gauges in a garden at Reading, Berkshire. Frontispiece to the 1868 edition of *British rainfall.*

A very early rain gauge was described in an Indian manuscript dating from 400 BC. It was a simple bowl about 18 in (450 mm) in diameter, and the writer suggested that sowing of seeds should be regulated according to the amount of rain registered in the bowl.

The first tipping bucket rain gauge which emptied itself when full, was made in 1662 by Sir Christopher Wren (1632–1723), the English architect. The design was later perfected by William Henry Dines (1855–1927), the English meteorologist.

Richard Townley, of Townley near Burnley, Lancashire, was the first person to keep a continuous record of rainfall in Great Britain, between the years 1677–1703.

George James Symons (1838–1900) was the first person to appreciate the value of a rainfall review over the whole country. His interest was stimulated by the drought years of 1854–8, and he started collecting rainfall statistics from observers in England and Wales. He had already published figures from 168 observers when he joined the Meteorological department of the Board of Trade in 1860. He extended his chain of observers to embrace the whole of the British Isles, and in 1863 resigned his job with the Board of Trade in order to devote himself entirely to rainfall work.

The British Rainfall Organisation was the title given to the body of 1500 rainfall observers who were contributing to Symons' annual publication *British Rainfall* at the time of his death in 1900. The organisation was taken over by the Meteorological Office in 1919 and the number of observers is now approximately 7000. Of these, one third are private individuals, reporting either to the Meteorological Office or to various water authorities. One family alone provided a continuous daily record of rainfall for 98 years, at Belleek, County Fermanagh, Ireland. John Beacom commenced readings in April 1879, his nephew Thomas Beacom, Jnr, took over in 1920, and when he died in 1950 his wife Lucy

continued with the observations. Lucy's daughter Margaret helped her mother in latter years when her eyesight was failing, and Margaret continued reporting rainfall after her mother died in 1973. Margaret Beacom died in hospital in February 1977, and the rainfall station disappeared from the climatological lists just short of completing its centenary.

Accurate rainfall measurement is not as easy as it might seem, a suspicion which was first confirmed by G. Heberden in 1769. He mounted a rain gauge on a roof 30 ft (9 m) high, and discovered that it caught only 80 per cent as much rain as a gauge set at ground level. A gauge on top of a 150 ft (45 m) tower caught only half the amount of rain that was collected at ground level. The discrepancy in rainfall was caused by wind eddies at the greater heights.

Rain gauge design and exposure became an absorbing hobby for many people, as exemplified by the Rev. C M Griffith whose garden at Reading, Berkshire, illustrates the 1868 edition of *British Rainfall*. It contains 42 gauges of different types and variously sited!

A natural syphon rain gauge was first patented by F L Halliwell in 1920. Rain falls through a funnel into a vessel, in which a float bearing a rod and pen traces on a rotating chart drum as it rises on the surface of the rainwater. Water is discharged by a syphoning tube when the container is full.

The standard specification for a modern rain-gauge is a funnel 5 in or 8 in (125 mm or 200 mm) in diameter with a sharp edged rim, bevelled outside to prevent run back into the funnel, and with walls falling vertically inside. The tube to the container which collects rain is narrow in order to minimise evaporation of rain already collected. The height of the rim above ground is 11·8 in (300 mm) which is enough to prevent splashback from the ground, but not enough to cause undue wind eddying. Exposure must be open on all sides.

Five-inch Snowdon type rain gauge made of copper and brass. (J Edson)

Rain falls unevenly, particularly from cumulonimbus clouds which have erratic but often strong vertical currents which have been known to reach 25 mph (40 km/h). Therefore it is not possible to interpolate with accuracy between two rain gauges very distant from each other to obtain a reliable estimate of rain at some intermediary place. A close network of cheap rain-gauges, even at the expense of some inaccuracies, gives a better picture of total rainfall than a sparse network of more expensive instruments.

Rain which is actually falling can be detected by radar and measured according to the echo received from the raindrops, which increases with the diameter of the drops. Radar has the special advantages of being able to give immediate warning of abnormal rainfalls which could cause flash floods.

A rain day is a period of 24 hours, usually starting 0900 h, GMT, during which 0·01 in (0·2 mm) of rain falls.

Point rainfall is the quantity of rain measured at one particular place. Rainfall quoted for a large area is the average of the various point rainfalls measured within the area.

Intensity of rain is classified as:

light – if falling at less than 0·02 in/h (0·5 mm/h)

moderate – if falling at 0·02–0·16 in/h (0·5–4 mm/h)

heavy – if falling at more than 0·16 in/h (4 mm/h)

A rain shadow is an area of below average rainfall on the leeward side of mountains which obstruct rain bearing winds. The forced ascent of air over the mountains intensifies rain on the windward slopes and on the summit, so that air is consequently drier when it starts its descent again down the leeward slopes. The drying out process is accentuated down steep mountains by adiabatic warming, so that rain may be almost unknown in some regions. The Atacama desert in Chile, along the western coast of South America is a rain shadow desert because prevailing winds are from the interior beyond the Bolivian Andes mountains.

Death Valley in California, USA, has a meagre 1·7 in (43·2 mm) mean annual rainfall, whereas San Francisco, only 250 miles (400 km) away but on the prevailing windward side of the mountains, manages an average rainfall of 22 in (559 mm). The Pacific coast about 800 miles (1290 km) to the north west receives approximately 140–150 in (3560–3800 mm) of rain per annum.

The rain bearing clouds are deep cumulonimbus and thick altostratus which occur separately or together in low pressure systems. Rainfall statistics therefore mirror the transient, seasonal or permanent location of low pressure, as well as the latitude and topography of an area. The lower the latitude, the greater the amount of vapour available for precipitation in warm air which has travelled far across the sea. The higher the mountain barrier, the greater the exaggeration of the meteorological factors which are squeezing the vapour out of air.

The most consistently wet place in the world is Mount Wai-'ale-'ale on the island of Kauai, Hawaiian Islands. The mountain is 5148 ft (1569 m) high and the island is situated at latitude 20° N, on the fringe of the equatorial low pressure convergence zone, at longitude 156° W, in the middle of the Pacific Ocean, and therefore constantly enveloped in warm moist air.

Rain falls on average 335 days per annum, sometimes as often as 350 days.

THE HIGHEST MEAN ANNUAL POINT RAINFALLS RECORDED	in	mm
Mt Wai-'ale-'ale, Kauai, Hawaii, 5148 ft (1569 m)	451	11 455
Cherrapungi, Meghalaya, India, site at 4307 ft (1313 m)	426	10 820
5-year mean at 3000 ft (915 m)	498	12 649

These annual totals are not significantly different from each other, nor do they exclude the likelihood that there are other wetter mountain tops where no rain-gauges are situated. The figures are not representative of the populated areas of the regions. Sea-level areas in Kauai only a few miles away from Mount Wai-'ale-'ale have as little as 20 in (500 mm) rain per annum.

The significant difference between the rain at Mount Wai-'ale-'ale and at Cherrapungi is that the former occurs all through the year, but the latter occurs mainly in the summer monsoon period. For that reason Cherrapungi holds all records for point rainfalls during long periods.

Record point rainfalls for periods of 15 days or more. Cherrapungi, on the crest of the southern range of the Khasi Hills, Meghalaya, India, receives rain in late spring or

summer during the SW monsoon. Lift over mountains is accentuated by additional squeeze through deep constricting valleys.

Cherrapungi	Point rainfall in	mm
2 consecutive calendar years 1860, 1861	1605	40 767
12 months (some overlapping of monsoon seasons)		
1 Aug 1860–31 July 1861	1042	26 467
1 calendar year 1861	905	22 987
6 months April–Sept 1861	884	22 454
31 days July 1861	366	9 296
15 days 24 June–8 July 1931	189	4 801

Record point rainfalls for periods between eight days and nine hours occurred on La Réunion Island, 400 miles (650 km) east of Madagascar in the Indian Ocean. The island is very mountainous and steep slopes up to 10 000 ft (3300 m) contain deep valleys up which wind can funnel fiercely giving extra lift to moist air. Minimum sea temperature, in March, is about 81°F (27°C) so there is always an abundance of moist warm air, and the heaviest rainfalls occur with tropical cyclones between November and May. Two such cyclones produced record point rainfalls at two reporting stations on the island.

Le Réunion Island	days	date	Point rainfall in	mm
Cilaos	8	11–19 Mar 1952	163	4140
	4	14–18 Mar 1952	138	3505
	2	15–17 Mar 1952	98	2489
	hours			
	24	15–16 Mar 1952	74	1880
Belouve	18	28 Feb 1964	66	1676
	12	28 Feb 1964	53	1346
	9	28 Feb 1964	43	1092

Seasonal rainfall with monsoon winds. *India* receives rain during the summer SW monsoon which blows across the Indian Ocean from the far side of the equator and into the low-pressure area over the warm continent. Rain starts at the end of May and continues for two to three months with only brief respites, often augmented by tropical cyclones.

Mean annual rainfall:

Delhi: 25·2 in (640 mm) of which 85 per cent falls between June and September.

Bombay: 71·2 in (1800 mm) of which 98 per cent falls between June and September.

Calcutta: 63·0 in (1600 mm) of which 84 per cent falls between May and October.

Northern Australia gets rain with the summer NW monsoon.

Darwin mean annual rainfall is 58·7 in (1491 mm), of which 80 per cent falls between December and March.

Chile, S America, has some winter rain.

Valparaiso, mean annual rainfall is 19·9 in (505 mm), of which 91 per cent falls between May and September.

A combination of moist monsoon wind, convergence and even a remote hurricane can produce rainfall which is exceptional even for wet regions. The Island of Luzon, Philippines, Pacific Ocean, experienced such a deluge in the middle of July 1972 when the vigorous typhoon *Rita* was 1500 miles (2400 km) away, just south west of Japan. Statistics for Manila and Mia Pasay City show that two to three times the average monthly rainfall fell during four days in the middle of the month, which had already been exceptionally wet. Drainage facilities were quite inadequate in such circumstances and disastrous flooding occurred.

| | Manila Port | | M⁷ Pasay City | |
	in	mm	in	mm
Average July	13·9	354·3	12·0	306·2
1–16 July 1972	10·2	261·1	9·8	249·4
17–21 July 1972	34·8	886·3	39·9*	1014·9*
22–31 July 1972	23·7	604·1	21·8	554·5
Total July 1972	68·9	1751·5	71·4	1813·8

* 18·6 in (472·4 mm) fell during 20 July.

Tropical cyclones and hurricanes often produce exceptionally heavy rain, particularly when they reach a coast and are influenced by heating of the land or by uplift over moun-

tains. The ferocity of the wind may then start to wane, but rain often intensifies.

Camille, 20 August 1969, bucketed 25–28 in (635–710 mm) of rain in eight hours over places in Virginia, USA, a couple of days after the hurricane had arrived at the Mississippi coast. Devastating damage was caused above ground and there was much erosion in underground caves by flood water. *Camille* caused more than 256 deaths, 151 in Virginia alone, and ranked as the most destructive hurricane, causing damage worth $1.42 billion.

Connie and *Diane*, 12–19 August 1955, poured 19 in (480 mm) rain into rivers from Virginia to Massachusetts, USA, causing widespread floods. These were worst in the Delaware Valley and Connecticut, where 187 lives were lost. Westfield, Massachusetts, received 19·4 in (493 mm) rain on 18–19 August.

Flora, 4–7 October 1963, jettisoned more than 60 in (1524 mm) rain on some places in Jamaica, West Indies. Six stations recorded more than 20 in (508 mm) in one day.

These amounts were more than twice the amounts which were precipitated from *Gilda* in four days 15–18 October 1973, but were probably equal to amounts which fell from a hurricane in 1909 for which details are not available.

Chance hurricanes give exceptional rainfalls even in normally arid country. Two hurricanes on average develop each year over the Arabian Sea, and 27 October 1972 was the first occasion for 75 years that such a storm travelled along the Gulf of Aden. There it caused 9 in (229 mm) of rain in Djibouti, (mean annual rainfall 5 in (127 mm)) and 6 in (152 mm) in Aden, (mean annual rainfall 1 in (25 mm)).

Exceptional point rainfalls of very short duration usually occur from individual cumulonimbus. These have strong vertical currents against which only the largest water drops can battle to reach ground, but they also have a small base area compared with the organised clouds of monsoon regimes, hurricanes and depressions. Such clouds develop in most parts of the world when conditions are unstable, and spectacular point rainfalls are therefore widely spread.

	Duration of rain minutes	date	Point rainfall in	mm
Holt, Montana, USA	42	22 June 1947	12·0	305
Curtea-de-Arges, Roumania	20	7 July 1889	8·10	206
Plumb Point, Jamaica	15	12 May 1916	7·80	198
Fussen, Bavaria	8	15 May 1920	4·96	126
Unionville, Maryland, USA	1	4 July 1956	1·23	31

Every possible check was made before accepting the Unionville 1 minute fall which was phenomenal (recorded on a Freiz Universal rain-gauge). Nevertheless, the storm produced only 2·84 in (72·1 mm) in 50 minutes which is considerably less than many recorded 50 minute falls. It is reasonable to suppose that other places may have had similar exceptional 1 minute falls without having the luck of a rain-gauge positioned to record them.

The most regular daily showers from cumulonimbus occur over land in equatorial regions, where there are consistent air masses, abundant vapour content in warm air and maximum solar radiation. In the basin of the Amazon River, Brazil, for instance, convection clouds build up regularly each morning, release heavy showers for a couple of hours in late afternoon and then disperse. The region never has less than 60 in (1520 mm) rain per annum and usually has 180 in (4570 mm).

Consistently light showers are characteristic of countries within the Arctic and Antarctic circle, where there is little vapour content in the cold air, and cumulonimbus tops do not reach great heights.

In temperate latitudes, showers are most frequent in unstable air streams moving from polar regions into warmer latitudes. They are heaviest over land during spring, when polar air streams are still at their coldest but land masses warm rapidly in the Sun. They are heaviest over the sea during autumn when the sea is at its warmest and provides the best heating source.

British rainfall viewed in the context of world extremes is not as heavy or prolonged as it is reputed to be. A wet day is defined as one which has 0·04 in (1 mm) rain. The wettest days of the year yield, on average,

1 in (25 mm) in south east England
2 in (50 mm) in hilly country in the west and north British Isles
3 in (75 mm) in high mountains in west and north British Isles.

Showers from cumulonimbus in deep unstable air are most frequent in spring; heavy downpours from cumulonimbus clouds in upper layers of unstable air occur mainly in summer; and rain from depressions is generally more frequent in winter than in summer. The following statistics reveal that these general rules merely exist to be broken!

AVERAGE FREQUENCY OF RAIN DAYS PER ANNUM

West Ireland, west and central Scotland, Shetland Isles	250
South west England, Wales and north England, central and east Ireland	200
Midlands, south and east England, east Scotland	175

GREATEST FREQUENCY OF RAIN DAYS

Ballynahinch, Galway, Rep. of Ireland in 1923	309

ANNUAL RAINFALL

	Average in	mm	Exceptional year	in	mm
Scotland	55·9	1420	1872	67·5	1715
N Ireland	42·5	1080	1928	51·1	1300
England and Wales	35·6	905	1872	50·7	1288

Note that none of these exceptional rainfalls *doubles* the mean rainfall, as has happened at the mountainous monsoon station at Cherrapungi.

Location of the 50 heaviest 2-hour rainfalls in Britain in 20th century:

Southern England	34
Midlands and N England	9
Wales	4
Scotland	2
N Ireland	1

Only two of these exceptional rainfalls occurred outside the warmer months of May–September, and those both occurred in October. The figures indicate that although northern mountainous areas of the British Isles have the highest annual rainfall, it is because they are most frequently near the centres of fast moving depressions.

Short period rainfalls happen mainly in southern areas where there is greatest thermal activity in summer, often accentuated by convergence in troughs of low pressure.

Freezing rain turns into **glazed frost,** and occurs during the transition period from a cold winter spell, usually high pressure, to a mild low pressure system, bringing frontal cloud. Rain falls from the advancing upper cloud into air near the ground which still has temperatures below freezing. The rain freezes on contact with all cold surfaces, making roads like ice rinks, and coating shrubs, telegraph wires, and all other exposed surfaces, in sheaths of ice. The condition usually lasts only a short time until the warm front arrives to engulf everything in a more mild air. Occasionally, high pressure re-asserts itself and blocks the advance of the mild air, prolonging the duration of freezing rain, which builds into deadly loads of ice.

Freezing rain fell over southern England and Wales from 27 January to 3 February 1940. Glazed frost accumulated until branches of old trees snapped off, supple trees bent to the ground, where they became welded by ice, and telegraph poles collapsed under the weight of tons of ice. Ponies on Plynlimon, Wales, were frozen to death in coffins of ice, and millions of birds died.

Rain sometimes carries extraneous matter, which has been swept aloft by strong air currents in shower clouds. Results are bizarre and often unpleasant.

Red rain is usually coloured by sand or dust transported on high level winds. In Europe such pollution usually originates from the Sahara desert in North Africa. Red rain fell in England on 21 and 22 February 1903, and there was a phenomenal fall of coloured precipitation in Switzerland on 14 October 1755: 9 in (225 mm) of blood red rain fell at Locarno, of which 1 in (25 mm) was estimated to be dust. Rain fell over an area of approximately 360 sq miles (936 km^2) and over the heights of the Alps the precipitation lay as red snow.

Rain brought minnow and smooth tailed sticklebacks to ground on 9 February 1859 at Aberdare, Glamorgan, during the middle of the morning. There were two showers at 10 minute intervals, after which the ground was covered with fish for an area measuring about 240 × 36 ft (80 × 12 m).

Rain carried spiders, of a species not known locally, to an area of Hungary in 1922.

A fall of maggots accompanied a heavy storm at Acapulco, Mexico, on 5 October 1968. Awnings, cockpits and dinghies assembled for the Olympics Yachting events were littered with maggots about 1 in (25 mm) long.

Trees in Gloucestershire weighed down with glazed frost in the first week of February 1940. (Crown copyright)

EXTREME RAINFALLS, ENGLAND AND WALES, SINCE 1873

Seasonal rainfalls

	Highest			Lowest		
	date	in	mm	date	in	mm
Winter (Dec–Feb)	1915	17·4	442·0	1964	3·3	83·8
Spring (Mar–May)	1947	12·1	307·3	1893	2·8	71·1
Summer (June–Aug)	1912	15·9	403·9	1976	3·1	77·0
Autumn (Sept–Nov)	1960	17·3	439·4	1947	5·7	144·8

Note that none of these exceptionally wet seasons occurred in 1872, which was the wettest year on record.

Monthly rainfalls

		Highest				Lowest	
		in	mm			in	mm
Oct	1903	8·3	210·8	Feb	1891	0·1	2·5
Dec	1914	8·0	203·2	June	1925	0·1	2·5
Nov	1929	7·7	195·6	Mar	1929	0·3	7·6
Aug	1912	7·3	185·4	April	1912	0·3	7·6
*Sept	1918	7·2	182·9	April	1938	0·3	7·6
Jan	1948	7·0	178·0	Sept	1959	0·3	7·6

* September 1976 rainfall was 6·2 in (160 mm), making the month the second wettest September on record.

Point rainfalls

	date	hrs	in	mm
Martinstown, Dorset	18 July 1955	15	11	279
Long Barrow, Exmoor	15 Aug 1952	12	8·9	228
Horncastle, Lincs	7 Oct 1960	5	7·2	182
Cannington, Somerset	16 Aug 1924	4½	8·5	216
Hampstead, London	14 Aug 1975	2½	6·7	170
Hewenden Reservoir, Yorks	11 June 1956	2	6·1	155
Wisley, Surrey	16 July 1947	1¼	4·0	102
Ilkley, Yorkshire	12 July 1900	1¼	3·75	94
Hemyock, Devon*	5 July 1963	1¼	3·1	79
		1	2·5	64
		¾	2	51
		¼	1	25

* Recorded on a Dines tilting rain recorder and probably representative of the worst British downpours.

	INCHES					MILLIMETRES		
Jan	Apr	July	Oct		Jan	Apr	July	Oct
0·6	3·2	1·8	2·5	Accra, Ghana	15	81	46	64
4·4	1·6	<0·1	3·1	Algiers, Algeria	112	41	<3	79
1·7	0·4	0·3	0·7	Alice Springs, Australia	43	10	8	18
3·2	1·2	0·7	1·9	Athens, Greece	81	30	18	47
0·3	2·3	6·3	8·1	Bangkok, Thailand	8	58	160	206
1·2	1·7	1·1	3·4	Barcelona, Spain	31	43	27	86
3·1	1·9	3·7	3·3	Belfast, N. Ireland	80	48	94	83
1·8	1·7	2·9	1·9	Berlin, Germany	46	43	73	49
2·4	2·7	4·9	2·8	Berne, Switzerland	61	68	119	70
0·1	<0·1	24·3	2·5	Bombay, India	3	<3	617	64
1·8	2·3	2·1	1·1	Bucharest, Rumania	46	59	53	29
3·1	3·5	2·2	3·4	Buenos Aires, Argentina	78	89	56	86
0·2	0·1	0·0	<0·1	Cairo, Egypt	5	3	0	<3
2·2	1·9	2·7	1·7	Christchurch, N. Zealand	56	48	69	43
0·6	3·9	5·6	4·4	Chungking, China	15	99	142	112
3·5	9·1	5·3	13·7	Colombo, Ceylon	89	231	135	348
1·9	1·5	2·8	2·3	Copenhagen, Denmark	49	38	71	59
15·2	3·8	<0·1	2·0	Darwin, Australia	386	97	<3	51
2·6	1·7	3·5	3·0	Dundee, Scotland	65	43	89	76
0·9	0·3	1·9	0·8	Fairbanks, Canada	23	8	48	20
2·2	1·7	2·7	2·9	Helsinki, Finland	56	43	68	73
2·1	2·0	5·3	2·6	Innsbruck, Austria	54	52	134	67
4·3	1·8	1·3	3·2	Istanbul, Turkey	109	46	34	81
4·5	1·5	0·3	2·2	Johannesburg, S. Africa	114	38	8	56
1·8	6·9	1·8	3·8	Kampala, Uganda	46	175	46	97
0·9	1·2	1·5	7·1	Kingston, Jamaica	23	30	38	180
4·4	2·1	0·1	2·4	Lisbon, Portugal	111	54	3	62
2·0	1·8	2·0	2·3	London, England	51	46	51	58
1·5	1·9	0·4	2·1	Madrid, Spain	39	48	11	53
9·8	8·7	2·3	4·2	Manaus, Brazil	249	221	58	107
1·7	1·7	0·4	3·0	Marseille, France	43	43	11	76
1·9	2·3	1·9	2·6	Melbourne, Australia	48	58	48	66
1·0	7·7	3·5	3·4	Mombasa, Kenya	25	196	89	86
3·8	2·6	3·7	3·4	Montreal, Canada	97	66	94	86
1·5	1·5	3·5	1·8	Moscow, USSR	39	39	88	45
1·4	2·5	5·8	6·5	Nassau, Bahamas	36	64	147	165
3·7	3·2	4·2	3·5	New York, USA	94	81	107	89
3·0	0·7	<0·1	1·0	Nicosia, Cyprus	76	18	<3	25
1·9	1·7	3·2	2·9	Oslo, Norway	49	43	82	74
1·5	1·3	0·1	3·0	Palma, Majorca	39	32	3	77
2·2	1·7	2·3	2·0	Paris, France	56	43	59	50
0·3	1·7	6·7	2·2	Perth, Australia	8	43	170	56
3·5	2·2	2·0	3·7	Reykjavik, Iceland	89	56	50	94
2·8	2·0	0·6	3·9	Rome, Italy	71	51	15	99
1·7	0·6	<0·1	1·1	Santa Cruz, Tenerife	43	15	<3	28
0·1	0·5	3·0	0·6	Santiago, Chile	3	13	76	15
3·2	1·7	3·9	3·9	Stockholm, Sweden	81	43	99	98
0·2	0·5	7·4	0·6	Tientsin, China	5	13	188	15
1·9	5·3	5·6	8·2	Tokyo, Japan	48	135	142	208

AVERAGE MONTHLY RAINFALL

CHAPTER 11

FLOOD AND DROUGHT

Tiros meteorological satellite

A flood is an accumulation of water which is too great to be disposed of by the normal means. The absolute quantity of rain is therefore less important than the duration or rate of fall compared with that normally experienced.

Soil is an important regulator for rain disposal. Water clings by surface tension to the top layer of soil particles and then is gradually forced downwards by the weight of further rain. Percolation is slow, so that soil acts most efficiently as a receptacle when the rain falls lightly but persistently, and least efficiently when rain falls very heavily. Soil becomes a blocked channel, and therefore a potential cause of flooding, when it is either baked hard by the Sun, frozen solid by frost or when it is already saturated with water. Any rain falling under such conditions runs off the surface as it would do from impermeable concrete. Soil is most receptive when it is moist.

Rivers and streams have been gouged by centuries of rainfall to cope with average quantities of water. The rivers with the biggest catchment areas in the wettest countries are as liable to flood as smaller rivers in dry countries, because any area of the world is liable to experience above average rainfalls occasionally. Many disasters occur because debris builds a dam across a river or stream, and then later bursts under the weight of accumulated water.

In urban areas drains carry rain water from impermeable surfaces and they are supposed to cope with *probable* heavy falls likely to be experienced over periods of 10, 25 or 50 years.

Flooding in Thames Ditton, Surrey, in September 1968. (*Surrey Commet*)

Bridge House at Colyton, Devon, after the floods of 10–11 July 1968. (K Sansom)

It is economically impractical to budget for every *possible* rainfall and therefore the gamble must fail sometimes. Blockage of drains by leaves and debris often causes floods which would not have been expected because of the quantity of rain alone.

Every flood is the 'worst ever' in the opinion of the particular individuals who suffered one. Undoubtedly Noah thought the same, but at any rate he did have time in which to build his Ark. A **flash flood** is one which occurs very suddenly, and little evasive action is then possible. The most notorious floods are those which comprise many individual 'worst floods', and pose exceptional rescue and recovery problems. A complete list of notorious floods would be endless, but a selection from recent years confirms that any area of the world may suffer.

Calama, Chile, situated in the rain-shadow desert of Atacama, enjoyed the reputation of being the driest place in the world, having had virtually no rain for 400 years. On *10 February 1972* the town lost its record when torrential rain fell during mid-afternoon, causing catstrophic floods and landslides. The

town was isolated by water, mud swept down from the hills and electricity supplies were short-circuited in the town and local mines.

Big Thompson Canyon, Colorado, USA 31 July 1976. A flash flood followed heavy rain which fell into two tributaries of the Thompson River and 10 in (250 mm) of rain fell in 4 hours at the high end of the Canyon, where peaks reach 9000 ft (2740 m). The rainfall was considered a once-in-100-years chance. Officials warned holiday-makers about the danger of a flash flood but they were not heeded. When the flood water arrived it cut a 15 mile (24 km) swath through the countryside, making it look like a refuse dump. Acres of trees were smashed, the road, where the canyon narrows to a gorge, collapsed to make a precipice 50 ft (15 m) deep, and 80 people lost their lives; 1000 people had to be lifted out of the canyon by helicopter.

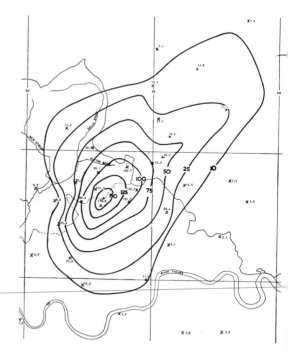

Isohyets (lines joining places having equal rainfall) for the Hampstead storm of 14 August 1975. Grid unit 6·2 miles (10 km). (*Journal of Meteorology*)

Stones and boulders, some weighing as much as five tons, being cleared away from the river at Lynmouth in July 1954, two years after the disastrous flood of 15 August 1952. (Syndication International)

Hampstead, London, 14 August 1975. At the end of a three week heat wave in south east England, a very local, but exceptionally heavy, storm caused 6·7 in (170 mm) of rain to fall in approximately 2½ hours. It was probably the biggest point rainfall in the last 100 years, and local drains were unable to cope with the water. Cars floated along the streets, basements and subways filled, and dozens of families had to be evacuated from badly damaged homes. One man was drowned and two struck by lightning.

Lynmouth, Devon, England, 15 August 1952. The town lies at sea level, immediately below precipitous heights rising 1000 ft (300 m) up to Exmoor, where the ground was already sodden after a wet summer. Then 12 hours continuous rain from a slow-moving depression caused 9 in (228 mm) of rain to accumulate in the rivers and streams lacing the moor. Torrents of water and debris in the East and West Lyn rivers shattered narrow bridges and then acted as battering rams against houses downstream. Approximately 200 000 tons of giant boulders

were carried down into Lynmouth by the swollen river, a total of 34 lives were lost and 3–400 people were rendered homeless; 28 bridges in the area were destroyed, 93 houses ruined or later demolished as unsafe, 28 cars were totally wrecked and 38 disappeared out to sea without trace.

Tunisia and NE Algeria, N Africa, 20–29 September 1969. A depression developed in the Mediterranean, along the junction between cold air from Europe and warm air from the Sahara on the southern side of the N African mountains. Rainfall in the ten-day period was several times greater than the mean rainfall for September.

Rainfall at Biskra, Algeria:

	in	mm
On 27 September 1969	3·4	88
On 28 September 1969	4·8	122
Previous record 15 November 1957	2·7	69·1
During September 1969	11·7	299·2
During an average September	0·7	17

Nearly 600 people died, $\frac{3}{4}$ million people were made homeless, mines were flooded, bridges which had stood since Roman times were washed away and there was enormous loss of livestock.

Florence, Italy, November 1966. Northern Italy had already had a very wet October, and on 3 November the river Arno was within a few feet of the embankment which protected the 14th century part of the city and its many artistic treasures. Continuous rain fell during 3 November, and in the early hours of 4 November the river overtopped its banks. Drains choked with debris, power supplies failed, art treasures became submerged in muddy filth. The water coursed through the town for 18 hours before subsiding, to leave many irreplaceable art treasures ruined and enough restoration work to occupy specialists for years. Floods also affected many other towns, including Venice and Pisa, and 170 lives were lost.

West Pakistan, India, August 1976. Particularly heavy monsoon rain had caused floods in Punjab by 2 August, and in Sind Province by the 3rd. Lahore experienced 6 in (150 mm) rain on the 7th; further floods in Punjab on the 10th left 109 dead, 6000 villages devastated and 3·5 million people homeless. These figures were increased during the next week, and by the 25th it was estimated that two million acres (800 000 hectares) of crops were damaged, 12 700 villages flooded and half a million homes destroyed. Over 200 people died in the latter part of the month alone.

The frequency of flood disasters is indicated by the following list, extracted by A J Thomas from newspapers and journals available in Great Britain over a period of four months. These floods are a small sample only of the total which probably occurred, but were not mentioned by the international news media.

September 1976

1–8   Monsoon floods persist in Pakistan. The Bolan dam gave way on the 6th, flooding villages in an area exceeding 3860 sq miles (11 000 km^2).

9   Typhoon *Fran* struck Okinawa with 50 ft (18 m) waves.

12   Flash flood in Petchabun Province, Thailand, killed 26 people.

13   Typhoon *Fran* reached Kyushu, Japan, giving 78 in (1950 mm) rain, a record for a single typhoon. There were 133 dead, 337 injured, 233 bridges washed away, 140 small boats and fishing vessels damaged or lost.

16–30   Monsoon floods in Bihar and Uttar Pradesh, India. Water flooded coal-mine in S Bihar drowning 10; 325 dead in both states.

23–26   Monsoon floods in N Bangladesh, 10 dead.

October 1976

1   Hurricane *Liza* hits Baja California, Mexico, giving nearly 12 in (300 mm) rain in 4 hours at La Paz. Several hundred killed and over 4000 injured.

2–3   Flooding in N Italy after violent storms.

15–17   Severe floods in New South Wales, Australia, especially in Queanbeyan.

25–26   Floods in S France and Corsica, where three people died.

29–31   Violent storms from Naples to Milan, Italy. Swiss–Italian railway cut by landslide north of Domodossola. High tides flooded Venice.

November 1976

1–6   Heavy rain and floods in Italy, damage in Lombardy put at £70 million.

5   Flash flood in Sicily struck Trapani after 5 in (127 mm) rain fell in 4 hours; 11 dead, 5 missing.

6–7   Torrential rain in N Honduras, three dead.

10   Severe half-hour storm in Sydney, Australia, caused extensive flooding and damage, mainly because hail blocked drains.

13–14   Floods along Rojali River, E Java, Indonesia, and also on Island of

Lombok, east of Bali; 136 dead, 50 missing, 4000 homeless.

29   Torrential rains in Kenya; bridge over R. Ngaineithia 136 miles (220 km) south east of Nairobi washed away. Locomotive and six cars of Mombasa–Nairobi express plunged into floodwaters; 24 dead, 60 injured.

December 1976

3–7   Tropical cyclone *Nora* hits central Philippines, causing floods, landslides and crop damage; 58 dead.

4–5   Thunderstorm causes floods near village of Matelot, Trinidad, destroying two bridges and carrying a river ferry out to sea.

19–20   Torrential rain, floods and landslips in Wellington, New Zealand: 10 in (260 mm) rain in places, two dead.

19–21   Cyclone *Ted* hit Mornington Island and North Queensland, Australia. Widespread floods and damage.

20   Floods in N Sumatra, 25 dead.

The Solway Moss Flood was one of the most unusual floods to have occurred in Great Britain, and was recounted to readers of *Weather* in the November 1971 issue by W Foggitt of Thirsk, Yorkshire. One of his ancestors actually experienced the flood, and another made extensive researches, which have been handed down to the present family in weather diaries and letters.

On 14 November 1771, rain started in the north of England and fell incessantly, so that by 19 November the River Tees had risen 20 ft (6 m). Floods swept away half of the north Yorkshire market town of Yarm, between Whitby and Barnard Castle; only one bridge out of 14 was left standing across the river Tyne; the village of Bywell, 6 miles (10 km) from Hexham was almost destroyed and three collieries in Sunderland were filled with water; 34 ships were wrecked on Sunderland Bar.

Ten miles north of Carlisle, near the Scottish border, lay Solway Moss, an area of moss covering a hill about 2–3 miles (3–5 km) in length and 1 mile (1·6 km) wide. The hill contained many springs which maintained the surface as a quagmire even in the driest summers and, during the reign of Henry VIII, tradition recounts that it sucked down a considerable part of a Scottish army. In the November rains of 1771 the moss swelled and breached the shell of solid earth which retained it at the eastern end of the hill. Moss and mud poured down into the valley, choked a stream at the bottom and formed a lake which extended one mile to the banks of the river Esk. Cattle and sheep were suffocated, salmon were killed in the River Esk and Solway Firth and about 14 farms, consisting of four or five houses each, were ruined. Although no human lives were lost, since the flood occurred at midnight when everyone was indoors, some 900 acres of good farming land were left covered in moss of depths varying from 2–20 ft (60 cm– 6 m), submerging all the hedges. An eyewitness wrote:

'Solway Moss itself, which before was a level plain on top of a hill, is now a valley; almost at the bottom of which runs, with considerable rapidity, a stream of black liquid peat earth. The surface of the hill gradually subsides, as the mud which supported it is discharged; and appears all over broken into fragments, so irregularly thrown together as to resemble a heap of ruins . . .'

Drought, in the meteorological sense, is lack of rain (or snow) and it is the predominant characteristic of high-pressure systems, called 'anticyclones'. Upper air subsides and warms over the centre of the anticyclones, thereby restricting the vertical development of cloud. When air is moist and suffers radiation cooling, shallow low cloud or fog may form, but there is no rain.

Meteorological definitions, used for statistical purposes, are as follows:

Absolute drought – a period of 15 consecutive days without rainfall of more than 0·01 in (0·2 mm).

Partial drought – a period of 29 consecutive days with *mean* rainfall of 0·01 in (0·2 mm) or less. Such a period may include a short duration of appreciable rainfall which disappears into insignificance when averaged over 29 days.

A dry spell – a period of 15 consecutive days, none of which has more than 0·04 in (1·0 mm) rainfall.

These definitions are geared for climates which can expect some rain at all times of the year.

In Great Britain, absolute droughts are relatively infrequent, as illustrated by figures from Rugby, Warwick, which is representative of central England. Rugby rainfall records have been kept since April 1871, and since that date there have been:

  128 absolute droughts of 15 consecutive days or more;

Of the above, 47 lasted 20 days or more
            17 lasted 25 days or more
            5 lasted 30 days or more
and the longest lasted 34 days: 4 August–6 September 1947.

No calendar month has been completely rainless since 1855.

Deserts are regions of the world where virtually no rain falls at all, either because of permanent high pressure or because of protection from prevailing moist winds by high mountain barriers (see rain shadow p. 134).
The principal deserts of the world are:

  the Sahara and Libyan deserts, stretching across north Africa, and the adjacent Arabian desert,
  the Gobi desert of central Asia,
  the Great Western desert of North America
  the Great Victoria desert of central Australia,
  the Kalahari desert of southern Africa,
  the Atacama desert and the Patagonia desert in South America.

A hydrological drought is an insufficiency of water supply to meet demand. This can occur anywhere in the world, because lifestyles have evolved on the basis of average rainfall and not absolute quantities of rain. For instance, an Indian monsoon is said to *fail* if it brings too little rain, or rain at too late a date, for the proper growth of the rice crop. Rice requires ankle deep water in the paddy fields at planting times, and it is needed by mid-June. There has never been an occasion when the monsoon has failed to bring *any* rain, but plenty of occasions (the latest in 1972) when the rainfall has been markedly below average, and insufficient for a good harvest. A hydrological drought in India, therefore, may appear strange when considered purely in terms of rainfall; 50 per cent of normal rainfall in Bombay, for instance, is approximately 35 in (890 mm) in four months, which is still much more than London gets on average in a whole year, 23 in (584 mm).

The natural reservoirs of water are:
● impervious basins of rock below ground, which retain water from which air is excluded; this is called 'groundwater'. The top level of groundwater is the 'water table', and its depth below surface varies according to local geological features and the wetness of the season. Groundwater is pumped to the surface at bore holes, and one of the problems during drought is that one cannot *see* how much water is left.
● springs, which are underground supplies rising naturally to the surface.
● lakes, streams and rivers which eventually discharge into the sea, and from which artificial reservoirs are stocked.
● snow, which is a refrigerated stock of water, released during spring.
● the soil, which is said to be at field capacity when it holds as much water as is possible, by surface tension and capillary action, as far down as the water table. Soil moisture deficiency occurs when water extraction is not compensated by rain or artificial watering. Waterlogged soil contains so much water that air is expelled from the soil and the level of the water table rises.

The most important water consumers are:
● The atmosphere, which evaporates enormous quantities of water each year, estimated

at 100 000 billion gallons over the whole world. A more comprehensible estimate expresses the evaporation of water over Great Britain as $\frac{2}{3}-\frac{3}{4}$ of the country's total annual rainfall. Evaporation occurs mainly during the summer months, and even a wet summer in Great Britain provides only for current needs and not for replenishing reservoirs.

● Vegetation, which consumes directly from the soil principally during spring and summer when evaporation is also at a maximum.

● Human beings, who have countless domestic, agricultural and industrial requirements for water at all times of the year, and particularly heavy demands in summer to make up artificially for what the clouds fail to provide.

Artificial reservoirs and irrigation channels are the means by which water authorities attempt to balance irregular supply of water with continuous voracious demand. It is economically impossible to cater for every *possible* drought and every *possible* increase in demand. Therefore hydrologists have the unenviable task of planning reservoir capacity on the basis of *probable* rainfall, and inevitably realistic compromises sometimes go awry.

The critical period of a reservoir is the time in which it will reach its lowest level, if not replenished by rain or from rivers. Most surface reservoirs in Great Britain have critical periods of nine months, but the largest have 18 months. In general, any numbers of dry summers can be accommodated without hardship providing the intervening winters are wet enough to replenish reservoirs.

The major high-pressure systems of the world shift seasonally in fairly regular manner, but their boundaries are by no means precisely defined. Sometimes they encroach further north, sometimes further south, and being sluggish systems they often persist longer than desired. Moreover, anticyclones seem to form cyclical habits of straying from their usual position, with consequent long-period abnormalities of rainfall. However, modern meteorologists are no nearer to defining the periodicity accurately than were astute weather observers in Biblical history.

One of the earliest predictions of drought, based on awareness of cyclical tendency, was that made by Joseph to King Pharaoh, and recounted in the Book of Genesis. He said that seven lean years would follow seven fat years, and he advised that corn be stored when it was plentiful, in order to cope with the food crisis which would follow in the drought years. There is no absolute validity to the period of seven years, but it does appear to be of the right order of magnitude for that part of the world.

A recent cycle of 'lean years' affected the Sahel, which is a marginal area situated between the rainless Sahara desert and the lush equatorial forests of west Africa. Average rainfall is 10–20 in (250–500 mm) – enough to encourage quick-growing sparse grass, which supports sheep and goats belonging to tribes who make a regular circuit from one grazing-ground to another. The Sahel had virtually no rain from 1973 until the autumn of 1976, because the subtropical high pressure belt stretched further south than usual. Many herds of animals died of starvation, and whole communities of nomadic people suffered famine. It was a measure of their plight that many accepted help in settling into communities in more hospitable areas, and many will never return to the Sahel again. Since the vagaries of the weather in such marginal desert zones cannot be controlled, it is all the more encouraging that the battle waged by charities, such as 'Save the Children Fund', against the fly causing river blindness is proving successful. The wetter region of the basin of the River Volga, where river blindness flourished, may therefore soon be safe for human habitation.

One of the most renowned droughts caused by monsoon failure resulted in the plagues visited upon the Egyptians prior to the exodus of the Israelites under the leadership of Moses, some time between the years 1290 and 1224 BC.

Egyptian agriculture depended upon heavy seasonal rain over the mountains of Ethiopia and in the region of Lake Victoria to flood the Nile all the way down to the sea. In Moses' time there were no controlling dams along the river. In the year of the plagues the shift of the high pressure belt must have so reduced rainfall in the source region that, by the time the northward flowing Nile had been further deplenished by evaporation, the Egyptians were left with nothing more than a trickle. Insects abounded in stagnant pools and carried disease among the population; algae made the water unfit to drink and coloured it red; and frogs, which usually bred only when the Nile floods receded, multiplied at a faster rate than the predatory ibis could cope with. It must have been an exceptional drought, even worse than the lean years described by Joseph.

In America the most infamous sequence of droughts occurred during the 1930s, when the great Dust Bowl was created in the central plains. The first serious drought occurred in the middle of 1930 and extended into the middle of 1931, by which time most of the northern and central plains experienced shortage of water. Every year thereafter till the end of the decade some region or other was affected by drought, and in 1934 and 1936 the area extended from Texas to the borders of Canada. Normal rainfall returned in November 1940.

Historical droughts in Great Britain which happened before the compilation of rainfall statistics can be glimpsed from written descriptions.

In 54 BC Julius Caesar was waging his second campaign in south east England and recounts in Book V of *de Bello Gallico* that his supply problems were much aggravated by the smallness of the autumn crops 'propter siccitates', on account of the dryness. He mentions persistent northerly winds, indicating a blocking anticyclone extending to Great Britain from the Azores.

The years 1252–53 sound remarkably similar to the years 1975–76. From the *Annals of Loch Ce* we know that the summer 1252 was so dry that people used to cross the river Shannon in Ireland without wetting their feet. In England, Matthew Paris wrote that after a dry April and May

'the sun rose to its solstitial culmination (June) and its immoderate and intolerable heat so burnt up the earth's surface and multiplied its warmth, that all the herbage withered away and the meadows denied all manner of food to the cattle. Moreover the heat continued into the night and generated flies, fleas and other injurious pests, and all things living endured a tedious life.'

In 1654, a Hampshire village appealed for relief for its inhabitants because on 9 May

'There happened a sudaine and lamentable fier in ye parish of Worting which being carried on by ye wind and exceeding heat, and drought of the weather burnt all that was combustible and melted even the church bells.'

The churches were repositories for fire buckets and fire hooks, used to pull thatch down from burning roofs, and frequent entries in church accounts for renewal or repair of fire-fighting equipment always accompanied periods of drought.

1665, the year of the Great Plague, began with a cold, dry winter and spring, and as early as 11 April King Charles reminded the Lord Mayor of London of the danger of fire because of wooden houses closely overhanging narrow streets. In south east England, every month from November 1665 to September 1666 was dry, and by August the River Thames at Oxford was a trickle. London buildings were as dry as tinder when the Great Fire of London started on 2 September 1666 and destroyed 13 000 houses, churches and public buildings. A rainy spell started on 9 September and there was almost incessant heavy rain for ten days early in October.

The worst drought in England and Wales since rainfall records began occurred during 1975 and 1976. Weather was dominated by high-pressure systems, which only withdrew occasionally to permit the approach of depressions bringing rain. Moreover these years followed the driest five-year period since the 1850s. 1971–5 having a mean rainfall of only 32 in (826 mm) per annum.

The calendar year 1975 was the fifth driest of the century. Rainless spells started in May and continued through to December, the only wet month being September. By June Herefordshire, Gwent, Dorset, Devon and Cornwall were all experiencing water cuts or restrictions, and South Yorkshire considered the drought to be the worst for 100 years. September rain fell on ground baked hard by the hot summer and was generally too late to be of use to farmers, and of no consequence for the reservoirs. It did, however, prevent a threatened water rationing in Sheffield. Stand pipes were in the streets of Barnsley, South Yorkshire, in December.

Most of England, from South Devon to Yorkshire, and also east Scotland had less than 70 per cent average rainfall during 1975.

The early months of 1976 were dry in many areas of England and Wales, although some northern districts had 150 per cent average rainfall. In particular, Sheffield's problems were alleviated by the wettest January since 1960. The crucial winter months in the Midlands and southern England passed without replenishment of reservoirs or ground water. April, which often produces heavy showers without suffering undue evaporative loss, also failed to live up to its reputation. May was changeable with heavy rain at times in the north. Southern areas had 15 or more days with some rain, but the total was still below average. June and August produced remarkably little rain over the whole of the British Isles which had an even hotter summer than 1975. Rain which did fall consisted mainly of spasmodic deluges from thunder storms. These swelled the climatological statistics recorded by rain-gauges, but did not materially affect the drought situation.

By the end of July, reservoirs in Devon and Cornwall were as low as 23 per cent capacity, the Mendip reservoirs in Somerset were losing water by evaporation at the rate of 5·5 million gallons (25 million litres) per day, and rivers

THE MOST SEVERE DROUGHTS IN ENGLAND AND WALES FOR SPECIFIED PERIODS BETWEEN 1820 AND 1976

Period	Year	Start month	Rainfall in	mm
3 month	1938	February	2·2	56
	1893	March	2·8	71
	1929	February	2·8	71
	1868	May	2·9	74
	1854	February	2·9	74
	1844	April	3·0	77
	1976	June	3·0	77
6 month	1921	February	7·0	179
	1976	March	8·1	208
	1887	February	8·7	221
	1929	January	9·0	230
	1870	April	9·4	241
	1826	March	9·8	249
12 month	1975/6	September	22·4	571
	1854/5	February	24·3	618
	1920/1	November	24·3	618
	1887/8	February	24·5	624
	1963/4	December	25·0	637
	1933/4	April	25·6	651
16 month	1975/6	May	29·8	757
	1854/5	February	31·9	811
	1933/4	April	33·6	855
	1887/8	February	33·7	857
	1920/1	August	34·6	880
	1873/4	April	35·3	899
18 month	1975/6	March	35·7	909
	1853/5	December	36·7	933
	1887/8	June	39·2	997
	1933/4	April	39·5	1005
	1873/4	February	40·5	1031
	1857/9	December	40·6	1032
24 month	1932/4	November	56·6	1439
	1853/5	October	56·6	1439
	1862/4	November	57·5	1461
	1887/9	February	58·7	1493
	1972/4	July	58·9	1497
	1974/6	September	58·9	1497

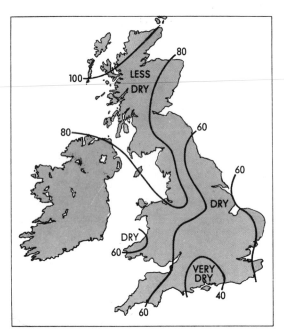

Rainfall over Great Britain for the period
October 1975–April 1976, expressed as
percentages of average rainfall. (Meteorological
Office, Bracknell)

were at record low levels. The source of the
Thames dried up for 9 miles (14 km) and water
at Molesey Lock, the last but one before the
tidal reaches, was being pumped *up-river* over
the lock. Even the Scottish River Spey was
14 in (356 mm) below normal summer level;
between the towns of Grantown and Crom-
dale, Grampian, a series of stones dated 1851,
1868, 1911, 1921 and 1955 record exceptional
low levels of the Spey in past years, and every
stone was clearly visible above the level of
water existing in August 1976. Stand pipes
were operating in South Wales and North
Devon, and general rationing was expected
by 15 September.

Guernsey, Channel Islands, had its driest
summer since 1843, and during June received
only 4 per cent average rainfall.

**Absolute drought in 1976 lasted for ex-
tremely long periods,** none of which con-

stituted a record, but which were phenomenal
because experienced over a widespread area.

*Duration of absolute drought at representative
places in different counties – in days:*

Teignmouth, Devon	44
Thorney Isle, Hampshire	41
Guernsey, Channel Isles	40
Aberporth, Dyfed	39
Guildford, Surrey	38
Edgbaston, Warwick	37
Sidcup, Kent	36
Scilly Isles	33
Valley, Gwynedd	29
Borrowash, Derby	28
Liverpool, Merseyside	27
Pickering, North Yorkshire	25
Hull, Humberside	24

The longest absolute drought in Great
Britain was 73 successive rainless days from
4 March–15 May 1893 at Mile End, London.

A Drought Bill was passed by Parliament on
15 July 1976, giving far-reaching powers to
local authorities to control the use of water.
For the first time ever, a Drought Minister
was appointed, Mr Denis Howell. On 25

Chelsea Reservoir at Walton on Thames, Surrey,
photographed soon after the 1976 drought had
broken. The base of the reservoir is clay and dries
out to an exaggerated form of soil polygon.
(Thames Water Authority)

August the Department of the Environment opened an emergency centre to advise on water problems. The National Water Council maintained that it would take a wet winter, a normal summer and a further wet winter to restore natural water resources to normal. It was the only sensible opinion in view of the impossibility of accurately forecasting quantities of rain.

Statistical evidence about rain following drought was not particularly encouraging.

There had been 17 summers since 1840 with average temperature greater than 60°F (15·8°C) and rainfall less than 7·8 in (200 mm), and only three were followed by wet Septembers, of which 1975 was one.

Between 1727 and 1840 there were 13 comparable summers, none of which was followed by a dry September. In the event, the highly improbable happened: rainfall in September 1976 was almost a record since 1871 and certainly a record to have followed upon such an exceptional drought.

	Year	in	mm
September	1918	7·2	183
	1976	6·3	160
Mid September–mid October	1976	6·8	172
	1935	6·7	171
October and September	1903	12·2	310
	1976	12·1	308

The first break in the 1976 drought came on 29 August, when heavy rain fell over the south of England. High pressure retreated to the Mediterranean, making up for a poor summer there by giving a fabulous early autumn. Great Britain was drenched in rain, much flooding resulted throughout September and October, and the succeeding months continued wet. By January it seemed certain that, if another hot dry summer should materialize in 1977, it could be faced with equanimity. By February, Chew Valley Lake and the Blagdon reservoir in Somerset were full to overflowing, and millions of gallons of water were running over spillways into the Rivers Chew and Yeo.

A blocking anticyclone is one which persists in latitudes normally travelled by depressions, which are therefore diverted into another direction. Hence drought in one area is usually adjacent to abnormally high rainfall in another.

There was a notable drought throughout north west Europe during 1976, exceptional dryness in Great Britain being mirrored by similar conditions in France, where many rivers, including some as fast flowing as the Loire, dried up. The blocking anticyclone diverted depressions southwards during July, causing the normally fine Mediterranean weather to be replaced by a wet summer more typical of Great Britain. Mediterranean rainfall in July 1976, expressed as a percentage of normal was:

Parts of southern Italy	150
Malta (record 18·9 in (480 mm) Jan–July	200
Parts of eastern Greece	800
Parts of southern Turkey	800
Algiers	2000
Parts of north western Algeria	3200

A surface pressure anomaly is a difference from normal surface pressure, and is expressed

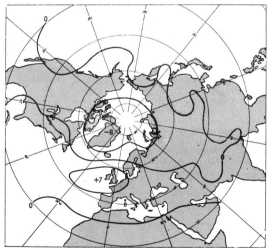

Pressure anomaly pattern for the period October 1975–April 1976. (Meteorological Office, Bracknell)

as a positive or negative number of millibars. For instance, during the crucial period October 1975–April 1976, when low pressure systems usually fill the reservoirs in Great Britain, the pressure anomaly was +7 mb, indicating much more anticyclonic weather than usual. At the same time, since nature has an extremely efficient, if complicated, method of balancing the atmosphere, the pressure anomaly over the Arctic region was −8 mb, abnormally low. The Arctic embraces Greenland and the northern boundaries of Canada, Europe and Asia, so that it is not surprising that high anomalies and abnormal weather in Europe should have been reflected by extraordinary weather on the other side of the world.

In the United States serious drought followed abnormally high pressure in the western states on the Pacific coast, resulting in only 40 per cent of normal rainfall during the years 1975 and 1976. Snow cover on the Rocky Mountains, a vital source of water in the spring, was only 25 per cent of normal at the end of March 1977, though the northern plains received helpful snowfalls in early March. In February farmers in the 400 miles (640 km) central valley of California, who provide half of the nation's vegetables and fruit, were warned that they might face cuts in irrigation water of 25–50 per cent during 1977. At the time of writing, it is impossible to say if the American drought will be relieved as quickly and as surprisingly as the British drought of 1975–6.

In China reports suggested that drought during the winter of 1976–7 had resulted in only 60 per cent normal soil moisture at the end of March. Winter wheat, the second most important crop after rice, which was planted in September and October failed to put on new growth and drought was accentuated by soil erosion in the wind. Weather conditions were a particular trial in northern China in the Tangshan area, almost destroyed by an earthquake in July 1976, and a campaign was launched for all available manpower to help irrigate by hand along the regions of the Yellow and Hwai rivers.

Cloud seeding is an experimental method of attempting to wring rain from clouds. Therefore it arouses tantalising but as yet unproven hopes amongst people in drought-stricken areas. Silver iodide crystals, solid carbon dioxide (dry ice) or salt are injected into clouds, by means of rockets or aircraft in order to speed the freezing or coalescence of super-cooled water drops, an apparently necessary preliminary to precipitation (p. 131). Experiments have been conducted both in England over Salisbury Plain and in America to seed clouds which have suitably low temperature. Results have been inconclusive because, whenever rain has fallen, it has been impossible to say with certainty that it might not have fallen unaided. There is no known method by which rain can be produced out of clear air.

CHAPTER 12

SNOW

ATS-3 Satellite

Snow activates a kind of love-hate relationship in people. It is beautiful when freshly fallen, and a superb playground for adults and children alike when it remains preserved in a dry state by cold temperatures. However, it causes chaos to transport and is an unmitigated nuisance when it is in a wet slushy condition or frozen into ice, so that people often wish it gone as soon as it has arrived. Moreover the manner in which snow often arrives in a blizzard, or departs by avalanche or thaw flood, means that snow must be considered a treacherous enemy.

Snow falls over every continent in the world, but in low latitudes only on the tops of high mountains. In such countries snow may be familiar only by hearsay, and millions of people still have to 'discover' snow personally. In high latitudes bulk snow is a familiar and

regular visitor, but the individual snow crystal is a comparatively recent discovery.

Claus Magnus (1490–1558), Swedish historian and Archbishop of Uppsala, was the first person known to have studied individual snow crystals. His drawings were reproduced by woodcut in a book published in Rome in 1555.

René Descartes (1596–1650), French mathematician, who lived in Holland, sketched some dozen different crystals.

Johannes Kepler (1571–1630) German astronomer, was the first to describe in a pamphlet in 1611 the characteristic six-sided symmetry of every snow crystal.

William Scoresby (1789–1857), English Arctic explorer, worked in the right environment to pursue the study of snow further, and he published a book with precise drawings of still more patterns of crystals.

Toshitsura Doi of Japan, published a book of 100 accurate drawings appropriately named *Snow Blossoms* and these, together with drawings by **James Glaisher** of England published in 1855, were the best portraits of snow crystals till the latter part of the 19th century.

William A. Bentley (1865–1931), was the first person to photograph ice crystals with a camera fitted with a microscope. He was an American farmer who was only 20 years old when his fascination with snow began, and he

Photographs of snow flakes taken by W A Bentley. (From the *Natural History of Ice and Snow* by A E H Tutter; courtesy Scott Polar Research Institute)

devoted the next 40 years of his life to building up a collection of 6000 photomicrographs of snow crystals, all being different. However, even this great number omitted many which he ignored because they did not conform to his particular idea of beauty. Bentley died in 1931, just before his book *Snow Crystals*, containing 2000 of his best photographs was published.

Ukichiro Nakaya of Hokkaido University, Japan, was the first to study snow with modern X-ray equipment and to explain, in 1954, that the hexagonal symmetry of individual crystals is due to molecular structure.

It was impossible to determine in the vast atmosphere exactly what conditions resulted in different shapes of hexagonal crystals, so research workers started to tackle the problem in the laboratory, by making ice crystals under known conditions, and discovering what shapes resulted.

Dr Vincent Joseph Schaefer (b 1906), American research chemist and meteorologist,

first made snow artificially in 1946. His earl attempts were unsuccessful because the super cooled clouds, which were easy enough t make in a freezer chest, tended to freeze o the sides rather than fall to the bottom as snow One day Schaefer put dry ice (solid carbo dioxide) into the chest in order to lower the ai temperature still further, and the super cooled cloud in the chest converted to ic crystals, which fell on to a black velvet cloth a the bottom of the chest like a miniature sno storm. The experiment was duplicated in th atmosphere in the same year, when an aircraf seeded clouds over Massachusetts, USA, wit pellets of solid carbon dioxide ('dry ice'), an caused snow flakes to fall from the cloud.

'Dry ice', which can cool a thin layer cloud to about $-94°F$ ($-70°C$) becam recognised as a suitable seeding agent fo promoting glaciation of a cloud in attempts t induce precipitation.

Every type of ice crystal has since bee manufactured under laboratory condition and they vary in shape according to the temperature at which they fall:

	°F	°C
Thin hexagonal	32 to 27	0 to −3
Needles	27 to 23	−3 to −5
Hollow prismatic columns	23 to 17	−5 to −8
Hexagonal plates	17 to 10	−8 to −12
Dendritic crystals	10 to 3	−12 to −16
Hexagonal plates	3 to −13	−16 to −25
Hollow prisms	−13 to −58	−25 to −50

These shapes are also dependent upon humidity. Needle crystals require moist air; plate crystals grow slowly when air is dry, but rapidly when air is moist; columnar crystals form in dry air, and the dendritic shapes require a moderately moist environment. The exquisite shapes which result are caused by complicated sequences of evaporation, condensation, sublimation and deposition in the micro-environment around each crystal in a super-cooled cloud. Growth is symmetrical about each hexagonal germ, but the pattern varies infinitely according to the layer of atmosphere in which the crystal grows, and the different layers through which it falls.

Dry snow consists of very cold crystals, which do not bond together by regelation and therefore remain small. The crystals may latch together if suitably shaped, though inevitably many crystals break under impact with each other.

Dry snow is typical of continental land masses well removed from the sea and, when freshly fallen, dry snow has a density of less than 0·1 gram per cubic centimetre. If driven by a strong wind, dry snow penetrates the smallest cracks in window and door frames, bringing a snow storm literally indoors. Moreover, particularly fine and powdery snow can even cause suffocation. The same consistently powdery quality makes dry snow amenable to clearance by 'suck-and-blow' machines, because it does not solidify by regelation under pressure inside the machines. Likewise, dry snow is an ideal surface on which to travel by ski because it does not clog on the under-surface.

Wet snow occurs at temperatures high enough to bond crystals into large snow flakes by regelation. It is typical of maritime borders of continental land masses between latitudes 40°–60°, where intensely cold air streams from inland can clash with mild airstream with abundant vapour from the sea. Fresh wet snow has a density of approximately 0·3 g/cm³. One m³ of newly fallen snow may therefore weigh 30 kg, and one cubic foot 1·87 lb.

Wet snow is ideal for making snowballs because the flakes bond together easily under hand pressure, but for the same reason it cannot be cleared away by a blower machine, only by snowplough or shovel.

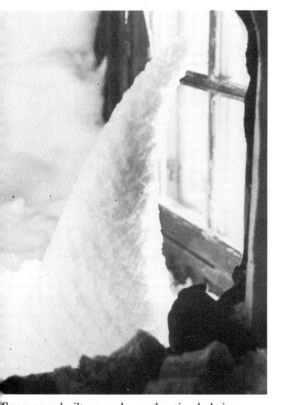

Snow cone built up underneath a tiny hole in a canvas passage alongside living quarters in Antarctica. Heat seepage from the lighted living room is causing the cone to melt nearest the window. (C. Swithinbank)

Digging out a car from wet snow after a blizzard over east Kent in December 1959. Note the drifts sculptured by eddies on the leeward side of the hedges. (Automobile Association)

Snow flakes may attain a size of several inches in diameter, and were reported 8 in × 12 in (200 mm × 300 mm) at Bratsk, Siberia, during the winter of 1971. Any snow flakes as large as that are probably caused by being swirled up and down within the cloud in air currents, accumulating more and more ice crystals, till they are in effect snow balls.

Graupel (German word for soft hail) is snow which has partly melted and refrozen, usually by being tossed in layers of different temperature, and falls to the ground as compressible pellets of thin ice with a soft core, rarely larger than 0·2 in (5 mm) in diameter.

The terminal speed of snow flakes is considerably less than the terminal speed of rain drops (p. 132) because snow presents a greater area of resistance to the wind. Large flakes having a diameter 0·4–1·6 in (10–40 mm) only reach a terminal velocity of 3–5 ft/s (1–1·7 m/s) which is not as fast as the speed of the smallest rain drops. The snow cover on the ground is therefore considerably affected by wind speed.

Snow lies evenly over the ground only afte falling in calm air or very light wind. It is the measured, as soon as possible after the fall, b graduated rule over a level surface well awa from obstructions which might have affecte the fall.

For purposes of climatological record depth of snow is translated into rainfall at th average rate of one inch rain for every one foo of snow (25 mm rain for every 300 mm snow

Actual rates, however, vary considerabl with type of snow. Very cold and feather snow, whose crystals interlock so lightly tha air constitutes 95 per cent of the snow cove may only yield one inch of rain for every thre feet of snow (25 mm rain for every 900 mr snow); whereas wet snow may give one inc rain for only seven inches snow (25 mm rai for 175 mm snow). A fresh, wet snow cove contains about 75 per cent air, but soon com pacts further.

The 'nuisance' value of level snow may b gauged from the following facts:

Motor traffic usually becomes disrupte

Snow sculptured by the wind. (Eidg. Institut für Schnee-und Lawinenforschung)

Miss Dorothy Redfearn and her sister Mary Alice measuring depth of snow at Forest in Teesdale, Barnard Castle, Durham, which is high up on the Pennine Chain. The sisters have supplied some 4 000 daily weather observations to the Air Ministry continuously since 1937. (*Daily Telegraph*)

with about 4 in (100 mm) level fall of snow.

Rail traffic becomes disrupted with about 6 in (150 mm) level fall of snow.

Cattle will nuzzle through 6 in (150 mm) snow, but not through 12 in (300 mm).

Sheep are able to walk through 12 in (300 mm) snow, but not through 24 in (600 mm).

The insulation value of a snow cover varies with its air content, and therefore is most efficient in newly fallen snow. Snow insulates the ground against excessively cold air temperature which may exist above the snow. It also prevents conduction of heat from the soil to the top of the snow cover. Air temperature within a snow cover varies according to distance from the extremes of temperature above and below. Corn germinated and grew to 3 in (75 mm) high beneath the sudden snow cover in the Devon blizzard of 1891, because the ground was warmer than normal for the season when the snow fell. Sheep can survive for several weeks if covered by snow because their own coats insulate them against loss of body heat until their small statures become completely covered by snow. Snow then melts near their bodies to form small caves in which

lambs are sometimes born and survive until rescued. Snow contains enough air for breathing until it compacts. Houses more readily retain the artificial heat generated indoors when they are submerged in snow and thus not exposed to icy winds.

Snow cover becomes more uneven as wind speed increases. In gale winds snow may remain in suspension in the wind to form a **blizzard**, and very little may settle upon open ground. Snow, however, accumulates in huge drifts in or around obstructions, making frozen sculptures which illustrate the normally invisible behaviour of wind. Snow piles up against windward surfaces; it is carried backwards in lee eddies and it traces aerodynamic flow patterns over slopes.

In the second week of March 1891, after a sudden blizzard over Dartmoor, Devon, England, narrow roads between hedges were filled to the top with snow but a few exposed fields had hardly any snow cover at all. The countryside lost all its usual topographical landmarks and those trudging the snow were as likely to find themselves walking over hedge tops as over roads.

Depth of snow drift gives an unrealistic value of total snow fall, but a very cogent impression of disruption of traffic.

After the blizzards experienced in Buffalo, New York, USA, during the end of January and the beginning of February 1977, the town was left with snow drifts 20 ft (6 m) high, which were compacted so hard by the wind that the blades of snow ploughs broke when trying to shift them.

During 1947, which was the snowiest winter in Great Britain in the 20th century, drifts accumulated to 15 ft (5 m) depth in many places, and farms and isolated villages were cut off for days on end.

Traditional reports in Devon, England, that the ravine Tavy Cleave on the west side of Dartmoor was filled with a giant drift 200–300 ft deep (60–100 m) during the March blizzard of 1891 are no longer considered to be a wild exaggeration, but a realistic possibility.

Wind flow patterns over roofs often cause irregular loading of snow, particularly on the lee side. British building specifications require that a roof pitch of less than 30° must be able to carry a load of 2 ft (0·6 m) of snow, but countries which have regular falls of heavier snow than occur in Great Britain make more stringent regulations. North Japan had an exceptionally cold January in 1977 and the heaviest snow for 14 years: over 200 roofs collapsed under the weight of snow.

A cornice is a wave shaped sculpture of snow projecting 6–9 ft (2–3 m) over a precipice, whether as low as a wall or as high as a moun-

A cornice of snow hangs over the leeward side of a mountain precipice in Switzerland. (Eidg. Institut für Schnee- und Lawinenforschung)

tain, without material support underneath. I is formed by violent lee eddies carrying snov backwards into the side of the obstruction after blowing strongly over the top surface.

A snow cushion is a mound of snow whic. forms in back eddying wind over lee slope: Windward slopes are frequently less snowy s that sheep are more likely to be able to nuzzl through to sustaining gorse. For this reasor Devon farmers do not burn gorse from th moors which face the east, the direction fror which the heaviest English snowfalls come.

Snow rollers are aggregates of snow flake which are driven along the ground by the win to form snow balls or cylinders.

A white-out blurs normal perception in snow storm, or over a snow cover, when clou merges into snow without a visible horizor Normally distinguishable contours of th landscape disappear, multiple reflection fror ice crystals and cloud prevents shadows, an all sense of direction and even of balance ma be lost.

Snow lies on the ground whenever air tem perature is below 37°F (3°C). It may reach th ground still frozen in air temperatures up t 44°F (7°C) but then melts at once.

When air temperature is near 32°F (0°C small differences in altitude make all th difference between snow and rain. On November 1958, rain fell on 34th Street, Nev York, while guards at the top of the Empir State Building at 1150 ft (350 m) were makin snowballs!

A snow cover lies for most of the winte wherever the temperature of the coldest mont is less than 27°F (−3°C). It lies intermittentl every winter wherever air temperatures ar 27° to 39°F (−3° to 4°C). Snow covers approx mately 23 per cent of the Earth's surface eith permanently or temporarily.

Between the poles and latitudes 66½° pr cipitation is nearly always in the form of snov but since there is little vapour content in th cold air, the quantity of snow is not very grea

An avalanche in Switzerland. (Eidg. Institut für Schnee-und Lawinenforschung)

Over Antarctica snowfalls are exceedingly difficult to measure because strong winds continually blow old snow and make it indistinguishable from new snow. The total annual amount is thought to be less than 5 in (125 mm) equivalent rainfall.

In latitudes lower than 40° snow falls wherever there are high enough mountains projecting above the freezing level of the upper air.

Among such mountain tops are Mt Fujiama, Japan, 33°N; Mt Teide, Tenerife, Canary Isles, 28°N; and, nearest to the equator, Mt Kenya, 17 058 ft (5199 m) Kenya, Africa, at latitude $\frac{1}{2}$° S.

At low altitudes, the occasional snowfalls in these latitudes cause considerable excitement. Snow fell at Mackay, Australia, 21° S, on 20

July 1965. It snowed in and around Riyadh, Saudi Arabia, 25° N, on 1 January 1973, clinging to the trees but not lying on the ground; and Jerusalem, 32° N, had a surprise accumulation of 39 in (990 mm) on 13 February 1920. Tampa, Florida, USA, 28° N, had enough snow for children to make snowballs in January 1886 and again in February 1899, when snowflakes were also seen in the air at Fort Myers, Florida, 26° N.

Within latitudes 40° and 66½° snow falls during the winter regularly, but in comparatively small quantities in the heart of large land masses. It also falls copiously if less regularly in maritime regions where moist air from the sea confronts cold air streams over the land.

Mountain barriers such as those of Scandinavia, central Europe, the eastern ranges of North and South America and the Southern Alps in New Zealand, all experience particularly heavy snowfalls because they are accessible to moist airstreams.

The world's greatest recorded snowfalls have all occurred in North America. The Rocky Mountains have an average annual snowfall of 300–400 in (7600–10 000 mm) and

Clearing snow after an avalanche. (Eidg. Institut für Schnee-und Lawinenforschung)

Paradise Ranger Station, Mt Rainier, Washington, has more snow than average.

	in	mm
Annual average snowfall at Paradise Ranger Station	575	14 605
Greatest 12 month snowfall, Paradise Ranger Station, 19 Feb 1971–18 Feb 1972	1224·5	31 102
Greatest five day snowfall, Thomson Pass, Alaska, 26–31 Dec 1955	175·4	4455
Greatest one day snowfall, Silver Lake, Colorado, 14–15 April 1921	74	1870

Exceptionally early snow in the western states of USA occurred in 1846. During October eight-day snow storms caused drifts of 40 ft (12 m) to accumulate in the Sierra Nevada Mountains, North California, trapping a party of emigrants in the mountains till the following February, by which time 40 of the original 87 emigrants had died.

The snowiest winter in the eastern states of USA in recent years was 1977. There were constant blizzards during the last two weeks of January, and by the end of the month a state of emergency had been declared in New York, New Jersey and Ohio. More than 60 people died in blizzards during January; transport was paralysed by snow drifts and the excessive cold had caused an acute shortage of fuel. After a brief respite, blizzards were renewed in the first week of February and it was not until the middle of that month that the 'Great American Winter' eased enough to permit a general return to work and to school.

By the end of February, Buffalo, New York, had recorded 183·1 in (4651 mm) snow, compared to its former record of 126 in (3200 mm) in 1909–10. Boonville, New York, one of the snowiest places, had 278 in (7061 mm) up to the end of February, and seemed set to surpass its previous record of 309 in (7849 mm) for a full season.

Snow drifts in many places were reported to be 20–30 ft (6–9 m) high, and they were so

hard that the blades of snow ploughs bent in trying to shift them. Even when the snow could be shifted, the problem was how to dispose of it before a thaw made it a flood hazard. Thousands of tons of ice hard snow was loaded aboard goods trains in Buffalo, to be taken out of the paralysed city for dumping wherever it would cause no trouble.

One of the least snowy winters in the western states of USA occurred during 1977, while the east was suffering from too much snow. The Rocky Mountains had hardly enough snow to provide a living for the regular skiing resorts, and Alaska was not thickly enough covered for the troops of the Army's Arctic Test Center to accomplish its usual manoeuvres. This had been a trend for the previous few years, and the Army is expected to move its Arctic training exercises to Watertown, New York, during the winter of 1978 in order to get 'proper' snow.

The average number of days with snow lying on the ground is considerably less in Great Britain than in North America.

	days per annum
South east Canada and north east USA	90–140
Southern states USA	1– 10
Scottish mountains	50–100
Inland and northern areas Great Britain	10– 20
Coastal and southern areas Great Britain	1– 10

Except where average figures are high the frequency rates are not very realistic. They indicate that very often no snow falls at all, but occasionally long periods of snow occur.

The most snowy winter in Great Britain in the 20th century was 1947. Between 22 January and 17 March snow fell every day somewhere in the country. There were several daily falls of over 2 ft (600 mm), drifts 15 ft (5 m) high were frequent, and the temperature remained at or near freezing level most of the ime so that snow accumulated over the whole period. Many areas were marooned for days on end, and the armed services were called in to drop supplies by helicopter to isolated farmsteads and villages, and to open up roads. An accumulated level fall of 60 in (1524 mm) was recorded in Upper Teesdale and in the Denbighshire Hills, Clwyd, Wales.

The winter of 1963 was even colder, and the snow cover lasted for many weeks then also, but the quantity of snow was slightly less.

In Great Britain, snow occurs most often between December and March, occasionally as late as May, rarely in June, and so exceptionally in July that reports are suspect.

17 May 1935	Devon and Cornwall 'looked like Christmas'.
17 May 1955	Southern counties had up to 2 in (50 mm) snow.
6 May 1578	Broad Chalke, Wiltshire, had such deep snow that bearers at a funeral had to carry the coffin over a field gate, and the attendant company climbed over hedges.
2 June 1975	Snow fell over the Scottish hills, the Pennines, the Isle of Wight and Cambridge, and provided unseasonal accompaniment to cricket at Buxton, Derbyshire and at the Lords cricket ground, London.
11/12 July 1888	Snow reported seen at Isle of Wight.
25 Sept 1885	Snow fell in London, – the earliest start to the snow 'season' known. On average the first fall of snow in London between the years 1811–1930 was between 18 and 25 November. During the period 1931–60 the average date of first snow was a little later: 8 December.

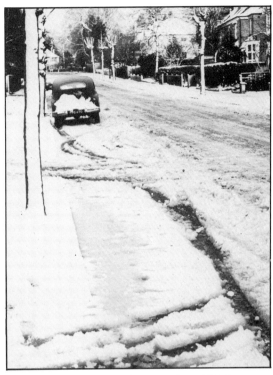

Typical road conditions in countries which have wet snow at temperatures near 32°F (0°C). Snow melts in the sunshine or under the pressure of traffic, and then refreezes to ice after dark.

The character of a snow cover on the ground continually changes by the same processes which determine the snowflakes which fall from the sky. Some crystals break, and others bond together by regelation. Some crystals melt, either because they are close to warm ground or because they are near a rock which is shallowly embedded in snow near the top and warms in sunshine. Convection, too, takes place within a snow cover, because air may be considerably warmer deep down near the ground, than it would be near the top and the icy winds. Warm air convects upwards; evaporation, condensation, sublimation or deposition takes place in the miniscule environment of each ice crystal. Gradually the ice crystals become more rounded and granular, they pack more closely, air is driven out of the layer until eventually it packs to solid ice with only occasional bubbles of trapped air.

Firn (a name of German origin) is old and well packed snow, containing less than 20 per cent of air. It is less white than fresh snow, because the closely packed crystals reflect less light, and it looks more like plaster.

A glacier is an extensive sheet of ice formed when permanent deposits of firn snow compress over hundreds of years. The process is accentuated by compression down constricting valleys, and glaciers become rivers of ice which travel slowly downhill. Glaciers cover 6 million square miles (15 million km²) of the Earth's surface. In warm latitudes they melt when they reach the appropriate latitude and feed rivers which might otherwise be dry.

The longest glacier in the world is the Lambert Glacier, discovered in Australian Antarctic Territory by an Australian aircrew during the summer of 1956–7. The glacier is up to 40 miles (64 km) wide and measures at least 250 miles (402 km) in length. Together with the Fisher Limb, the Lambert Glacier forms a continuous ice passage of 320 miles (514 km).

Geike Glacier, South Georgia, Antarctica 1972, terminating in Cumberland West Bay. The folds and crevasses have been caused by centuries of slow movement of the ice. (Crown copyright; courtesy HMS *Endurance*)

There are also large glaciers in the Himalayas, India, the longest being Siachen, 4 miles (76 km), in the Karakoram range. Two others, the Hispar and the Biafo, combine to form an ice river 76 miles (122 km) long.

New Zealand has several glaciers creeping down the Southern Alps and finishing as sluggish streams in warm forests.

The Glacier National Park, British Columbia, USA, contain 60 separate glaciers which are fed by winter storms and maintained by the subarctic temperatures at the high altitude. The largest, Sperry Glacier, covers about 300 acres (121 hectares). There are many glaciers in Central Europe, whose average speed is about 6–15 in (150–380 mm) per day, and which melt at an average altitude of 6000 ft (1830 m) above sea level into turbid rivers.

In contrast, permanent snow in Great Britain is confined to a small number of gullies on Ben Nevis 4406 ft (1343 m) in Scotland, and a few small beds of snow on Mt Snowdon 3560 ft (1085 m) in Wales. Rock formations worn smooth by travelling ice indicate that glaciers did exist in Britain centuries ago. In order that semi-permanent snow beds in Scotland should become glaciers about 25 summers with temperatures 4°F (2°C) lower than the present average would be needed, and there is no evidence that this is about to occur.

An avalanche is a mechanical break in a snow or ice cover caused by a weakness in one particular area or layer. Snow may slide over a film of melt water or roll over granular crystals or accelerate as if on lubricated ball bearings if both conditions apply. A cornice overhanging a precipice is particularly liable to crash to ground as a result of even the slightest fissure in its structure.

A slab avalanche is a whole layer of snow which breaks loose along a weak boundary leaving a break-off wall.

A loose snow avalanche is a mass of snow which breaks from a particular weak point and fans outwards into a pear-shaped track downhill.

Avalanches can become *air borne* and jump dense timber barriers, particularly when the snow is dry and powdery, and when a strong wind is blowing. Steep slopes frequently avalanche in heavy snow storms because of the additional weight of snow falling upon them. Gentle slopes manage to carry a greater quantity of snow before avalanching, but worse damage is caused when the final break occurs. Attempts are sometimes made to cause frequent but less damaging avalanches by means of explosives.

The speed of avalanches may reach 50 mph (80 km/h) along the ground, and thereafter the snow tends to become airborne. Speed increases whenever falling snow is channelled down narrow gulleys.

One of the fastest measured avalanches occurred at Glärnisch, Switzerland, on 6 March 1898. Snow travelled down a 44° slope at a mean speed of 217 mph (349 km/h), achieving a distance of 4·3 miles (6·9 km) in 1 minute 12 seconds. After crossing a valley more than one mile in width the avalanche ran a considerable distance up the opposite slope before returning into the valley. Snow dust took 7 minutes to settle.

Avalanches occur most frequently in spring, or during winter when there is a sudden change to milder air stream. They occur wherever there are snow covers and slopes and most happen unnoticed in uninhabited areas.

The most dangerous aspects of an avalanche are:
● weight of snow, particularly in a wet snow avalanche.
● risk of suffocation within a dry powder airborne avalanche.
● risk of suffocation when buried within snow.
The risk is greatest in wet snow, and least after a slow-moving avalanche of dry snow which retains air pockets. Twenty minutes is the average time in which rescuers must trace the tell-tale coloured threads carried by skiers in order to rescue victims alive. An Austrian

postman once survived three days buried in snow, but that was exceptional.
● the pressure wave which builds up ahead of a fast moving avalanche, enough to demolish houses before they are engulfed in snow.
● the explosion of air within the avalanche when it is suddenly brought to a halt.
● the partial vacuum behind a fast-moving avalanche which attracts a violent inrush of air, enough to carry a man along with it, even though he escapes the forward blast of the avalanche.
● temporary adiabatic heating on the descent, so that snow melts but refreezes at once when brought to a halt.

A man was once carried along by an avalanche and covered in melt water which froze immediately when the avalanche came to rest. His life was saved by the lucky presence of people who were able to assist him out of his prison of ice.

Disastrous avalanches in the particularly snowy regions of the **Cascade and Rocky Mountains, USA,** have been relatively infrequent. This is not because avalanches do not happen there, but because the mountains have not been inhabited to any extent, except during the gold rush, which started about 1860. In 1874 a mining camp near Alta, Utah, was almost entirely destroyed by an avalanche, and in the next 35 years, 67 more persons were killed.

The deep valleys of the **European Alps** however, contain many farms and villages, so that this region suffers disastrous consequences from the frequent avalanches.

On 13 December 1916 more than 100 avalanches occurred in the Dolomite valley of Northern Italy: 10 000 Austrian and Italian troops were reputed killed and bodies were still being found in 1952.

January and February 1951 witnessed many avalanches after massive quantities of snow fell between 19–21 January, when warm air from the Atlantic converged with cold polar air over the Alps. Houses were crushed at Andermatt, Zermatt, and Vals in Switzerland,

and at Innsbruck and Heiligenblut in Austria. A train in the eastern canton of Grison, Switzerland, was blocked up in a tunnel by simultaneous avalanches at either end. Over 100 people were killed by snow that season, and many forests were destroyed.

The winter of 1970 was just as disastrous. In January an avalanche in northern Italy caused much damage to local industry, and several avalanches in the French Alps resulted in 60 deaths. In Teheran, Persia, snow entombed cars and lorries on 28 January and killed more than 50 people. This disaster followed a snowfall of 1·3 in (33 mm) during the night (a total only exceeded six times in the previous 70 years) and then a sudden change to relatively mild air which loosened the snow on the slopes. Before the winter was gone, three more disastrous avalanches occurred in the French Alps. On 10 February a chalet was buried at Val d'Isère, killing 39 people; eight persons lost their lives near Mont Cenis on 24 February; and on 15 April a sanatorium was engulfed in snow at Plateau d'Assy resulting in 72 deaths.

The only disastrous avalanche in England occurred on 27 December 1836, in the unlikely place of Lewes, Sussex. Heavy snow started to fall on Christmas Eve, and easterly gales were blowing over the top of Cliffe Hill

The Snow Drop Inn, Lewes, Sussex, site of the only disastrous avalanche in England on 27 December 1836.

and slamming backwards in vicious eddies over the 200 ft (60 m) chalk precipice at the far end. A cornice of snow gradually built outwards so that it overhung a row of houses which stood below. Next day, when the inhabitants of the houses saw what had happened they merely regarded the cornice as a snow sculpture to be admired and not as a serious threat to their safety. On 27 December bright sunshine caused a fissure in the cornice, which was noticed by one man who gave the alarm. The inhabitants ignored the warning, and the snow broke away in two separate avalanches, one in the morning and the other in the afternoon. The houses were demolished and eight people were killed.

The chalk cliff was excavated to a safer distance from the road, and a public house was built on the site of the old houses and named 'Snow Drop Inn' in commemoration.

Notorious ice avalanches: On 14 August 1919 an estimated one million tons of ice broke off from the glacier near **Chamonix, France,** and plunged over precipitous rocks. A flood of ice and stone resulted, 2500 ft long, 70 ft wide and 60 ft deep (760 × 21 × 18 m), in which nine visitors from Paris were engulfed without any hope of rescue.

On 10 January 1962 an estimated four million tons of ice avalanched from the 22 205 ft (6768 m) peak of **Nevado de Huascaran, Peru,** S America. The ice richochetted from side to side of the valley below and buried four mountain villages and the town of Ranrahirca. As the avalanche continued downhill it gathered up rocks and mud as well, travelling a total distance of 11 miles (18 km) at an estimated speed of 60 mph (100 km/h) in about 15 minutes. Seven villages, one town and about 3500 persons were wiped out in this short space of time, as well as an estimated 10 000 livestock.

Ablation is the general term for the conversion of snow and ice back to vapour and water, which is thus returned into the world's water cycle once more.

Sunshine is not very efficient at thawing a thick snow cover because of the high reflectivity of snow. Some melting occurs on the surface in warm sunshine, but the water often refreezes again at night. Curious shapes may result from uneven melting in sunshine.

Snow penitents are pillars of firn or ice, which sometimes form when there is high insolation over a snow cover, and when air is below 32°F (0°C) and dry. Small amounts of surface snow melt wherever the snow density is least and form tiny hollows in the snow. These hollows concentrate the Sun's rays like a concave mirror and increase the absorption of heat at the bottom of the hollows. The air temperature in the micro-environments of the depressions rises, and more snow melts. This reduces the depth of snow over the soil or rock

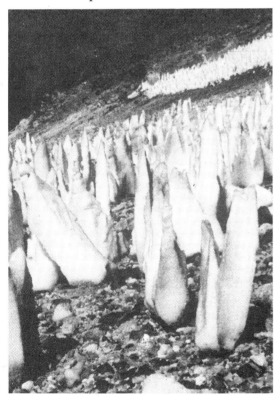

Snow penitents on Mount Demavand, Iran. (B A Benander; courtesy *Weather*)

surface below, which heats in the sunshine and induces still more melting of snow. Eventually, the ground is uncovered at the bottom of the depression, while the edges remain standing as columns of ice projecting into the cold air above. Once the soil between the penitents is cleared, the bases heat by radiation from the ground. The penitents become undercut, they lean towards the Sun and eventually collapse.

Warm air is more effective than sunshine at thawing large quantities of snow. In Great Britain a sudden change from cold easterly winds to mild Atlantic air streams of temperature 40°–45°F (4°–7°C) may melt snow at a rate of 2·5 in (65 mm) per day. If warm air is accompanied by sunshine the rate of ablation may be as much as 7 in (175 mm), and falling rain increases the rate to something like 10 in (250 mm) per day.

The 'snow eater' is the name often given to very dry föhn winds which descend on the lee side of mountains and evaporate a snow cover as rapidly as 2 ft (600 mm) per day.

Countries with the least to fear from thawing snow are those like Switzerland, which have regular snow every year, so that centuries of excessive water during spring have carved streams and rivers of adequate width. Mountain streams become torrents of rushing water in spring, but often dry out by the end of summer awaiting the next spring floods.

Countries with the most to fear from thawing snow are those, like Great Britain, where heavy snow is infrequent and rivers have been gouged by the persistent fall of rain all through the year. Drainage generally keeps pace with the rate at which rain falls, and rivers and streams are narrower than they would be if they had to cope with a huge stockpile of snow released suddenly in spring. Consequently, an abnormally snowy winter may result in a greater press of water during the thaw than rivers can accommodate. The worst snow thaw floods in England and Wales in the

20th century occurred after the severe winter of 1947. Warm air and rain nudged its way into south west England on 10 March, flood waters covered vast areas of southern England by 11 March and inundated low-lying areas by 13 March. A severe SW gale on the night of 16 March drove flood waters ahead, and caused many breaches of dykes in the fenland. Vast areas of the east coast from Yorkshire to Essex were submerged in water till the end of the month.

The eastern states of USA also suffer serious thaw floods after exceptionally severe winters. Among the worst were floods which started on 17 January 1937, after a sudden thaw accompanied by unseasonal and very heavy rain. The Ohio River flooded along its entire length, the Mississippi basin was awash, complete towns were engulfed in water, and ten states became emergency areas. Louisville was entirely marooned and Cincinnati had flood water 80 ft (24 m) deep in places. Over 100 people lost their lives, and more than $1\frac{1}{2}$ million people were driven from their homes. Memories such as those encouraged the authorities of Buffalo, in February 1977, to attempt to move snow out of the town by train, to be dumped in locations where it could melt without danger.

Snow cannot thaw in very high latitudes, where air temperature does not rise above freezing level. Small annual quantities of snow accumulate for centuries into dense sheets of firn snow and ice, and then gradually inch their way downhill towards the sea:

The largest expanse of permanent sheet ice, 85 per cent of the world's total, covers the mountainous continent of Antarctica over the south pole, which is an area equivalent to the size of Europe and USA together, or twice the size of Australia. In the northern hemisphere, Greenland has the greatest expanse of permanent ice, about 10 per cent of the world's total. It is estimated that in the unlikely event of these ice sheets melting, they would together raise the level of the oceans

approximately 225 ft (70 m). Fortunately there is little likelihood of this happening.

Ice sheets creep downhill at speeds which vary from 50–1500 ft (15–450 m) per annum. They crack open into crevasses when moving over rock obstructions, portions may be lifted above the general level of the ice sheet and become domes on top of underlying rocks; eventually these thick sheets reach the coast.

Ice shelves are ice sheets which have reached the coast line and then continue floating out to sea. Once the ice shelf gets into deep enough water the movement of the sea causes it to fracture and break away at an ice front. Ice shelves vary in thickness from 450 ft (140 m) at the seaward edge, where it has suffered considerable melting, to 4000 ft (1200 m) at the shore boundary. Average thickness of the ice sheet over Antarctica is estimated to be 6500 ft (1980 m) and the greatest measured thickness over Antarctica is 14 000 ft (4267 m).

Tabular icebergs are broken sections of shelf ice and are peculiar to Antarctica. They are flat topped, the striations of individual annual snowfalls are clearly visible throughout the depth of the break line and they have a white lustre colour like plaster of Paris. They float with four-fifths of their volume below water, and present a sheer cliff of ice 90 ft (27 m) above the sea on average.

Captain Robert Scott, British explorer, sighted a tabular berg 138 ft (42 m) high on his last expedition in 1911.

Many tabular bergs measure 20–30 miles (30–50 km) in length. A tabular berg 208 × 60 miles (335 × 100 km) was sighted by the USS *Glacier* 150 miles (240 km) west of Scott Island on 12 November 1956. Two adjacent giants were photographed by satellite in the Weddell Sea during January 1969. They measured 25 × 55 miles (40 × 90 km) and 38 × 100 miles (60 × 160 km) and were separated by only a few miles of open water. They travelled 300 miles (480 km) in four months.

The remains of a tabular berg was sighted as far north as 26° 30′ S, 25° 40′ W in 1894 by a Russian ship *Dochra* on 30 April 1894.

A tabular iceberg in Marguerite Bay, Antarctica, makes an ideal landing area for a Whirlwind helicopter launched from HMS *Endurance* in February 1973. Note the striations of countless years of snowfall. (Crown copyright; courtesy HMS *Endurance*)

Fast ice is that which has broken from the ice shelves and grounded in shallow water. It offers anchorage to sea ice and extends in a belt around the continent as far as the 900 ft (300 m) depth of sea contour, beyond which the ice floats free to roam the ocean. In some areas, notably between longitude 136° W and 158° W around Antarctica, fast ice may be persistent and extend over a width of about 60 miles (95 km).

Glaciers 'calve' into icebergs of irregular shape when they reach the sea, and these often contain crevasses which the sea and wind open up into caves. Icebergs themselves often calve again and may capsize because of a new centre of gravity.

A ship approaching the continent of Antarctica during summer expects to see approximately 300 bergs before reaching the coast, the first visible evidence of their proximity being a dampening down of the sea to give an oily appearance.

Glaciers in Greenland calve into the sea as ice bergs, and many drift into the Atlantic via Baffin Bay.

Glacier ice bergs are generally flat white in colour, but occasionally dazzling white when the right conditions of light reflect from air bubbles near the surface. They are more dense than tabular bergs, and resist weathering better. Black bergs are dark coloured because of mud and stone embedded within, or because of final expulsion of air in the melting process.

Bergy bits are remnants of large ice bergs which are still visible above the sea.

Growlers are small remnants of ice bergs, which are almost entirely submerged beneath the ice, but which cause considerable damage to ships when dashed by heavy waves.

The worst accident caused by an ice berg in the North Atlantic was the sinking of the *Titanic* at 41° 16′ N 50° 4′ W, on the night of 14/15 April 1912, during her maiden voyage. – The night was dark, the ice berg was one of the black variety, and it was not seen until about 500 yd (450 m) away. The *Titanic* was holed in collision with the ice berg, and 1503 people out of the 2201 aboard were drowned.

Today a radar monitoring system keeps track on travelling ice bergs, and reports their presence to shipping.

Iceberg in the uncharted waters off Rothera Point, Adelaide Island, Antarctica. (Crown copyright, courtesy HMS *Endurance*)

CHAPTER 13

HAIL

STATE OF QATAR دولة قطر

Launching of a meteorological satellite.

Hail was one of the traditional weapons of wrath in the armoury of the gods. –

'And the Lord said to Moses, stretch forth thine hand towards heaven that there may be hail in all the land of Egypt, upon man, upon beast and upon every herb of the field.' (Exodus 9.)

Despite more worldly explanations, hail is still regarded as a major plague.

Hailstones are ice crystals, which have been tossed up and down by the strong vertical currents in a cumulonimbus cloud, acquiring one coating of ice after another until they are heavy enough to fall to ground. Crystals attain coatings of clear ice when in contact with large super-cooled water drops which only freeze slowly, and get covered in rime when amongst small super-cooled drops. Hailstones are usually round or conical in shape, depending upon distortion during travel.

Soft hail or graupel is small and opaque, having frozen speedily enough to trap air within the ice. It has a soft nucleus, surrounded by a coating of clear ice where the freezing process has been slowed down by the release of latent heat.

Large hailstones have alternate rings of clear and opaque ice. Cross sections reveal the details of the hailstone's journey up and down in the cloud as clearly as concentric rings in the trunk of a tree reveal the weather conditions during growth. Twenty-five separate layers have been counted in one hailstone.

In equatorial regions hail is mainly a problem over mountainous country where altitude ensures a temperature low enough for hail to remain frozen until reaching the ground.

In polar regions hail does not occur because cumulonimbus do not develop to great heights, and temperatures within the clouds are too low to contain large super-cooled water drops.

In middle latitudes, during the warmer months of the year, hail forms mainly over large land masses. Thermal up-currents in cumulonimbus are then at their strongest, and contain an abundance of super-cooled water drops on which small ice crystals can feed.

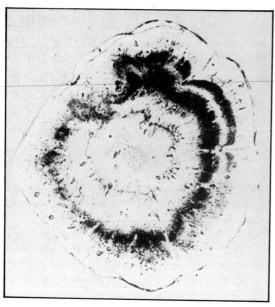

Cross section through a typically shaped hailstone.
(Meteorological Office, Bracknell)

Hailstone diameter is usually between 0·2–2·0 in (5–50 mm), anything over 0·4 in (10 mm) in diameter being termed 'large'. Any stones which are larger than 2·0 in (50 mm) are usually conglomerates of smaller stones, bonded together by regelation in the same way as ice floes bond together into pack ice.

The largest recorded single hailstone fell at Coffeyville, Kansas, USA, on 3 September 1970, and weighed 1·67 lb (758 g). It measured 7½ in (190 mm) in diameter and 17½ in (444 mm) circumference when photographed in the hands of the two boys who found it, and could have been as big as 8 in (200 mm) in diameter when first picked up.

Other notable hailstorms and stones:

17 Aug 1830   Mexico City, Mexico: hail fell to a depth of 16 in (400 mm).

30 April 1888   Moradabad and Beheri, Northern India: hailstones as large as cricket balls fell, killing 246 people, and more than 1600 sheep and goats.

22 Dec 1907   Port Said, Egypt: destructiv hail fell, and samples colle ted weighed 53–194 oz (15C 550 g). Hailstones 1½ in (38 mn diameter fell in Cairo on th previous evening, 21 Decem ber.

8 May 1926   Dallas, Texas, USA: hailston the size of cricket balls cause damage worth 2 million dolla in 15 minutes.

6 July 1928   Potter, Nebraska, USA: hai stones measured, reached diameter of 5½ in (140 mm) an weighed 1½ lb (680 g).

19 June 1932   Western Hunan Province, S China: a hailstorm killed 20 people and injured thousands

17 Nov 1949   Durban, S Africa: hailstone weighed 5½–8 oz (156–227 g and caused damage wort £500 000.

14 July 1953   Alberta Province, Canada hailstones as large as golf ball covered an area 140 × 5 mile (225 × 8 km). Thousands o birds were killed, many havin their skulls crushed by th hail.

27 May 1959   Delhi, India: hailstones esti mated size of 8 in (200 mm diameter or more batterec holes 10–15 in (250–375 mm diameter in an aircraft.

3 June 1959   Selden, NW Kansas, USA: hailstorm lasted 85 minutes and covered an area of approxi mately 9 × 6 miles (14 × 10 km in hailstones to a depth o 18 in (450 mm).

Unusual hailstones fell in the northern suburbs of Sydney, Australia, on 3 January 1971. They consisted almost entirely of clear ice, but had small opaque centres. The knobbly stones had icicle extensions of about the same length as the diameter of the central sphere, about 0·8 in (20 mm).

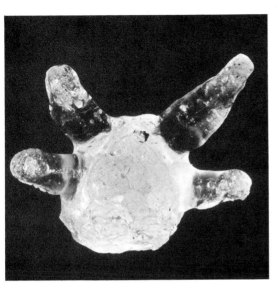

Hailstone which fell at Sydney, Australia, on 3 January 1971. The scale is in centimetres and the greatest dimension across the horns is 4·5 cm (1·8 in). (S C Mossop)

At Dubuque, Iowa, USA, on 16 June 1882, hailstones up to 5 in (125 mm) in diameter fell during a 13 minute storm, and in two stones small living frogs were found. They had been carried up in the vertical currents of the storm, and acquired coatings of ice before becoming heavy enough to fall to the ground.

Tragic human 'hail' occurred on two occasions in Germany over the Rhön mountains. In 1930, glider pilots, caught in a thundercloud, baled out of their gliders and were carried up and down within the super-cooled cloud till they fell to earth frozen within ice prisons. Only one man out of five survived the ordeal. One glider pilot died in a similar manner in 1938.

In Great Britain, the largest hail is usually considerably smaller than that suffered elsewhere in the world. Moreover, small stones often melt before being noticed, so that the frequency with which hail occurs is hard to assess. Many hailstones bounce out of the apertures of rain gauges, and those which fall inside melt and become indistinguishable from rainfall. However, a simple hail indicator can be made by stretching uncreased aluminium foil tightly across a frame or an open tin, and leaving it in an unsheltered exposure. Hailstones which strike the foil make readily visible imprints.

The oldest known hailstone imprints are fossilised, and date from about 160 million years ago. They have been discovered in the cliffs of north east Yorkshire, south of the Peak Fault at Ravenscar. Hail fell originally into mud of plastic consistency, soft enough to give way under the falling hailstones, but stiff enough to retain the impressions of the stones after they had melted.

In Great Britain hail does not usually remain on the ground for long because surface air temperatures tend to be above melting level. Nevertheless, on 6 August 1956, hail which fell in Arundel, Sussex, to a depth of 2 ft (60 mm) in places, was swept aside by road sweepers on to a grass verge beneath a dense cover of large trees. The hail survived in this shade for more than three days, despite maximum screen temperatures locally of 65–74°F (18–23°C). The hail became steadily more disguised as dirt was thrown over it by passing traffic.

Heavy falls of hail often appear very dramatic and a recent storm on 14 August 1975 at Hampstead, London, was described by Patricia Beckman in the Journal of Meteorology.

'Gardens and playing fields were completely covered by a heaving off-white crust of hail nearly one foot in depth, looking like a winter snowscape. As continuing hail tore to earth, this ever-swelling crust was forced by the lie of the land into waves which slowly rippled down hill like a sea of icy porridge.'

The heaviest recorded hailstone in Great Britain, weighing 5 oz (141 g), fell at Horsham, West Sussex, on 5 September 1958. Though this seems puny compared with the 1·67 lb (750 g) hailstone which fell at Coffeyville, USA, the country has experienced many hail storms of damaging proportions. Most of the stones of exceptional size are measured by domestic rulers or tape measures, rather than being weighed, or they are described by comparison with known objects.

Examples of notable hail storms in Great Britain:

24 July 1818   Orkney Isles: hailstones as large as goose eggs fell to a depth of 9 in (225 mm).

3 July 1883   Barton, Lincolnshire: hailstones 5 × 3 in (125 × 75 mm), some weighing $2\frac{1}{2}$ oz (70 g) broke 15 tons of glass in the town.

8 June 1957   Camelford, Cornwall: during one half hour in the afternoon an estimated equivalent of 1 in (25 mm) rain fell as hailstones, which could not be measured by local rain gauges because they were bouncing 3 ft (1 m) high and 12 ft (4 m) horizontally. It had been wet all day, total rainfall 7·1 in (180 mm), and the hailstones were washed along in flood water, coalescing into masses of ice in the same way that frozen peas tipped into cold water in a saucepan bond together. The inn yard at Camelford was piled knee deep with solid blocks of hailstones.

13 July 1967   West Wiltshire and its borders with Somerset and Gloucestershire: hail with a diameter 0·5 in (13 mm) fell over the Mendips and, by the time the storm reached Melksham, was as large as golf balls. Hail of approximately 3 in (75 mm) diameter was reported near the village of Gastard, Wiltshire. Such large hail is rare in Great Britain, and on this occasion it caused much damage to greenhouses and growing crops.

The annual frequency of large hail in Great Britain is indicated by the following reports from various newspapers during 1975:

12 January   Clay Coton, Northamptonshire: hailstones fell for a few minutes at 1330 GMT 'as big as a man's fist'.

23 May   Chulmleigh and Chawleigh, Devon: hailstones often 'as large as marbles' accumulated to depths of 4 in (100 mm).

8 July   Westone, Northampton: hail fell between 1830 and 1900 GMT, average diameter 0·5 in (12 mm).

14 July   widespread hail in west and north Midlands. Sizes variously reported as 'big as golfballs', greater than 1 in (25 mm), 'a good half inch across', 'up to 3 in (70 mm) in diameter'.

17 July   Stretton-on-Dunsmore, Warwick: hail 'the size of large marbles'.

5 August   Coventry, Warwick: $\frac{3}{4}$ in (18 mm) diameter hailstones, maximum diameters over 1 in (30 mm).

14 August   Hampstead, London: largest hailstones nearly $\frac{3}{4}$ in (20 mm) diameter.

Hail is the worst enemy of many agricultural communities. It can strip leaves from vineyards and tea plantations, it can batter crops of cereals to a useless pulp, and can cause irremediable damage to young citrus fruits. Therefore, farmers have been trying throughout history to devise methods of preventing hail.

Primitive tribes used to shoot arrows into clouds, in order to frighten away the evil spirits, which they thought inhabited the clouds and were making hail.

Christian communities started ringing church bells in the 8th century in order to exorcise the evil spirits in the clouds. It was a dangerous procedure, because hail is often accompanied by thunder and lightning, and, before lightning conductors were invented,

Cartoon from the *Brisbane Courier*, c 1901, showing Clement Wragge, Queensland Government Meteorologist and the Stiger gun with which he hoped to release rain from clouds. (R J Gourlay)

ped with cast-iron muzzle loading mortars. These had 3 cm bore, were 20 cm long, charged with 180 g powder and mounted on stout wooden platforms to fire vertically. Metal smoke stacks were mounted above the muzzles to act as sounding boxes and to make more noise. The following year, 1897, there was no damaging hail at all in the valley, and the gun defence attained immediate fame. By

church towers were vulnerable to lightning strikes. However, despite an unfortunately high number of deaths, bell-ringing remained popular as a hail prevention method.

Cannons were first fired into clouds over central Europe during the 16th century, but there were no conclusive results from the experiments. There was considerable wrangling about whether storms were merely diverted from one satisfied vineyard owner to another aggrieved one.

The Stiger Gun was introduced in 1896 by Albert Stiger, burgomaster in the Steirmark district of Austria, after a series of disastrous hail-storm years. In order to protect the valley, 36 stations were established and equip-

Stiger gun mounted in the public gardens at Charleville, Australia. The inscription on the gun is in error, the name being Stiger not Steiger; he was Mr, not Professor; there were 6 guns, not 10; and the Mayor of Charleville fired the guns on that date and not Mr Wragge. (M G Soutter)

1900, 7000 stations protected north Italy alone, and Stiger guns had been sent to Russia, Spain and America. The protection method was not without its dangers, and was the direct cause of eleven deaths and 60 serious injuries in just one year, 1900.

The Stiger Gun attracted attention also in Australia where the problem was drought. Clement Wragge, Queensland Government Meteorologist, thought the explosion in a vapour laden cloud might release rain, and in September 1901 trials started with a Stiger Gun in the Botanic Gardens, Brisbane. Result – one fractured gun, no rain, a wet season at the end of 1902, and consequent wane of interest.

Meteorologists were divided in opinion about whether the whole idea was nonsense or not, and a conference on the matter was held in Graz, Austria, in July 1902. The Austrian and Italian governments set up two test areas, which were equipped for even bigger barrages, but within two years both areas had disastrous storms. The idea was discredited once more, but all that had really been proved was that the method was not infallible. Rockets continued to be fired experimentally in various parts of the world.

In July 1963, rocket trials started in the Kericho area of Kenya, Africa, where the tea plantations on high ground (6700 ft (2042 m)) suffer badly from hail. Results showed that despite a higher than usual incidence of storms, hail caused less damage since it was often 'mushy'.

In 1969, the Russians claimed to have reduced hail damage by up to 80 per cent in selected agricultural test areas of the Caucasus by introducing cloud seeding chemicals by artillery shells into hail-bearing storms. The size of hailstones was reduced from an average 2 in (50 mm) diameter to an average 0·4 in (10 mm) diameter.

Possible explanations for the success of some rocketry experiments to prevent hail:
● Nuclei introduced into clouds, either by the rocket's own explosives or special chemical seeds, encourage more super-cooled drops to freeze, and thus they remain small.
● Pressure waves from the rocket explosion may cause cracking of large hailstones which contain air pockets. Such stones have been known to explode with loud reports when falling to the ground.
● Shock waves may speed the freezing of water drops and increase the proportion of soft hail in a cloud.

Overhead cover provides more practical protection for the orange groves in Sorrento, Italy. Permanent vertical pallisades shelter the groves against the wind and these are surmounted by a horizontal framework of cross bars. Tidy piles of rush mats sit astride the framework at intervals, capped with two mats at an angle, like the roof of a dovecot. At the first indication of hail, the mats are spread

Pile of rush mats in Sorrento, Italy, ready for laying across the horizontal framework as protection against hail for the orange grove below.

out over the framework to make a roof for the orange trees below. The hail melts and seeps through as valuable water instead of being destructive ammunition.

Hydro meteors or ice meteors is the name given to large chunks of ice which have been known to fall from the sky, and which cannot be explained. They usually occur singly.

Two examples from the 19th century, and ten since 1970, indicate the nature of the mystery.

15 June 1829	Flammarion wrote about a block of ice weighing 4·4 lb (2 kg) which fell out of the sky at Cazorta, Spain.
13 Aug 1849	a single mass of ice reported to be 6 ft (2 m) in diameter was reported to have fallen in Ross, Scotland.
16 Aug 1970	a huge lump of ice crashed through the conservatory roof of a house in Isleworth, Greater London, where a family of four was asleep.
25 June 1971	a block of ice weighing 2 lb (900 g) crashed into a flower bed in Rouen, N France, just missing a man working in a garden.
23 Jan 1972	a block of ice more than 3 ft square (1 m²) smashed into the ground near a house in Shirley, Surrey.
9 Jan 1973	a block of ice weighing 10 lb (4·5 kg) fell out of the sky shattering a porch at West Wickham, Kent.
22 Sept 1973	a ball of ice crashed through the roof of a bungalow at Wombwell, Yorkshire.
25 Mar 1974	a mass of ice about 18 in (450 mm) diameter crashed on to a car which the owner was cleaning, at Pinner, Middlesex. Ice smashed roof tiles nearby.
June 1974	(exact date not known), a block of ice weighing about 2 lb

(900 g) fell into the lawn of St Patrick's Hospital, Cashel, Co Tipperary, Eire, making a dent 1½ in (38 mm) deep.

24 Jan 1975	a 48 lb (22 kg) ice bomb damaged the roof of a house in Fulham Road, London.
15 May 1976	several lumps of ice hit houses in Reading, Berkshire.
2 Jan 1977	a block of ice weighing about 110 lb (50 kg) smashed through the roof and into a bedroom in a house in Ponders End, Middlesex.

Possible explanations for ice meteors:

● Breakage from an aircraft of ice which originally formed by flying through super-cooled cloud, or by waste water seeping from the internal domestic installations of the plane.

Sometimes this explanation is substantiated by discovery of pollution in the ice, sometimes it is refuted by denials that any planes have been in the area, or that they could even fly with such weights of ice aboard.

● Congealed masses of hailstones, – a reason often disproved because the ice has no concentric ring patterns.

● A possible consequence of powerful lightning strokes on the water constituents of a cloud by some method not yet known.

However, an American study in 1960 of ice meteors showed that in about one third of the cases, no clouds were closer than 600 miles (1000 km) of the ice fall site.

The most closely scrutinised ice meteor was one which providentially dropped at the feet of R F Griffiths, a lightning observer for the Electrical Research Association, who was immediately aware of the importance of the sudden evidence from the sky. On the evening of Monday, 2 April 1973, strong northerly winds were blowing in the Manchester area, and the sky was half covered with clouds whose base was about 2000 ft (600 m). At 1954 GMT there was one very bright flash of lightning – and one only – which was seen over a wide area of Manchester. About 10 minutes later a huge

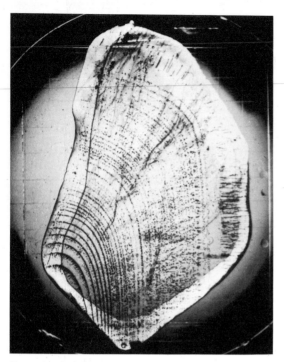

Cross section, longest dimension 4·7 in (120 mm), of the ice meteor which fell at Manchester on 2 April 1973, viewed by transmitted light. (R F Griffiths)

lump of ice fell to the ground in Burton Road, Manchester, mostly shattering into small pieces; but one large lump remained, which

Mr Griffiths hurriedly took home and put into the freezer. Later, in laboratory tests, thin sections of the block were cut and photographed by both reflected and transmitted light. They were found to have 51 layers of clear ice separated by thinner layers of trapped air bubbles. The fragment was 5·5 in (140 mm) in length, weighed 20 oz (567 g) and appeared to have broken off at the nucleus of growth, which was less than 0·4 (10 mm) in diameter. It was estimated that the complete ice meteor might have weighed 2–4 lb (1–2 kg), thus comparing favourably with the Coffeyville, USA, record authenticated hailstone weighing 1·67 lb (750 g). Analysis of a sample of meltwater from the ice meteor indicated that it was composed of cloud water. Close questioning of personnel at the nearby air port revealed that none of the aircraft in the vicinity of the ice meteor drop had experienced any icing of such a nature, and no other hail was reported nearer than Wilmslow, several miles away. The origin of the meteor remains a mystery.

Research continues, and for all interested weather observers there is one golden rule to be followed if an ice meteor is found. Consign it quickly into the deep freeze compartment of a refrigerator and report the find to a local meteorological office.

CHAPTER 14

ELECTRICITY IN THE ATMOSPHERE AND THUNDERSTORMS

Thor the Thunderer brings the storm

Electricity is the hallmark of modern living, yet the word itself derives from a substance whose electro static properties were known even to the philosophers of Ancient Greece.

'Elektron' is the Greek word for amber – a fossilised resin – which used to be much prized as a material for making into ornaments. From the writings of Thales, a philosopher of the 6th century BC, we know that the Greeks were aware of the fact that amber, when rubbed, acquired the property of attracting small particles of light weight. This fact did not at the time appear to have any connection with thunder and lightning, which were considered to be the visible and audible expressions of

displeasure by the gods. Aristotle (384–322 BC) attempted a more materialistic explanation, suggesting that thunder was the noise made by air which was ejected from one cloud and then hit another, and that lightning was the ejected wind burning.

Dr William Gilbert (1540–1603), English physician, discovered that many other materials besides amber acquired the ability to attract small particles when rubbed. In 1600 he published a treatise *De Magnete* (things which attract) in which he introduced the terms 'electrics' and 'electricity'. He distinguished two kinds of 'electrics': vitreous electrics produced when glass was rubbed with silk; and resinous electrics produced when amber or sealing wax was rubbed with fur. Gilbert noted that the presence of moisture lessened the attracting abilities of the substances which were rubbed. 'Non-electrics' were defined as materials which remained unaffected by rubbing.

Other scientists continued the experiments, and by the end of the 18th century it was known that similar electrics repelled each other and dissimilar electrics attracted each other. Moreover, electrics tended to collect more easily around points or curved contours of the substances rubbed.

Benjamin Franklin (1706–90), American scientist and statesman, was convinced that lightning was a form of electricity. One day, in July 1752, on a suitably cloudy day which, experience told him, might result in a thunderstorm, he flew a kite made of a silk handkerchief stretched taut over two crossed sticks. Near the end of the anchoring hemp twine he attached a metal key, and, between the key and his hand, he used a silk ribbon which he kept dry by standing inside a shed doorway. However, weather does not arrive to order and Franklin found that many clouds passed overhead without providing him with the evidence he wanted. Eventually rain fall, the kite twine became wet and a few loose threads of twine moved apart from each other, as if containing similar 'electrics'. Franklin stretched his hand towards the key and sparks jumped the gap between. He had proved that 'electrics' had been collected from the cloud, but without the rubbing of vitreous or resinous substances. The old descriptions of the two kinds of 'electrics' became inappropriate and Franklin renamed them positive electric charge (+ve) instead of 'vitreous electric', and negative electric charge (-ve) instead of 'resinous electric'. The two together are known collectively as static electricity or electrostatic charges. Non-electrics were later renamed conductors when it was discovered that current electricity would flow through them.

Michael Faraday (1791–1867), English chemist and electrical engineer, discovered that electrostatic charges always collect on the outside of a hollow object. His own experiments were carried out with a cage, but any hollow object may be described as a 'Faraday cage' when its reaction to electrostatic charge is discussed.

Sir Joseph John Thomson (1856–1940), Scottish physicist, discovered the electrical nature of the atom. Every atom consists of a nucleus of particles called 'neutrons' (without electric charge) and particles called 'protons' which have positive electric charge. Electrons are negative electric charges, which revolve around the nucleus like planets round a sun, and which are equal in number to the protons in the nucleus. The electrons of some materials can transfer their allegiance when stimulated

by heat or friction. Atoms which gain electrons then have more negative charges than positive, and are said to be 'negatively' charged. Atoms which have lost electrons then have more protons than electrons and are said to be 'positively' charged. Insulating materials have electrons, which are firmly bound to their own atom and cannot move independently.

Separation of electric charge by friction occurs all the time, by people walking over the ground, by particles rubbing together in the air, and by road vehicles or aircraft travelling rapidly over the ground and through air and cloud. Normally, charge separation is small and one charge leaks to earth unnoticed, while the other is neutralised gradually by ions in the air.

Ions are particles in the atmosphere which have acquired separated charge by various natural processes. There is a concentration of these particles in the ionosphere, the region above 40 miles (60 km) above ground, but they also occur in the troposphere, up to 10 miles (16 km) above ground, which is the region where weather occurs. Any electric charge of small amount which collects on objects attracts ions of opposite charge, and they neutralise each other. When the collected charge is greater than normal, for instance at the sharp point of a conductor, a more violent discharge occurs with a visible spark. This is often accompanied by a crackle or hissing noise, and the whole phenomenon is called a 'brush discharge'.

Brush discharge, as defined above, has become a particular feature of daily living ever since synthetic materials, which are nearly always insulators, started to predominate over natural fibres and leather which are usually conductors. Clothes fizz and spark when pulled off quickly, gyrate around the hand, and become so attracted to each other that they are hard to separate.

The most usual 'shocking' situations for human beings are when sliding across seats to enter or leave cars. The separated charge clings to the body, because it cannot leak quickly through synthetic fabrics, but then discharges painfully when a pointed finger stretches to lock the door or insert the ignition key. Remedy – keep hold of the metal car body the whole time while entering or leaving so that the charges conduct away as they form.

Busy secretaries, scuffing their feet across synthetic carpets, often accumulate a large electrostatic charge which discharges painfully on stretching a hand towards a metal filing cabinet. Remedy – approach closely in order to discharge through the broad area of the body before offering a finger for point discharge.

Dogs acquire an electrostatic charge when stretched in front of a fire on a synthetic carpet. The charge jumps painfully from wet nose to caressing hand of an owner, but can be avoided by placing the flat of the hand on the broad side of the dog to achieve discharge.

Relative humidity is a pertinent factor in determining indoor brush discharge. The lower the relative humidity the smaller the chance of electrostatic charges leaking away to the air. The worst problems arise in very cold climates, such as endured by Whitehorse Yukon, Canada. Air temperature outdoors is often below $-30°F$ ($-34°C$), relative humidity usually above 80 per cent. When such air is heated indoor to a comfortable $70°F$ ($21°C$), relative humidity falls to around 5 per cent. Even humidifiers cannot raise relative humidity enough to solve 'shocking' problems.

St Elmo's Fire is a brush discharge which happens in the atmosphere when there exists a strong electrical field. The discharge occurs from protuberances, such as ships' masts, wind vanes or aircraft wing tips, and is usually blue-green in colour, or sometimes whitish. The Fire is often occompanied by a crackling noise.

This brush discharge has traditionally been regarded as an omen of good fortune, and was at one time called 'the fire of Castor and Pollux', sons of the Greek god Zeus. Later,

the fire was named after St Elmo, who was Bishop of Gaeta, Italy, in the 4th century, and became the patron saint of fire whose protection was much invoked by mariners.

In the late 12th century, St Elmo's Fire appeared at the masthead of a ship in the fleet of Richard I and was thought to be an apparition of the Virgin Mary. More recently, on 21 December 1976, the Prefects of Dover Boys Grammar School were playing their annual football match against the Masters, a day in which convection cloud was rapidly building upwards to cumulonimbus. At 1210 GMT lightning was seen over Dover, followed almost immediately by thunder. One of the masters F G Thomas, reported that

'the football match stopped, because the hair of three of the players was glowing and standing up. The electrical charge was presumably a type of St Elmo's Fire and surrounded the heads only. The players did not feel anything and were happily quite unhurt but they reported hearing a popping sound like the repeated snapping of fingers.'

Andes Glow or Andes Lights is a brush discharge, sometimes seen in the vicinity of mountain peaks. Observations come mainly from the Andes mountains in South America, but sightings have been reported in the European Alps, Mexico and Lapland. The light takes the form either of a single flash, intermittent flashes or regular flashes, and sometimes the light reaches above the peaks as a beam. The phenomenon is usually seen when relative humidity is low. Weather is often cloudless, but sightings occur mostly towards dawn when a strong temperature inversion often exists, a factor which may be contributory to the discharge.

Brush discharge can be dangerous in the presence of inflammable vapour, and has been suspected of causing explosions in tankers during vigorous cleansing of empty tanks.

One of the worst disasters, attributed to brush discharge, happened on 6 May, 1937. The German air ship *Hindenburg* had crossed the Atlantic and was close to the mooring mast at Lakehurst airfield, New Jersey, USA, with her lines already thrown out ready for tying up. There was a sudden flash, an explosion, and in moments the whole airship was ablaze: 35 people were killed, or later died of burns, but 62 people miraculously survived. The cause of the explosion was never proven, but St Elmo's Fire had been seen playing around the airship during its flight against strong head winds. It was suggested that the charge had jumped violently across to the mast tip, and ignited some leaking inflammable gas.

A thunderstorm is the most powerful electrical phenomenon in nature. Extremely high electrical differences build up in deep clouds and eventually discharge as lightning. Thunder is the sound made by the violent expansion of air, which is heated along the line of the flash.

Thunder rumbles because the sound waves echo from intervening obstructions. Freak reflections or bending of sound waves may cause silent zones quite near to the storm, while the noise is being heard very far away. Thunder can usually be heard 10 miles (16 km) away, but it has been heard as far distant as 40 miles (65 km).

A thunderstorm day is defined as one on which thunder is heard even if the listener is too far away to suffer the weather effects of the storm. Statistics of thunderstorm days therefore do not necessarily imply that a storm has been overhead, merely that it has been in the neighbourhood.

The separation of electrical charge within a cloud is complicated and still not fully understood. Friction and also the processes of water transformation play their parts. Water drops which break apart acquire positive charge on the larger fragment, and negative charge on the finer spray. Supercooled water drops which freeze to rime acquire negative charge on the rime, and positive charge on any tiny ice splinters shed in the process. There is a charge transfer between ice crystals of different temperature and between ice crystals which

rub together. All these processes, and probably others not yet discovered, contribute to the electrification of a cloud.

Cumulonimbus are the principal thunderstorm clouds, because they contain violent and disruptive winds, a plentiful supply of supercooled water drops, and the glaciation stage of development triggers off large electrical charge separation. It has been proved that positive charge collects at the top of a cumulonimbus and negative charge near the base, usually in the region of the 14°F (−10°C) isotherm, with a small positive charge area low down in the cloud in the region of heavy rain. The negatively charged base of the cloud attracts a positively charged 'shadow' on the ground below, which follows the cloud along the highest contours available in an attempt to meet the attracting charge above.

Thunderstorms occur in two types of cumulonimbus clouds: those with low bases, probably less than 2000 ft (600 m) above ground, which develop in air streams which are unstable from the ground up to great heights; and those with high bases at 6000 ft (1800 m) or more above ground, which develop from castellanus cloud in an upper layer of unstable air during a heat wave. The necessary atmospheric conditions for thunderstorms to develop are therefore the same as the conditions necessary for the formation of cumulonimbus clouds (see also Chapter 9).

Thunderstorms of short duration occur at any time of the year when conditions are suitable for the development of low base cumulonimbus. They are most frequent in late spring and summer, but they can occur in winter and often accompany vigorous cold fronts. Winter thunderstorms are sometimes called 'freaks', but they are really quite normal occurrences. However, they usually pass quickly, with perhaps no more than one or two loud claps of thunder, and therefore they do not live in the memory as do the long and awe-inspiring high level thunderstorms of summer.

Low-base thunderstorms travel with approximately the same speed and direction as the wind at 10 000 ft (3000 m) above the ground, and this is usually fairly strong in an unstable air stream. There is only a germ of truth in the tradition that 'thunderstorms travel *against* the wind'. An approaching cumulonimbus affects surface wind in much the same way as a vacuum cleaner, pushed across a carpet, affects the particles of dirt lying there. They are sucked *towards* the cleaner in the opposite direction from that in which the cleaner is being pushed. Similarly, surface wind alters temporarily as it gets sucked towards the base of an approaching cumulonimbus which is nevertheless moving inexorably towards an observer.

Thunderstorms of long duration occur in high base cumulonimbus, which develop after the accumulated heat of summer breaks from a lower stable layer of air into instable air above. These high-base clouds also travel on the upper winds, but these are usually light at the end of a summer anticyclone. Moreover, the tradition that 'thunderstorms move in circles' is no worse than a slightly inaccurate description of high level storms. Each storm cell probably lasts no longer than 30–40 minutes and does not have time to move in a circle. However, each down draught from one dying thunder cloud provides the impetus for another to form within the self-contained region of unstable air aloft. Hence self-propagated thunderstorms may be observed in all directions during a whole night of thunder activity, giving the impression that one storm only has been moving in a circle.

The most frequent thunderstorms occur in regions with regular development of cumulonimbus, which is within equatorial regions.

Kampala, Uganda, Africa, has an average 242 thunderstorm days per annum.

On the mountainous island of Java, Indonesia, an average 322 thunderstorm days per annum were recorded at Bogor for the period 1916–19. Even allowing for the fact that this figure included days when thunder was heard in the distance but no stormy weather materialised, Bogor is probably the most thundery place in the world. It has at least 25 severe storms each year, when cloud-to-earth lightning occurs within a half mile distance at least every 30 seconds for a period of at least 30 minutes.

Thunderstorms are virtually unknown in polar regions because cumulus clouds do not develop to any great height, and there are no intense heat waves. These regions, however, have many spectacular electrical displays, caused by friction between ice crystals in snow blizzards, or by solar discharges which are organised into waving curtains of light by the Earth's magnetic field. (See Aurora).

In middle latitudes thunderstorms are most frequent over land masses providing a strong thermal heat source. In the United States of America the frequency of thunderstorm days varies from three per annum along the west coast, to approximately 45 per annum in the central states and up to 70 per annum in Florida. In Great Britain, the Midlands have an average 20 thunderstorm days per annum, and the south-east of England has a relatively high number of 15 thunderstorm days because cumulonimbus are often 'imported' on south-easterly winds from France. The remaining coastal regions of the country have on average only four thunderstorm days per annum. Experienced observers reported 38 thunderstorm days at Stonyhurst, Lancashire in 1912 and at Huddersfield, West Yorkshire in 1967. Possibly other places could have equalled these records, if it were not for the difficulty of detecting distant thunder amidst all the other noises of urban life.

Lightning is the discharge of an electric field which has developed within a cloud; the discharge may occur within the cloud, from one cloud to another, or between cloud and ground. However, since air is normally non-conductive, discharge can only occur after channels of ionised air have been established.

A leader stroke is a channel of ionised air, formed when electrons are accelerated by the intense electrical field. The stroke darts downwards from the cloud base in progressive steps of about 150–300 ft (50–100 m) until it establishes an open conductive channel to the ground. The first leader-strokes are normally invisible but the final stepped leader which reaches ground is visible, and looks like an illuminated river with tributaries. The speed of the leader-stroke varies enormously, from as little as 100 miles/s (160 km/s) to as much as 1000 miles/s (1600 km/s).

The return stroke flashes up this channel from ground to cloud, and is the faster bright flash which is usually referred to as lightning. The speed of the return stroke may reach up to 87 000 miles/s (140 000 km/s), which is nearly half the speed of light itself. The flash, therefore, lasts a mere millionth of a second, but persistence of the image on the retina of the human eye makes it appear to last longer. There is evidence that the temperature of the air in the channel of the return stroke may reach 54 000°F (30 000°C), which is more than five times greater than that of the surface of the Sun.

A typical lightning flash consists of three or four leaders each followed by a return stroke, but one flash sequence was photographed which had 26 strokes. The width of the channel is seldom more than 1 in (25 mm).

Lightning appears forked when the leader stroke and the return stroke are visible without obstruction from other clouds.

Sheet lightning is forked lightning which is obscured by other cloud, and therefore only seen as reflected illumination.

The distance of a lightning flash from an observer can be estimated by the difference between the almost instantaneous receipt of the light signal by the eye and the delayed receipt by the ear of the more slowly moving sound signal of thunder. Sound travels at approximately 1 mile per 5 seconds (1 km per 3 seconds). Therefore, if T is the time in seconds between the flash seen and the thunder heard, the distance of the flash is:

$$\frac{T}{5} \text{ miles } \left(\frac{T}{3} \text{ km} \right).$$

Sferics are directional fixes on lightning flashes, received by aerial and registered on cathode ray tubes at observing stations which are at some distance from each other. Thousands of electrical discharges occur in the atmosphere every second, but only relatively few reach the ground as a strike. In Great Britain there is an average six lightning strikes per square mile (4 per km²) per annum.

Lightning causes damage or death in various ways:

● *By vapourisation*, so that moisture in any container expands suddenly and causes an explosion. Damp brickwork may shatter, road surfaces with underlying moisture can be ripped up and trees explode.

In Australia, eucalyptus trees of a variety known as 'Darwin Woolly Butts' are particularly prone to explosion. Many trunks are piped up the centre with termite nests, giving a moist core of honeycombed mud and humus approximately 3 in (75 mm) in diameter, which reacts like a bomb when struck by lightning.

● *By melting and fusion :* For instance, lightning which strikes sand may create small particles of vitrified rock or fulgurites, which are thin tubes of glass enclosing sand grains. Nails in brickwork may melt and fall out of their holes and metal joints may fuse, sometimes in extraordinary circumstances. On 10 August 1975, a man who was umpiring a cricket match near Berwick on Tweed was struck by lightning which welded solid an iron joint in his leg.

● *By burning* – a particular hazard at the end of summer heat waves when the countryside is especially dry. The USA is particularly prone to thunderstorms in summer, and lightning is a severe menace in creating forest fires. On 15 August 1967, lightning started a fire in Idaho state, which spread in strong wind to encompass 90 square miles (240 km²).

Firebrands were carried in the wind 10 miles (16 km) ahead of the flame front.

On 28 October 1975, lightning fired and destroyed a Greek oil-tanker at Jurong, Singapore.

● *By conduction* along wires or overhead cables, which are not intended for discharge of lightning, so that explosions occur at the end of the conductor, for instance in television sets or electric power installations. Surge arrestors and suitably placed lightning conductors can do much to prevent damage to electrical installations, but the problem is similar to that encountered when seeking protection against other types of weather excesses. Complete protection costs more money than people are willing to pay for an occasional risk. A particularly thundery day, which interrupted the 1975 summer heat wave, was 8 August. Storms began in Devon and Cornwall in the early morning and lightning blew out several transformers and telephone installations. Storms spread during the day to most of Great Britain and in the evening set fire to an electricity substation at Bradford on Avon, Wiltshire, where the accompanying photograph was taken. A person can be protected against arcing from a television set, or explosion within a set, by pulling out the plug connected to the electrical circuit. This will not, however, prevent lightning from travel-

Lightning at Bradford on Avon, Wiltshire, 8 August 1975, which blew out several transformers and telephone stations. (G Bodman; courtesy *Journal of Meteorology*)

ling via the aerial into the electrical circuit or other parts of the house – but that risk is small. The aerials projecting above houses in urban areas are relatively insignificant features of a generally rough surface contour, and it is only the lone high rise building which soars above all others which suffers particular risk from a lightning strike.

● *By compression and decompression of air* near a lightning flash, which may blast the clothes off a person, or knock them down as if by sledgehammer. On 28 June 1976, lightning knocked down six golfers playing at Oakbrook, Illinois, USA, but caused them no injury.

● *By direct lightning strike* to the human body, most likely to kill when it passes close to the respiratory centre in the lower part of the brain, or when passing close to the heart. The most dangerous lightning flash is therefore one which strikes the head and passes close to these sensitive regions, en route for the feet and earth. However, lightning does not seek out these organs and many lucky escapes have occurred because the flash travelled from shoulder to leg, or arm to arm, and bypassed the head or heart. Every year all over the world there are the lucky persons and the unlucky ones. The chances of being killed by lightning are many times less than the chances of being killed by a traffic accident. Among the lucky people in 1975 were two golfers playing in the Wills Masters Tournament at Melbourne, Australia on 24 October. They were walking along the fairway under umbrellas which attracted lightning and struck them. They were shaken, but unhurt.

The only man in the world to have survived a lightning strike seven times is Park Ranger Roy C Sullivan (USA). He lost a big toe nail in 1942, lost his eyebrows in July 1969 and was burnt on the left shoulder in July 1970. His hair was set on fire in April 1972 and August 1973. In June 1976 his ankle was injured and on 26 June 1977 he suffered chest and stomach burns.

● *By a potential difference and current* from one point on the ground to another, caused by temporary rearrangement of electric charge over the surface as the lightning strikes. A human being may experience this current up one leg and down the other and the shock will be greater with his feet far apart. Hence it is safer for a person caught in an open field in a thunderstorm to crouch down low, with feet together, than to stand upright and walk with long strides. Cattle are more prone to be killed by this type of lightning strike than humans, because their legs are further apart and a strike from one leg to another necessarily passes close to the heart. On 22 July 1975 several cows were killed by lightning at Congleton, Cheshire; and another storm on 8 August 1975 near Huddersfield, Yorkshire, so frightened cows that they stampeded and trampled a woman to death.

Thunderbolts do not exist in the way many people believe, ie as solid objects ejected from a thunderstorm cloud. However, a lightning flash does make a loud cracking noise when it strikes ground and throws up a plume of steam when striking water, and either of these occurrences registers in the mind as the more usual circumstance of a heavy object falling. On 4 August 1975, lightning struck ground at Hampstead, the highest point in London, and an observer nearby reported that the noise sounded like machine-gun fire.

Ball lightning may, or may not, exist. Many people, including some meteorologists, think it is all imagination, and are possibly influenced by the fact that such fireballs cannot be explained, and have not been artificially produced in a laboratory. On the other hand, reports of ball lightning have been made throughout history, often by people who have not previously heard of the phenomenon and have no obvious reasons for concocting false evidence. The general picture, which builds up from the many reports, is that ball lightning is spherical or pear shaped, often has fuzzy edges and a diameter 4–8 in (100–200 mm). Fireballs can be seen in daylight and have the intensity of a domestic lamp bulb, and are either stationary or wander with slow erratic movement. Some-

times they move along conductors such as metal window frames; they have been known to enter houses by chimneys and disappear through doors, both silently and explosively. A few cause damage, but others hardly raise alarm in the people who witness them. The accounts of ball lightning rarely mention any sensation of heat. Among disastrous balls of lightning was one which occurred at Little Sodbury Manor in Gloucestershire, and was reported in Sir Robert Atkyn's *History of Gloucestershire.*

'In 1556 died Maurice Walsh Esq, together with seven of his children, occasioned by a fiery sulphureous globe rolling in at the parlour door at dinner time, which struck one dead at the table and caused the death of the rest. It made a passage through a window on the other side of the room.'

A similar experience, but which was not fatal, was recounted in volume 63 of the *Philosophical Transactions,* printed in London in 1773, and reported by the vicar of the lightning prone village of Steeple Ashton, Wiltshire (p. 186). The Rev Mr Wainhouse of Steeple Ashton and the Rev Mr Pitcairn of Trowbridge were in the parlour of the vicarage talking together about a loud clap of thunder which had just occurred when they saw a ball of fire between them at face level. It was the size of a 'sixpenny loaf' and surrounded with a dark smoke; and it burst with the sound of firing cannon, filling the room with a suffocating smoke and a disagreeable smell, resembling 'sulphur, vitriol and other minerals in fusion.' Mr Wainhouse was not hurt, but Mr Pitcairn was struck on the shoulder and briefly stunned. He remembered having seen the ball of fire for a few seconds *after* he was struck, and he mentioned a great quantity of fire of different colours vibrating swiftly, both backwards and forwards.

Vibrations were also mentioned by Mr E Matts of Coventry, Warwickshire, when he reported in the journal of the Royal Meteorological Society, *Weather,* a happening on 10 November 1940.

'I was working at the far end of my garden, the weather was normal, no rain, no sign of thunder. Suddenly I seemed to be in the centre of intense blackness and looking down observed at my feet a ball about 2 ft across. It was of a pale blue-green colour and seemed made of a mass of writhing strings of light, about $\frac{1}{4}$ inch in diameter. It remained there for about 3 seconds, and then rose away from me, just missing a poplar tree about 8 ft away. It cleared the houses by about 20 ft and landed at the rear of the Weavers Arms on the Bell Green road, a distance of about $\frac{1}{4}$ mile. There was a loud explosion and much damage was done to the public house. I felt no alarm whatever.'

Evidence of damage presumed to be caused by ball lightning comes from the University of Edinburgh, where on 8 June 1972 an almost circular hole of 1·9 by 1·8 in (49 by 46 mm) was made in the window of the Meteorology Department. An irregular crack ran across the bottom of the pane, which broke when being removed. The remainder of the hole was photographed, and the missing circle of glass was found intact inside the room. The edge of the piece, and that of the glass surrounding the hole, had a fused appearance on the inner side of the pane and was smooth to the touch. An earthed radiator close to the bottom of the window pane may explain why the lightning was attracted to that spot. A similar hole in a pane of glass was photographed and published in 1921 in a book entitled *Meteorology* by A E M Geddes. The size of that hole was 2·5 by 2·3 in (64 by 58 mm).

Lightning has been known to strike out of a clear sky, a fact which complicates attempts to explain lightning as a phenomenon produced in clouds. In September 1966, a lightning flash from an apparently clear sky felled 30 workers, who were picking peppers at Alfrida, Arizona, and killed three of them.

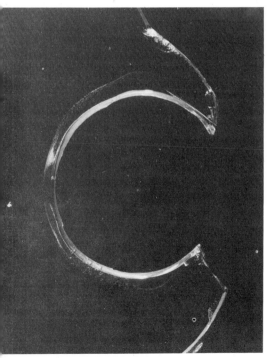

Damage by lightning to window of the Meteorology Department, University of Edinburgh, on 8 June 1972. (D H McIntosh)

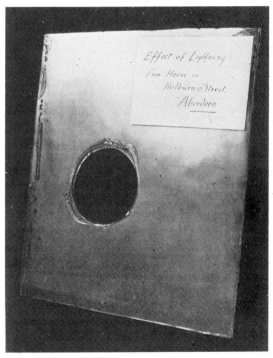

Photograph from *Meteorology* by A E M Geddes, published in 1921, showing window damage by lightning in Aberdeen. (D H McIntosh)

On 2 June 1976, a single blinding flash of lightning, occurred at Myrtleford, Victoria, Australia, on a cloudless night. A fireball was seen to explode over three houses, a television set blew up and telephones were put out of order. Iron sheds fused together, wire fencing welded, and there were three football-sized marks burnt into the ground near the houses. A 66 000 volt powerline fused, blacking out a large area, and one shed had a burn hole as large as a tennis ball and looked as if made by a laser beam.

Lightning chooses the highest point available by which to discharge to earth. On a landscape with only a few prominent peaks, these will therefore be most prone to damage by lightning. Hence, the tradition that lightning never strikes twice in the same place has been frequently confounded, particularly before the invention of the lightning conductor. Churches with high towers or spires used to be particularly vulnerable targets.

Amongst English churches permanently scarred by lightning was the Church of St Mary the Virgin in Steeple Ashton, Wiltshire. It was originally built in the early 13th century, a tower was added in the 15th century and surmounted by a steeple 93 ft (28 m) high. The steeple was ruptured by lightning on 25 July 1670, workmen set about repairing it almost at once, and by October were putting the finishing touches to their work. On 15 October there was another thunderstorm, the steeple was again struck and this time collapsed. Two workmen were killed and the falling spire damaged the main structure of the church, which took another five years to repair. The steeple was not renewed. Taking into consideration also the fireball incident at the vicarage in the village (p. 184) it was perhaps tempting providence to live in Steeple Ashton, when bearing the name of Bolt. On 26 June 1973 an 84 year-old pensioner, Mr Bolt, was thrown across his kitchen when a flash of lightning wrecked a hay barn some few yards from his house.

A particularly disastrous lightning strike occurred at Widecombe in the Moor, Devon on 21 October 1638. Afternoon service was in progress in the parish church when a severe thunderstorm occurred with consequences which were described by Richard Hill, the village schoolmaster at the time. His florid verse is still displayed on boards in the church and indicates that a huge storm cloud wielded all the powers at its disposal.

A crack of thunder suddenly, with lightning hail and fire
Fell on the Church and tower here, and ran into the Choir.
A sulphurous smell came with it, and the tower strangely rent,
The stones abroad into the air with violence were sent. . . .
One man was struck dead, two wounded so they died a few hours after. . . .
One man was scorched so that he lived but fourteen day and died,
Whose clothes were very little burnt. But many there were beside
Were wounded, scorched and stupified. . . .
Some had their skin all over scorched, yet no harm to their clothes
One man had money in his purse which melted was in part,
A key likewise which hung thereto, and yet the purse not hurt
Save only some black holes so small as with a needle made. . . .
The Church within so filled was with timber stone and fire
That scarce a vacant place was seen in church or in the choir.

It is highly likely that there was also a tornado associated with the storm, because a pamphlet issued by the Puritans some time later, in which the tragic story was recounted as a punitive manifestation from the Lord, was illustrated with a cloud over the church from which a funnel cloud descended. There were approximately 60 casualties from the storm, including four dead.

Benjamin Franklin invented the lightning conductor as a result of his kite experiment in July 1752 (p. 177), and two months later xed one to his own home in Philadelphia. 'he conductor consisted of a pointed iron rod , collect the charge, reaching about 9 ft (3 m) ove roof top. Connected to the rod was a pper strip down the outside wall of the ouse, which led to a metal plate bedded ft (2 m) into the ground, the whole conductor roviding an easy route to earth for lightning. 'ranklin arranged similar protection for two f the public buildings in Philadelphia, and e published a description of his invention in ovember 1752, claiming no patent rights r the idea. Americans adopted lightning nductors with enthusiasm, except in some arts of New England, where the idea was eemed an interference with Divine Providence. 'ranklin's invention also met with marked lack of enthusiasm in Europe, partly for religious reasons, and in Britain simply because it was American and the political scene was somewhat strained at the time.

In 1753 the Russian scientist Georg Wilhelm Richman was experimenting during a thunderstorm with collecting charge on an iron rod when he placed his head too near the rod and the flash leapt across the gap to his head, earthed down through a leg, bursting his shoe and killed him. Even that warning example did little to promote lightning conductor safety in Europe.

The first public building to be protected by lightning conductor in Europe was the Church of St Jacob in Hamburg in 1769; and in Great Britain the first was St Paul's Cathedral, Lon-

. Ford Capri, with two intrepid occupants, being struck by artificial lightning at the high tension istallation of the University of Mannheim, Germany. (Ford Motor Co Ltd)

don, in 1770, – 18 years after Franklin first invented the lightning conductor. Dr William Watson, Vice President of the Royal Society, London, set an earlier good example by fixing a conductor on his own home at Payneshill, London in 1762.

A well earthed lightning conductor is considered to give reliable, though not certain, protection within a conical volume, whose vertex is the top of the conductor, and whose base area is a circle of radius equal to the height of the conductor.

Horizontal lightning conductors are now known to be as effective as vertical rods, provided they are properly bonded to roofs or chimneys and incorporated with conductive metal strips, guttering or drain pipes into an earthed protective ring around the house.

Lightning can jump a gap between its initial strike path and an alternative route close by. It can jump from the outside of a roof to a water tank close to the roof inside; it can jump from a solitary tree top to complete the journey to earth through a person standing beneath; or it may jump from an extended car aerial to a person standing outside the car and about to put the aerial down into its sheath. It is cer-

tainly safer to have the aerial retracted durin a storm in case it conducts lightning inside t. car, but this should be done at the first sign approaching storm cloud and not during t. storm itself.

One of the safest places in a thunderstor is inside a metal car, particularly when one not touching the sides. The car acts like Faraday cage (p. 178), and any lightning fla travels over the outside surface and runs earth through the tyres. Although these a usually made of rubber, which is an insulatin material, there are enough other constituen in the fabric to make tyres excellent conductor especially on wet roads. Nevertheless, it is frightening experience to be inside a thin met cage with blinding lightning flashing all aroun and thunder and heavy rain falling on the ro making a deafening noise. In order to convin people of the inherent safety of a car to ligh ning flashes, intrepid volunteers from both t Ford Motor Company and Mercedes Benz L sat in cars, which were bombarded by artifici lightning at two million volts generated at t Siemens High Tension Centre, Mannheir Germany. The lightning struck the cars wi a roar like thunder, but neither the cars nor t occupants were hurt.

CHAPTER 15

WHIRLWINDS, TORNADOES AND WATERSPOUTS

00TH ANNIVERSARY OF THE WORLD METEOROLOGICAL ORGANIZATION

eus, father of the gods and a radascope.

he whirling motion of a vortex is the most
ficient method devised by nature for remov-
g fluids in a hurry. Opposing currents in
rbulent rivers resolve their collisions by
.eans of a whirlpool, just as water running out
rough the plughole in a bath rotates rapidly
.to a hollow funnel as the last quantities dis-
ppear.

ortices in the atmosphere serve to move
.r from one place or altitude to another in
rder to achieve the necessary balance of heat
ver the whole world. The major distributors
f energy are the spiralling cloud systems of
epressions and hurricanes, but smaller and
.ore intense vortices assist them in the task.
ome originate at ground level on cloudless
ays over very hot surfaces, and their winds
.tate in either direction according to chance
ircumstances which start the spinning motion.

Larger vortices originate within clouds and
develop downwards to the ground and these
usually, but not invariably, rotate in the directions laid down in Buys Ballot's Law for the
major low-pressure circulations – anticlockwise
in the northern hemisphere and clockwise in
the southern hemisphere. All these air vortices
develop suddenly, cannot be predicted, are
too transient to appear on weather maps and
have very low pressure centres.

Whirlwind is a general term, covering all
rotating wind storms which originate on the
ground and spiral upwards, but in popular
parlance a whirlwind usually implies sufficient
strength to cause damage. Less vigorous
vortices are called 'land devils' or 'water
devils' according to the surface over which
they originate; or they have names describing
the particles which are carried along in the
whirling wind.

Sand pillars form over hot desert surfaces,
where the temperature of the air close to the
sand may be many degrees higher than air a
few feet above. Air tries to obey the buoyancy
rules and rise, but since the whole surface
layer cannot rise at the same time, the desired
result is achieved by small individual cells of
rising air. If a horizontal wind is blowing, these
cells of rising air may be set spinning into
vortices carrying sand. They rise to a few feet
high, travel a short distance and then collapse
again in the general turbulence of the pressure
wind, their temporary job of transporting heat
accomplished. Sand pillars constantly form
and disperse along the sandy hills of the Namib
Desert along the coast of south west Africa as
cool winds from the sea blow onshore.

Dust whirls have been studied closely by meteorological personnel in north-west Libya, where small wind vortices often form during the hot months of the year on the plain between the Mediterranean and the Jebel Hills. Air temperature close to the ground may be 16°F (9°C) higher than that at 4 ft (1·2 m) above ground. The dust whirls are shaped like inverted cones and tilt forward by 5°–15° from the vertical along their path of movement, as if anxious to reach their destination. They often reach a height of 200 ft (60 m), but a whirl reaching 400 ft (120 m) has been observed with a tilt of nearly 40° from the vertical. The dust whirls sometimes move in procession down wind of particular hot spots at an average speed of 10 mph (16 km/h), but the life span of each individual whirl is a matter of minutes only.

The most spectacular land devils form over the dusty desert of south west Arizona, USA, where on hot summer days the ground temperature may heat to as much as 150–160°F (65–70°C). This results in an extremely unstable layer of air within the first few feet above ground, and rising air is set spinning by the general horizontal wind into dust devils which often reach a height of 300 ft (100 m), and have been known to reach 3000 ft (1 km). They are visible because of the dust they pick up into the circulation, and because of condensation in the upward soaring air. However, the environment air is usually too dry to sustain convection and produce cloud. The majority of Arizona dust devils last for only three or four minutes, and the slightest interruption to the rising air causes them to collapse. However, larger devils have been known to last for 30 minutes, and some can be as destructive as narrow tornadoes. On 29 May 1902, a livery stable in Phoenix, Arizona, was demolished, and on 2 June 1964 a church under construction was destroyed by tornado-like dust devils.

In Great Britain, land devils occur during summer, usually originating over particularly sheltered surfaces heating in the sunshin[e]. When the pressure wind is more than 10 m[ph] (16 km/h), turbulence alone achieves t[he] disposal of the heated air which rises into t[he] horizontal air stream. But when the horizont[al] wind is very light, the rising air over the h[ot] spot may be set spinning. Land devils may b[e] visible because of the dust which they suck u[p,] but sometimes they are invisible and a[re] detectable only by sudden inexplicable burs[ts] of wind, often accompanied by a hissing nois[e.]

Fine weather whirlwinds of destructi[ve] proportions do occur in hot summers [in] Great Britain. On 30 June 1975 there was [a] whirlwind at Warmley, Bristol. It was said [to] have roared like an express train as it moved [a] shed 30 ft (10 m) long through a distance [of] 4 ft (1·2 m), while workers at the facto[ry] concerned were actually watching. The si[de] of the roof blew off and landed on a car in th[e] car park 120 ft (40 m) away. The day was war[m] and cloudless, and the temperature of the a[ir] at 1500 h when the damage was caused, wa[s] 72°F (22°C).

Water devils are vortices of air over a wat[er] surface. They usually form over land an[d] travel thence on to water when they quick[ly] collapse, but they occasionally form over [a] warm water surface which is suddenly overru[n] by cold air. This can happen, for instanc[e] when a cool sea breeze penetrates inland durin[g] a summer afternoon and passes across a lak[e] which has been steadily heating over a lon[g] heat wave. The rotating winds in water devi[ls] lift spray into the circulation and may caus[e] undulation on the surface.

Water devils have been less often reporte[d] throughout history than have water monster[s] which has prompted G T Meaden to sugge[st] in an article in the *Journal of Meteorolog[y]* that water devils and monsters may be one an[d] the same thing. For example, an occurrence i[n] Aberdeenshire, Scotland, at the end of the 18t[h] century was reported by a meticulous weath[er] observer in matter of fact terms, but coul[d] equally have been described as a sea monst[er.]

by anyone without knowledge of the ways of the weather:

'The 2nd June (1779) sitting by the water we saw a pillar of water rise as high as the tallest tree, and fall down again, after which it rolled along for a considerable space in large rolls as if a cask had been under the water, (and out of those rolls sprung up small strings of water, rising pretty high, as out of the strup of a razor). The noise it made was such as a firework of powder makes when first set off, but much louder. The day was clear, fine sunshine and not a breath of wind.'

Sea monsters are by no means the prerogative of the British, whose biggest mystery is the Loch Ness Monster. In British Columbia a legendary water serpent called 'Ogopogo' inhabits Lake Okanagan; the lakes of Kashmir are supposed to house mysterious monsters and the Chinese and the Arabs have many stories about sea monsters. The common denominator of them all could be the physical laws governing vortices.

Fires can spawn whirlwinds as the heated air tries to escape upwards. Vigorous whirlwinds were seen around the cloud of ash erupted from the volcano which formed the new island of Surtsey off Iceland in 1965. Over 120 vigorous vortices occurred over the fire following the Tokyo earthquake of 1923. The most terrifying man-made whirlwinds occurred in the firestorms which resulted from bombing in the 1939–45 World War. On 7–8 September 1940 enemy bombing produced the first firestorm of the war in Quebec Yard, Surrey Docks, Southwark, London, when rapidly convecting air sucked in replacement air with the aid of whirlwinds. Hamburg, Germany was bombed on 27 July 1943 on a sultry night, when violent convection and whirlwinds helped to burn out 8 sq miles (20 km^2) of the city. In a raid on Dresden, Germany, on 13–15 February 1945, whirlwinds of such intensity developed that people attempting to escape from the fires were instead carried into the fires by the spiralling winds.

Tornadoes are bad-weather vortices, whose exact causes are still imperfectly understood. They are auxiliaries to intense depressions, hurricanes or large cumulonimbus clouds and consist of very violent vortices of spinning air which lower from the base of the main cloud. The visible symptom of a tornado is a funnel cloud, which tapers from a broad exit at the main cloud base down to a narrow tip; this sometimes reaches ground and causes damage, and at other times remains harmlessly above ground. A tornado funnel may retract from or lower to ground several times during its travel across country, leaving intermittent trails of damage to mark its leapfrog progress. The funnel cloud may be deflected by the wind, sometimes almost towards the horizontal, and, when descending from a cloud whose main base is high above ground, appears like a living, writhing reptile. Several funnel clouds may extend downwards at the same time from a vigorous storm cloud, presenting an awesome impression on a fertile imagination. The prophet Ezekiel (c. 590 BC) had probably never seen such a sight before, when he recounted in the first chapter of his book in the Old Testament his experience near the river of Chebar in the land of the Chaldeans. He looked and saw:

'a whirlwind to northwards, a great cloud and a fire infolding itself . . . out of the midst thereof came the likeness of four living creatures . . . and everyone had four wings . . . and their feet were straight feet and the sole of their feet was the sole of a calf's foot . . . and they went every one straight forward . . . and they turned not when they went . . . Their appearance was like burning coals of fire . . . it went up and down among the living creatures and the fire was bright and out of the fire went forth lightning.'

Ezekiel's account is embellished by further elaborate interpretations of the phenomenon which he could probably only see dimly in the half light of the storm, but the meaning is clear. There was a storm, four tornadoes which progressed steadfastly with the main cloud, and there was lightning associated with them. 'The sole of a calf's foot' may be a picturesque reference to a suction mark.

Suction marks are often left in soft ground by a funnel cloud, which has extended right down to the surface. When such a cloud is tilting forwards, and particularly when traversing an upward slope, the suction is greater at the forward edge than at the back, resulting in a semicircular impression, rather like a horse's hoofmark. The account of a tornado which occurred at Scarborough, Yorkshire in August 1165, was written by a monk who referred to it as the 'old enemy' and 'the black horse'.

'The footprints of this accursed horse were of a very enormous size, especially on the hill near the town of Scardeburch, from which he gave a leap into the sea; and here for a whole year afterwards they were plainly visible, the impression of each foot being deeply graven in the earth.'

Lightning accompanies tornadoes. The prophet Ezekiel saw from a distance the illuminated tornadoes, but Frank Lane in his book *The Elements Rage* quotes a Kansas farmer who lay on the ground and was able to look straight upwards into the hollow funnel of cloud.

'There was a hollow opening in the center of the funnel, about 50 or 100 ft in diameter, and extending straight upwards for a distance of at least one half mile, as best I could judge under the circumstances. The walls of the opening were of rotating clouds and the whole was made brilliantly visible by constant flashes of lightning which zigzagged from side to side. Had it not been for the lightning I could not have seen the opening, nor any distance up into it anyway. Around the lower rim of the great vortex small tornadoes were constantly forming and breaking away. These looked like tails as they writhed their way around the end of the funnel. It was these that made the hissing noise.'

There is still doubt as to whether the lightning is a *result* of the tornado, or whether it plays some part in the *production* of the tornado.

Wind direction in tornadoes usually, but not invariably, obeys the rules propounded by Buys Ballot for depression and hurricanes; anticlockwise in the northern hemisphere and clockwise in the southern. However, subsidiary vortices whirling around tornadoes may rotate in either direction, set spinning by some chance factor in the same way that land devils

originating above a ground surface may sp in either direction.

Wind speed in tornado circulations is difficu to measure, because ordinary anemomete cannot withstand the onslaught. Electron measurement, based upon radar echoes from moving funnel cloud, can be obtained, but th problem is to have an instrument positione in the right place at the right time. On 10 Jur 1958 radar recorded a wind speed of 206 mp (331 km/h) in a tornado at El Dorado Kansas USA, but it is considered that wind speec more than twice that amount are usual.

A tornado inflicts damage in various way
● *By the direct impact of wind,* whose force proportional to the square of wind speed. wind of 300 mph (480 km/h) in a tornado w exert a direct force 100 times greater than th force exerted by a wind speed of 30 mp (48 km/h), and this may amount to pressur of 200 lb per ft^2 (980 kg/m^2).
● *By twist* due to unequal wind speeds with the very narrow band of the circulation. Wind which blow in a tornado of small cross sectio are often so much greater on one side of a tre than on the other, that they screw off the tre top as easily as a person twists off the stalk a ripe pear.
● *By explosion* when a tornado passes direct over a building which contains air at norm atmospheric pressure. Barometric pressure h not been measured at the centre of a tornad because few barometers happen to be in th right place at the right time and none surviv the ordeal. However, a barometer close to tornado at Newtown, Kansas, USA, has bee known to record a fall of 25·7 mb in 10 minute followed by a rise of 31·8 mb in 17 minute and another barometer at St Louis, Missour USA, once fell to 912·3 mb near a tornado. is thought that pressure gradients of abo 60 mb may exist across the narrow circulatio which would result in a momentary inequali of pressure between the outside and inside of building equivalent to an outward thrust several tons. Roofs are sucked off and wal

A Rolba snow plough sucks up dry snow in Switzerland and blows it to the side of the road.
(Rolba AG)

Crevasse in the Forno Glacier,
Graubünden, Switzerland. Many
years of compression have driven all air
from the clear ice in the depths of the
crevasse. (Dr G Frei)

Tornado over the Akrotiri peninsula of Cyprus, 22 December 1969. (D Imrie)

Two land devils over the dusty desert of south west Arizona, USA.
(S B Idso)

explode outwards. The advice given in tornado safety rules in the USA, is to open doors and windows on the opposite side of the building from that of the approaching tornado, so as to facilitate the equalisation of atmospheric pressure.

● *By lift and drop* in the vertical currents within the tornado. An upcurrent of 150 mph (240 km/h) was indicated by a film taken in Dallas, USA, on 2 April 1957, and lesser currents can fill tornadoes with light debris to make them look like travelling junk shops. Sheds, cattle and human beings have often been carried high into the air, sometimes suffering injury when falling to ground again; but often they are lowered gently without harm on the outer rim of the circulation, where upcurrents only just fail to maintain the weight aloft.

Tornadoes achieve prodigious feats of levitation and penetration, by using a combination of all the above mentioned powers:

On 4 February 1842, small pieces of board with blunt ends were driven into turf to a depth of 18 in (450 mm) by a tornado in Ohio. In 1931 a tornado in Minnesota lifted an 83-ton rail coach and 117 passengers 80 ft (25 m) into the air before dropping them into a ditch; and on 12 June 1957, a tornado passed over a steel air port hangar in Dallas, Texas, USA and pulled the concrete piers out of the ground. In Great Britain, on 26 September 1971, a tornado moved a 90-ton engine 150 ft (50 m) along a railway track near Rotherham, South Yorkshire, and lifted a 40 gallon (180 l) empty metal drum 3 ft (1 m) above the ground.

The destructive diameter of a tornado varies from a few feet to about one mile (1 m–1·5 km). The wider swaths of damage often occur without any sight of elongated funnel clouds, indicating that the main cloud base is low enough to sweep the ground with the wide top of the vortex. In contrast, elongated funnels with narrow tips often pick their way with such precision that one house may be damaged, but another next door may remain unscathed: On 26 June 1973 a tornado at Cranfield, Bedfordshire, ripped the roof off the laboratory buildings, belonging to the Environmental Science Research Unit, while considerately leaving untouched the houses on an adjacent estate. An anemometer and wind vane, situated 300 ft (100 m) away from the wrecked building, recorded 85 mph (136 km/h) before the pen lifted off the chart and electricity supply was disrupted, and the wind direction fluctuated violently.

The distance travelled by tornadoes varies so much that average figures are meaningless. In the central states of the USA, uninterrupted flat plains provide minimum disturbance to the progress of tornadoes. On 26 May 1917 a verified single tornado travelled 293 miles (471 km) across Texas with only occasional leaps off the ground. It travelled at speeds between 55–75 mph (88–120 km/h), lasting for 7 hours 20 minutes. In contrast, a tornado in Wyoming in 1954 had a track of only 45 ft (15 m), and a tornado in Dakota was once observed to remain stationary in a field for 45 minutes.

In Great Britain, the longest recorded distance achieved by a single tornado was 100 miles (160 km) from Great Missenden, Buckinghamshire, to Blakeney, Norfolk, at

Tree split by the tornado at the gardens of the Royal Horticultural Society, Wisley, Surrey, on 21 July 1965. (R P Scase)

an average speed of 25 mph (40 km/h). A short-lived but intense tornado occurred on 21 July 1965 in Surrey, travelling 2 miles (3 km) in 10 minutes across the grounds of the Royal Horticultural Society at Wisley to the main road.

The most frequent devastating tornadoes occur over the mid-west and continental plains of North America, mostly between April and June, when cool dry air from the north or north west conflicts with warm moist air from the Gulf of Mexico. Under such contrasting conditions of temperature, humidity and wind, vigorous cold fronts and storm clouds develop. The states bordering the Gulf of Mexico tend to have tornadoes rather earlier in the year, during February or March, but none of the dates mentioned are exclusive. Tornadoes occur at any time of the year, on several days in succession when suitable conditions persist, and often in swarms when associated with intense depressions or hurricanes. The United States suffer hundreds of tornadoes each year, and probably many occur in remote areas which go unrecorded. In 1965 a total of 899 tornadoes were recorded, but 1919 was a lucky year with only 64. Swarms of tornadoes are difficult to count, but 60 or more may occur on a single day, and it is estimated that as many as 115 may have been spawned by the hurricane *Beulah* in 1967. On Palm Sunday, 11 April 1965, 37 tornadoes afflicted the mid-west states when 271 people were killed and more than 5000 injured.

One of the worst disasters in the USA occurred on 18 March 1925, when a series of at least eight separate tornadoes in the central states of Missouri, southern Illinois and Indiana spread a trail of death and damage, which in places was almost 20 miles (32 km) wide. The principal tornado developed in the early afternoon, and travelled at speeds between 55–75 mph (88–120 km/h), cutting swaths of destruction through towns, before anyone had time to realise what was happening. One of the worst hit towns was Murphysboro, where children were still in schools and workers

concentrated in offices and factories. Three miles of buildings collapsed and 200 people died in that town alone. The width of the main tornado was approximately a mile (1·6 km) in places, but less than half that amount elsewhere. The tornadoes retracted from the ground occasionally, so that during a day in which there were 695 deaths and 2027 injuries four small towns were almost wiped out, yet others were entirely untouched.

An almost equivalent series of devastating tornadoes occurred on 4 April 1973, sweeping through the south and mid-west states. Some small communities in Ohio and Kentucky were almost wiped out and at least half the town of Xenia, Ohio (25 000 inhabitants), was destroyed as if by bulldozer. More than 300 people were killed that day and 4000 were injured. Seven states were declared disaster areas and yet, in the usual capricious manner with which tornadoes travel, some towns were unaware of the fact that anything dreadful was happening elsewhere and were quite unharmed.

Devastating tornadoes occur all over the world, even though no other country is as badly afflicted as the United States of America. A few examples from the 20th century indicate their strength.

● 30 June 1912: a tornado in Regina, Saskatchewan, Canada, killed 28 and injured one hundred.

● 11 September 1970: a tornado in the Gulf of Venice, Italy lifted a steam yacht with 60 persons on board and sank it near the island of Santa Elena, killing 36 people. The same furious wind circulation destroyed a camping site nearby, killing 11 people and injuring several hundred.

● 10 May 1976: a tornado demolished a church at Arahura, near Kokitika, New Zealand, lifted a bus shelter and its occupant into the air and deposited it, together with a signal box, on to the railway line. Debris from the church penetrated 18 ft (6 m) into a cliff alongside the railway cutting. A piece of sheet iron which was hurled across the power lines caused disruption of electricity supplies.

● 30 November 1976: the worst tornado in Belgium for many years moved across open country near Houwaart. The tornado reached ground three times, when it uprooted small trees, felled a large tree across the main road, damaged roofs and destroyed most of the glass in a greenhouse factory.

● 1–2 April 1977: there were violent tornadoes in Bangladesh, India, particularly in the Madaripur district, 80 miles (128 km) from Dacca; 500 people were killed and more than 6000 injured, while hundreds of thousands were left homeless.

In Great Britain, tornadoes occur more frequently than was at one time thought. They usually happen within an area stretching from the north Midlands southeastwards to Kent and few have been reported from Scotland. Tornadoes are most likely to occur in July and August when summer thunderstorms are most frequent, but they also occur at any time of the year in association with intense depressions. The vortices may pass unnoticed in the general hubbub of a strong gale and under cover of darkness, but the swath-like path of destruction cut through towns provides evidence afterwards of their existence:

On 15 January 1968 a deep depression crossed central Scotland during the night, and average wind speed in Glasgow was 61 mph (98 km/h) with gusts up to 102 mph (164 km/h). The wind was blowing from WSW generally, but was considerably disturbed in the Glasgow area by the mountains to windward. Enormous damage was done in the city but, when the army started to make temporary repairs to roofs with tarpaulins, they remarked that their roof top view indicated definite paths of damage. A resident in the highest part of the city commented that there were four distinct bursts of exceptional violence during the night, accompanied by noises like an express train approaching, which suggests that the depression was accompanied by tornadoes.

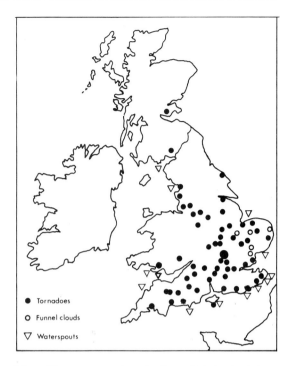

Map of known tornadoes in Great Britain during 1974. (*Journal of Meteorology*)

Tornadoes which are spawned by depression or hurricanes usually occur in the forward part of the systems. On 26 November 1703 there occurred the nearest to a true hurricane that the south of England has known (p. 85). The storm reached a peak in the west country some hours before midnight, but already in the afternoon gale winds were blowing, and a tornado was experienced in Oxfordshire. Daniel Defoe received the report from a witness when he was writing his account of the storm.

'A spout marching with wind like the trunk of an elephant snapped the body of an oak, sucked up water in cart ruts, tumbled an old barn and twisted its thatch around in the air. A quarter of a mile away it knocked down a man.'

The frequency of tornadoes in Great Britain has been closely researched in recent

THE TORRO TORNADO INTENSITY SCALE

TORRO Force	Name	Characteristic damage on a tornado scale
FC	FUNNEL CLOUD or INCIPIENT TORNADO	No damage to structures, unless to tops of tallest towers, or to radiosondes, balloons, and aircraft. No damage in the country, except possibly agitation to highest treetops and effect on birds and smoke. Record FC when tornado spout seen aloft but not known to have reached ground level. A whistling or rushing sound may be noticed.
0	LIGHT TORNADO	A. Loose, light litter raised from the ground in spirals. B. Temporary structures like marquees seriously affected. C. Slight dislodging of the least secure and most exposed tiles, slates, chimney pots or TV aerials may occur. D. Trees severely disturbed, some twigs snapped off. Bushes may be damaged. Hay, straw, and some growing plants and flowers raised in spirals.
1	MILD TORNADO	A. Heavier matter levitated include planks, corrugated iron, deckchairs, light garden furniture, etc. B. Minor to major damage to sheds, outhouses, locksheds, and other wooden structures (such as henhouses, outhouses). C. Some dislodging of tiles, slates and chimney pots. D. Hayricks seriously disarranged, shrubs and trees may be uprooted, damage to hedgerows, crops, trees, etc.
2	MODERATE TORNADO	A. Exposed, heavy mobile homes displaced; light caravans damaged. B. Minor to major damage to sheds, outhouses, lockup garages, etc. C. Considerable damage to slates, tiles and chimney-stacks. D. General damage to trees, big branches torn off, some trees uprooted. Tornado track easily followed by damage to hedgerows, crops, trees, etc.
3	STRONG TORNADO	A. Mobile homes displaced, damaged or overturned; caravans badly damaged. B. Sheds, lock-up garages, outbuildings torn from supports/foundations. C. Severe roof damage to houses, exposing much of roof timbers, thatched roofs stripped. Some serious window and door damage.

years by individual meteorologists and close scrutiny of old letters, journals and newspapers has revealed 112 tornadoes between the years 1001 and 1800, 208 tornadoes in the 19th century and 419 from 1901–75. Obviously the discrepancy in figures arises not because of lack of tornadoes in the early years, but because of lack of reports, smaller populated areas to suffer damage and a greater chance of tornadoes passing unseen. It is estimated that as many as 50 tornadoes may occur in a year; 20 tornadoes occurred during 11 days in 1971, and 33 during 16 days in 1974, while 41 occurred during 11 days in 1966.

The intensity of tornadoes in Great Britain compared with those elsewhere in the world can only be gauged by descriptions of the damage they cause. G T Meaden of the Tornado and Storm Research Association has suggested a tornado intensity scale as an extension to the Beaufort wind scale and has graded the known British tornadoes accordingly.

TORRO Force	Name	Characteristic damage on a tornado scale
		D. Considerable damage (including twisted tops) to strong trees. A few strong trees uprooted or snapped.
4	SEVERE TORNADO	A. Caravans and mobile homes destroyed or gravely damaged.
		C. Entire roofs torn off some frame/wooden houses and small/medium brick or stone houses and light industrial buildings leaving strong upright walls.
		D. Large well-rooted trees uprooted, snapped, or twisted apart. The ground possibly furrowed by tornado spout to a depth of about 1 metre.
5	INTENSE TORNADO	C. More extensive failure of roofs than for force 4, yet with house-walls remaining. Small weak buildings, as in some rural areas (or as existed in mediaeval towns), may collapse.
		D. Trees carried through the air.
6	MODERATELY DEVASTATING TORNADO	A. Motor vehicles over 1 ton lifted well off the ground.
		C. Most residences lose roofs and some a wall or two; also some heavier roofs torn off (public and industrial buildings, churches). More of the less-strong buildings collapse, some totally ruined.
		D. Across the breadth of the tornado track, every tree in mature woodland or forest uprooted, snapped, twisted, or debranched.
7	STRONGLY DEVASTATING TORNADO	C. Walls of frame/wooden houses and buildings torn away; some walls of stone or brick houses and buildings collapsed or are partly beaten down. Steel framed industrial buildings buckled. Locomotives and trains thrown over.
8	SEVERELY DEVASTATING TORNADO	C. Entire frame houses levelled; most other houses collapse in part or whole. Some steel structures quite badly damaged. Motor cars hurled great distances.
9	,,	C. Many steel structures badly damaged. Locomotives and trains hurled some distances.
10	INTENSELY DEVASTATING TORNADO	C. Entire frame/wooden houses hurled from foundations.
11	,,	C. Steel-reinforced concrete buildings severely damaged.
12	SUPER TORNADOES	

Sub-divisions A, B and C apply mainly to urban situations and sub-division D to rural situations.

STRONGEST TORNADOES	Probable Torro Force
In Great Britain, in the 1970s	4–5
in the 20th century	6–7
ever recorded, in 1091	8
In France and Germany	9
In USA, in an average year	9
ever recorded	10–11

The worst tornado to have occurred in Great Britain was possibly that which struck London on 17 October 1091, graded TORRO force 8. The roof of the church St Mary le Bow was lifted off and killed two people, while four rafters 26 ft (8 m) long were driven into the ground with such force that barely 4 ft (1·2 m) protruded above ground. Various chroniclers, however, recount that 600 houses were demolished and other churches ruined, which suggests that there were also strong winds blowing, contributing to the widespread scale of destruction.

A severe tornado typical of Great Britain, TORRO force 4–5, was associated with a summer thunderstorm in May 1141, at Wellesbourne, Warwickshire. During the storm hail the size of pigeons eggs fell and killed a woman. John of Worcester recounts in his Chronicles that:

'a very violent whirlwind sprang up, a hideous darkness extended from the earth to the sky and the house of the priest whose name is Leoured was violently shaken and all of his outbuildings were thrown down beyond the river Avon. And about 40 of the houses of the peasants were overturned in a similar way and rendered uninhabitable.'

The longest tornado track recorded in Great Britain occurred on 21 May 1950. The tornado was first sighted at 1600 hrs near Great Missenden, Buckinghamshire, and it travelled nearly 100 miles (160 km) in 4 hours across country to Blakeney, Norfolk. It caused the worst damage in Linslade, Bedfordshire, where two roads of houses were entirely unroofed, television aerials were twisted like corkscrews and some poultry plucked clean as if ready for the oven. (This latter phenomenon is frequently reported in accounts of tornadoes, and may be due to the difference between pressure outside and that inside hollow feather quills.) The tornado did not touch ground all the time, but its path was minutely tracked by H H Lamb of the Meteorological Office by its erratic trail of scattered trees, burst sheds and unroofed houses.

A recent swarm of tornadoes occurred over East Anglia on the night of 1–2 December 1975, when a cold front moved south east across the area. Evidence was pieced together following an appeal on Anglia Television and suggests that at least seven tornadoes, TORRO force 3–5, accomplished the total damage sustained. A caravan was tossed 120–130 ft (40–50 m) across a field, a car was lifted from one side of the road to another, a substantial brick wall was levelled to the ground, turnips were pulled out of the ground, and a piece of heavy-gauge iron roof 7 ft (2·1 m) long blew against a thick farm house door and split it as

if by the thrust of a javelin. A barn roof, estimated to weigh 2 tons, was lifted and rotated through 45° while the walls collapsed outwards.

Water spouts are similar to tornadoes, but they form over the sea. A funnel lowers from the main cloud, and even before it reaches the surface of the sea the spiralling winds start a vortex agitation on the water. Spray rises as a broad foot towards the narrow funnel cloud which both join together to form a continuous column of water drops. Water spouts have a short life, usually no more than 20 minutes and, although they can cause damage, they are not as violent as tornadoes. They occur with deep cumulonimbus clouds and vigorous cold fronts, but also with relatively shallow cumulus when there is an abundance of warm moisture to feed the unstable air.

Waterspouts can be seen frequently in summer over the coastal waters around Florida, USA. On 2 September 1967 four students of meteorology happened to be on an aerial flight from Miami when they witnessed six separate water spouts. They had cameras with them and Joseph H Golden wrote an account for the Royal Meteorological Society in *Weather* describing what they saw.

The diameters of the spouts varied from 40–80 ft (12–24 m), but the largest had a diameter of about 100 ft (30 m). The parent clouds had a base of 2200 ft (670 m) above the sea, measured by altimeter, but the tops of the clouds were estimated to be no more than 20 000 ft (6000 m), though still growing. None of the parent clouds were precipitating. A spray vortex on the surface of the sea, with well-defined wake trailing behind, gave prior indication of the spout a few seconds before the ropelike funnels became fully visible. The nearest spout was rotating in an anticlockwise direction and the spray near the sea surface was being whirled outwards with a speed of about 115 mph (185 km/h). One spout exhibited a strange pulsating outer sheath of condensation, which rotated around the better defined inner funnel and then moved upward into the

Water spout seen from HMAS *Melbourne* off the coast of Queensland, Australia, on 16 June 1974. (H L Daw; courtesy *Weather*)

base of the cloud. The larger spout was later discovered to have caused considerable damage after crossing the shore, uprooting bushes and trees, lifting a 2-ton car a few feet above ground, and causing cupboards inside houses to pop open because of reduced pressure. The wind that day was light SW at ground level, but meteorological upper air soundings revealed that wind veered with height although remaining less than 16 mph (25 km/h) all the way up to 20 000 ft (6000 m).

A waterspout in the southern hemisphere was observed only 300 ft (100 m) away from HMAS *Melbourne* on 16 June 1974, while she was operating off the coast of Queensland, Australia. Lieutenant Commander H L Daw reported that the spout was transparent, rotating in a clockwise direction and was about 30 ft (10 m) in diameter, with a rather broader diameter near the sea and near the cloud base. The column was 2500 ft (750 m) high and upright at first, but after 5 minutes it wavered, bent, divided and disappeared. Three other spouts were sighted in the distance, and all appeared to be forming beneath the leading

edge of cumulus clouds whose bases were estimated to be 2500 ft (650 m) and tops 9000 ft (3000 m), still growing.

Waterspouts occur in British waters, and since the funnel clouds may writhe and trail in the wind in the same manner as tornado funnels, it is not surprising to discover flamboyant accounts of early water spouts. In June 1233 it is reported that:

'two huge snakes were seen by many along the coast, fiercely battling in the air and after a long struggle one overcame the other and drove it into the depths'

The greatest frequency of water spout sightings occur around the south and south east coast of England. A particularly active day in recent years was 18 August 1974, when several groups of three to six spouts in the English Channel were seen by the same observers. At least two water spouts formed off the Isle of Wight, at least six formed between Selsey Bill and Beachy Head, with a further five off Hastings. The reports were studied by Mr L P Stevens of the Southampton Weather Centre, who described the weather conditions as overcast but warm, with a light north easterly wind subject to considerable shifting of direction, and a calm sea, except where agitated by water spouts. Cloud base was generally 1000 ft (300 m), but there were reports of lower stratus down to 100 ft (30 m) and some thunderstorms were reported.

Waterspouts also occur in the coastal water of northern England and Scotland. On 15 April 1903 a waterspout crossed Lerwick harbour, Shetland Isles, travelling at considerable speed and damaging shipping in the harbour. Waterspouts were seen in Kirkwall Bay, Orkney and in Eday Sound, Orkney in the summer of 1933, and more recently, in November 1975, a column of water 150 ft (50 m) high and 100 ft (30 m) wide was seen in the Moray Firth, Scotland. It was spinning at terrific speed with the base on the sea like a boiling cauldron, and it travelled towards Lossiemouth for 2 miles (3 km) before suddenly disappearing. The wind that day was fresh north easterly.

Waterspouts which cross land have been known to cause damage on land, before collapsing. On 22 August 1975, one of several waterspouts which formed off East Anglia ripped tiles and guttering off houses in Kessingland, Suffolk; another which struck the harbour at West Mersea, Essex, hurled a dinghy into the air and carried it 450 ft (150 m) before dashing it to ground.

Close proximity to a water spout can be an extremely unpleasant experience when protected by nothing more substantial than a small yacht. Mr B Kenyon of Winchester described in *Weather* an encounter with a waterspout off Portland Bill, Weymouth. The sea was lumpy and uncomfortable, the sky was overcast and lightning could be seen over the land. Wind was freshening and :

'about this time a column, Admiralty grey in colour, was seen to starboard of us. It dawned on us that this was the same shape as the whirlwind in the Wizard of Oz. We dropped the foresail and secured it to safety rails as quickly as we could and lashed ourselves with the spare sheets (ropes) into the cockpit. Rain was now coming down heavily and the spout approached closer. Time was about 0530, and the wind was now so heavy that it was difficult to keep our eyes open and keep watch. The spout increased in size (or came nearer) and it appeared on recollection to be anticlockwise, water turbulent at the base. The water could be seen rising into the column, the colour of the base was a muddy green-brown, though as you looked up the column it became more bluey green. Without an horizon it was difficult to give any indication of the height. From the detail that could be seen it was between 250 and 350 yards away passing us down the starboard side and astern. At the same time an extremely severe electric storm was lying around the boat and forked lightning striking the water. The width of the lightning was quite frightening appearing to be a yard or more in width. We kept our hands away from all metal parts, said nothing to each other but were both rather shaken.

CHAPTER 16

OPTICAL PHENOMENA

ris, rainbow goddess and a
Weather balloon

The silent and weird optical phenomena which
esult from the passage of light through the
atmosphere, have been as much feared or
evered throughout history as the noisy and
violent manifestations of weather.

The sudden loss of light during an eclipse
of the Sun is terrifying to primitive tribes, who
do not understand that the Sun is merely
shaded temporarily by the Moon. But even
educated people, who know that there are
perfectly natural explanations for displays of
light in the atmosphere, find something
uncanny about the precise geometric designs
which occur.

The rules governing the path of light in
the atmosphere are somewhat contradictory.

Light travels in straight lines – but only
within a homogeneous medium, and when

there are no obstructing small particles. The
'straight' lines of light are really wave motions
of very small length and amplitude. Light
bends when encountering small particles or
when passing through a medium, such as air,
which changes density gradually. Light bends
abruptly when entering and leaving a boundary
between air and another transparent medium,
such as water or ice.

**Light rays are partly reflected and partly
absorbed** by any materials on which they fall.
The smoother the surface on which the rays
impinge, the more the light is reflected, but
all materials, however rough, reflect some
light. In this way sunshine is diffused, (ie
spread about) to provide illumination outside
the vicinity of direct sunbeams.

The laws of reflection are straightforward.
The *normal* is defined as a line perpendicular
to a surface on which light impinges, the *angle
of incidence* is the angle which the approaching
light ray makes with the normal, and the *angle
of reflection* is the angle the light ray makes
with the normal after reflection.

The angle of incidence equals the angle of
reflection.

Transparent materials are those which
permit absorbed light rays to pass right through.
If the light strikes the surface at an oblique
angle, more is reflected than transmitted. If
the light strikes vertically more is transmitted
than reflected. On entering or leaving a
boundary surface between transparent media
of different density, light rays bend, a process
called *refraction*.

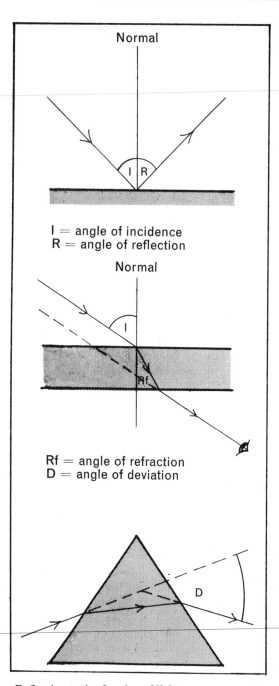

Normal

I = angle of incidence
R = angle of reflection

Normal

Rf = angle of refraction
D = angle of deviation

Reflection and refraction of light.

The laws of refraction of light were postulated in 1621 by Willibrod Snell, Professor of Mathematics at Leyden University, Holland.

The angle of incidence is the angle the light ray makes with the normal *before* entering the new medium, and the *angle of refraction* is the angle it makes with the normal *after* entering.

A light ray entering a denser medium (eg from air into water), bends *towards* the normal so that the angle of refraction is less than the angle of incidence. On emerging from the denser medium the light ray bends *away* from the normal so that the angle of refraction is greater than the angle of incidence. The angle of refraction can therefore sometimes be greater than 90° when light reaches a less dense medium.

Total internal reflection occurs when a light ray tries to escape from a dense to a less dense medium, but impinges on the boundary at such a large angle of incidence that the angle of refraction is more than 90°. The light then *reflects* from the surface instead of passing through.

The angle of deviation is the angle which a ray of light makes with its original track, when it emerges after having passed right through a transparent substance. If the light passes through parallel boundaries (eg a rectangular block of ice or glass), the ray emerges displaced but parallel to its original track, and without change in appearance. When light passes through transparent boundaries which are set at an angle to each other, then the whole appearance of the emerging light may be transformed.

Sir Isaac Newton (1642–1727), English physicist, was the first to demonstrate the coloured nature of light. He concentrated a beam of white sunlight on to one face of a 60° prism of glass, and placed the prism so that the light which emerged on the far side fell on to a white wall. The result was a display of colours which ranged from red on the top to violet at the bottom. He concluded that white light consists of many superimposed colours, which bend by different amounts on entering a transparent medium.

The spectrum of light is the name given to all the colours which make up white light. These colours are violet, indigo, blue, green, yellow, orange and red, and their wave lengths range from 0·4 microns (violet) to 0·7 microns (red) – (1 micron is a millionth of a metre.) When entering another transparent medium, the shorter wave lengths bend more than the longer wave lengths, but the colours are only separated enough to be recognisable when refracted more than once in the same direction on passing through a transparent medium.

The angle of deviation is least when light passes symmetrically through two boundaries at angles to each other, and this is when colour separation is most pronounced.

Diffraction is the bending of light rays around particles or water drops which have approximately the same wave length of light. The longer wave lengths (red) are liable to greater diffraction than the shorter wave lengths (violet).

Scattering is the change in direction of light rays produced by the molecules of air itself. Scattering is greater for light rays of shorter wave length (violet) than for the rays of longer wave length (red).

The sky appears blue and the Sun yellow when light from the Sun travels through a depth of atmosphere which is clean and dry. Then the shortest wave band of the visible spectrum, blue, is scattered by the molecules of the atmosphere, and the remainder reaches the eye. Scattering only affects a very small proportion of light emitted from the Sun, which therefore appears pale yellow or whitish in the blue sky. The bluest skies in Great Britain occur when the Sun shines through a vigorous air stream from the north, in which thermal activity and showers have cleansed the lower atmosphere of dirt.

The sky appears white and the Sun red when light from the Sun travels through a considerable thickness of atmosphere which contains water droplets or dirt, scattering light in all the wave bands. Residual light rays reaching the eye from the Sun are then all in the higher wave length: red. These conditions most often occur towards sunset in quiet high-pressure weather when a fine cloudless day is starting to degenerate into a misty or foggy night.

The Sun may appear red when seen through a particularly dirty atmosphere, and apparently glowed weirdly red through the pall of smoke which enveloped London during the Great Fire in the first week of September 1666. The Sun also appears red when high in the sky and shining through the ash erupted by volcanoes.

A blue Sun or a blue Moon can occur when particles of critical size scatter red light more than blue. It occurred in Great Britain on 26 September 1950, when smoke particles from forest fires in Alberta, Canada reached the country on winds at 6–8 miles (10–13 km) altitude. However, the phenomenon does not happen often, hence the expression 'once in a blue moon'.

A green flash sometimes accompanies the last or first glimpse of the setting or rising Sun. It is caused by the greater refraction of the green wave band, the shortest after the blue and violet which are scattered by the molecules of the air. The flash is momentary only, but a prolonged green flash was seen on 6 December 1970 in special circumstances: a Boeing 707 aircraft was descending towards a sheet of cloud just as the Sun was starting to rise above it. The navigator saw a green flash for about 5 seconds and then, after a 2 seconds' return to normal coloration, he saw the flash again for a further 3 seconds. The aircraft was descending at a rate balanced by the rate of rise of the Sun.

A red flash from the wave length with least refraction angle has occasionally been seen as the lower segment of the Sun appears below a cloud bank on the horizon.

Visibility is the distance of the furthest objects on the ground which can be seen at a specified time. Observers gauge visibility by known landmarks of predetermined distance. Topography and obstructions on the horizon are a limiting factor, so that good visibility often cannot be expressed more accurately than for instance, 'greater than 30 miles' (50 km). However, there are always close landmarks by which to gauge short visibilities. 'A hand's length' indicates impenetrable fog, though it is reported more prosaically in number of metres by meteorological observers.

Visibility depends on the quantity of obscuring particles of dirt or moisture in the air through which one is looking.

Visibility in middle latitudes is best when wind blows from high latitudes to low. These are occasions of brisk thermal activity to carry dirt upwards from polluted areas near the ground, or wash it down to ground in showers. In Great Britain the best visibility is approximately 130 miles (210 km), and the Antrim Hills, Northern Ireland, whose highest point is 1817 ft (553 m), can frequently be seen from Ben Nevis, Highland, Scotland (4406 ft (1343 m)).

The Wicklow Hills, Rep. of Ireland, highest point 3039 ft (926 m), were seen from Coniston Old Man, Cumbria, 2633 ft (803 m), in 1965, approximately 160 miles (257 km) distance. The Mourne Mountains, Co. Down, Northern Ireland, highest point 2796 ft (852 m), were seen from a height of 500 ft (152 m) in Cumbria in July 1968, 120 miles (193 m) distance.

The worst visibility, excluding water drop fog which may be totally obscuring, occurs in high pressure weather when a temperature inversion keeps pollution and moisture droplets trapped within a shallow layer of the ground. The sky may then appear as ominously dark, as if there were a storm cloud approaching. The oblique visibility from an aircraft on approach to a landing field may be very low, even though an observer standing vertically below can see the aircraft plainly through the shorter distance of polluted air.

Visibility in polar regions is often extremely good because of lack of pollution in the air. On cloudless days and nights shadows cast by the light of the Moon or Sun bring into relief every undulation of the white landscape. There are however, particular visibility troubles on cloudy days caused by the multiple reflection between white cloud and snow.

Whiteout is the confusion of normal optical senses, which occurs when light (from the Sun or Moon) is diffused through thin cloud and diffused back again from a uniformly white snow surface. All the normal standards, such as shadows, coloured objects and the horizon by which the human eye judges distance and perspective, disappear into a universal whiteness. It is difficult to know if one is standing on head or heels, and the sense of balance is affected. It becomes dangerous even to walk because snow covered hummocks of ice or snow drifts are invisible contours over which to stumble.

However, cloud sheets are often thick enough to serve better as reflectors than transmitters of light, and the intensity of light reflected from large areas in polar regions is not always the same. Then clouds become valuable mirrors.

Ice blink on the horizon. (C Swithinbank)

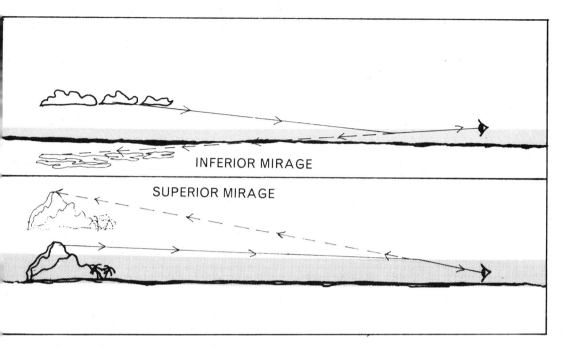

nferior and superior mirages.

ce blink is a whitish glare on the horizon reflected from ice on to the underside of cloud. ce blink has subtle tints of yellow or grey which can even indicate to experienced travellers the type of ice over which the blink is seen.

Water sky is the grey reflection cast on the underside of cloud by open water below.

A cloud map or land sky is the alternating white and grey colours reflected on to the underside of cloud by a variable surface below of water, snow or ice. It is an invaluable navigation aid to travellers who are saved long journeys only to find their passage blocked at the end. Eskimos, travelling by kayak, dodge expertly through leads of open water, and recognize the permanent headland by which they navigate in the cloud map above. Those who travel across the snow using sledge and dog avoid the water leads and can often journey for days at a time without seeing water.

The images of very distant objects, like the stars, are always slightly displaced from their real position, because light bends gradually on travelling through progressive layers of air of different density.

An inferior mirage is seen below the real object, when light refracts and internally reflects at the abrupt boundary of an intensely hot layer of low density air, such as exists over the desert or over a tarmac road in summer. The image seen is always in the direction along which light enters the eye, irrespective of previous distortion, so the reflection of the sky appears on the ground. It shimmers, because of the convection activity near the ground, and the brain reacts by thinking that the reflection of the sky must be the more usual phenomenon of water. The message has proved tantalising and disappointing for many people wandering thirsty in the desert. Since internal reflections only occur when the angle of incidence is oblique, mirages are usually seen in the distance, or along an inclined surface.

A superior mirage is an image seen above the real object, because the light from the object bends downwards when travelling through a layer of very cold dense air before reaching the eye. The effect can bring into view objects which are normally below the horizon and accounts for repeat sunsets in polar regions.

Sir Ernest Shackleton wrote in his diary on 15 April 1915:

'The sun set amid a glow of prismatic colour on a line just above the horizon. A minute later Worsley saw a golden glow which expanded as he watched it, and presently the sun appeared and rose in a semi diameter clear of the horizon. A quarter of an hour later, the sun set a second time.'

In another entry he writes:

'I had taken the sun for the last time and said we would not see it again for 90 days. Then after 8 days it got up again, risen by refraction. On other days we watched the sun set, come up again and set, over and over until we got tired of it!'

Refraction not only brings objects below the horizon into view, it sometimes appears to project them high into the sky. Phantom mountain-ranges often appear in Antarctica weirdly grey, but with the recognisable contours of ranges below the horizon.

Ghostly mountains often appear in the sky over the Gulf of California, an hour or so before sunset. The 10 100 ft (3078 m) mountain peak Cerro La Encantada, on the peninsula of Baja California, Mexico, is not normally visible from Puerto Penasco, 116 miles (186 km) away on the other side of the Gulf. About an hour or so before sunset, the sea breeze ceases, and cold air settles over the bay, and about 45 minutes before sunset a mirage of La Encantada looms high into the sky. The contours are quite recognisable, and it is as if the real mountain had grown to four times its true height.

Fata morgana is a complicated superior mirage caused by distortion of light, both vertically and horizontally, when passing through several layers of air of different density. The resulting mirage bears little resemblance to the viewed object, and is more like a fairy landscape. Fata morgana usually occurs over water, and the name originated from Italy where the mirage is often seen over the Strait of Messina.

Looming is the impression of huge size, close distance, associated with superior mirages or with the Sun or Moon when low on the horizon. Opinion is divided about whether this is a genuine magnification process or not. could be caused by varying densities atmosphere acting like a lens, or it may be psychological reaction of the mind to what knows is impossible: the setting Sun is not *really* sitting on the horizon, or nestling between houses, and mountains do not really stand in the sky. The only certain thing is that most observers are conscious of magnification or looming closely. Ptolemy, too, commented in the 2nd century that any object viewed across land looked larger than the same object viewed across empty space.

Circular displays of light occur in the atmosphere, when dust particles of uniform size or symmetrically shaped ice crystals and water drops change paths of light by diffraction refraction and reflection. Light from the Sun and Moon are so far away that all rays entering a sheet of dust, ice crystals or water drops can be considered parallel to each other. Light rays passing through the sheet and diffracted reflected or refracted by fixed amounts therefore also emerge parallel at a fixed angle of deviation. The eye can only detect those rays which reach it from that angle, ie, from points on a circle.

A circular or part circular display of light is therefore measured by the angle of deviation of light passing through the sheet of water drops or ice crystals.

All optical displays are unique to each observer, because they are determined by light rays which enter the observer's eyes

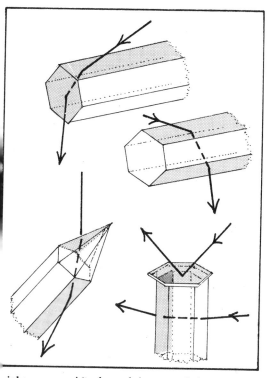

light rays passing through ice crystals in such ways as to produce optical phenomena.

...nd his alone. Distant phenomena, like rain-...ows or haloes, *appear* to be the same to several ...bservers standing alongside each other, be-...use it is not possible to discern the tiny ...ifferences by means of the points of reference ...ormally available on the landscape or in the ...ky.

halo is a ring of coloured light around a ...ght source, caused by the refraction of light ...hen passing through ice crystals which are ...ndomly organised. Red is on the inside with ...ellow and blue on the outside, but sometimes ...e colour is faint and the halo then appears ...hitish.

Halo displays are often seen around the ...ower plants at Fairbanks, Alaska, where ...ected water vapour crystallises immediately ...outside air which is often below −22° F ...30° C).

The most familiar haloes, however, are those seen around the Sun or the Moon, when they are obscured by a thin sheet of ice crystal cloud, cirrostratus. The light from the Moon is not usually strong enough to produce a halo, except near the time of full-moon.

An approximate measurement of the size of a halo can be made with a pair of dividers, held so that the hinge is close to the eye. Position one point on the centre of the Moon, and open the other arm until its extremity reaches the halo. The angle between the two arms is the angle of the halo.

A halo round the Sun should *never* be measured directly by eye, even through a cloud of ice crystals, but should be viewed by reflection in a piece of dark glass, or alongside an obstruction which masks the Sun centre.

In practice, a very rough measurement provides an accurate answer to the size of a halo, because the three possible sizes are so different from each other.

The 22° halo is the most common, and is formed when light passes through two alternate longitudinal faces of ice crystals.

The 46° halo occurs occasionally, when light passes through one longitudinal face of an ice crystal, and the end section at right angles to it.

The 8° halo is very rare, and occurs when light passes through one longitudinal face of a crystal, and its prism end. This halo may be

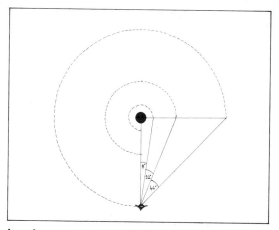

Angular measurement of haloes.

less rare than is thought, but it is so close to the Sun that it is difficult to detect.

Parhelia, mock suns, or sun dogs are images of the Sun formed by refraction of light through ice crystals aligned with their axes vertical. Such crystals are usually surmounted by hexagonal plate crystals, which act rather like parachutes to keep the crystals suspended vertically. Parhelia are at the same elevation as the Sun and on either side of it. They are positioned on the halo when the Sun is near the horizon, but a little way outside the halo when the Sun is high in the sky. Parhelia are whitish with a red tinge on the side nearest the Sun.

Parry arcs form above and below a halo when hexagonal crystals lie with their main axis and two opposite sides horizontal.

Circumzenithal arcs form by refraction through the 90° edges of vertically aligned crystals. They are vividly coloured, red towards the Sun, and are seen alone or above the 46° halo, convex to the Sun.

The parhelic circle is a whitish bright circle around the Sun, parallel to the horizon, caused by reflection from the top surfaces of ice crystals whose axes are vertical.

A sun pillar is a column of light above or below a low elevation Sun, and is caused by reflection in ice crystals which are inclined slightly to the horizontal. Being reflected light, a sun pillar has the same colour as the Sun. It is often best observed when an obstruction blocks out the view of the Sun itself, but the sun pillar may remain visible for a short time after the Sun has sunk below the horizon.

Sun crosses are seen when sun pillars intersect with an incomplete parhelic circle.

A sub sun is a reflection of the Sun seen from a mountain or an aircraft, and projected on to a cloud of systematically aligned ice crystal surfaces.

The Arc of Lowitz was named after th astronomer who first saw and described it in halo display over Petersburg on 29 June 179

The Arc is a downward extension of th mock sun, caused by oscillation about th vertical of ice crystals whose axes are arrange symmetrically. It is a very rare phenomeno but was believed seen by Professor Scorer an G Nicholson at Teddington, Middlesex, o 11 May 1965 at 2015 GMT.

A spectacular halo display was witnesse at Saskatoon, Canada on 3 December 197 and photographed by W F J Evans, of th University of Saskatchewan. The theoretic whole display was sketched and the portion enclosed within dotted lines were photographe

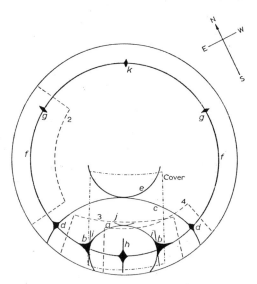

Fig. 1.   The celestial sphere showing the coverage of the photographs in relation to the halo display. The main halo features observed were:
a   the 22° halo
b   the parhelia of the 22° halo
c   the 46° halo
d   the parhelia of the 46° halo
e   the circumzenithal arc
f   the parhelic circle
g   the paranthelia of 120°
h   the sun pillar
i   lateral tangent arcs to 22° halo
j   upper arc of contact to 22° halo
k   anthelion, reported by several observers but not visible at Saskatoon when the photographs were taken

The halo display over Saskatoon, Canada, on 3 December 1970. Sections within dotted lines were photographed. (W J Evans; courtesy *Weather*

Part of the halo display at Saskatoon,
Canada, on 3 December 1970. (W J Evans)

Primary (inner) and secondary (outer) rainbows, seen at Tavistock, Devon, 22 December
1973. (K B Shone)

Brockenspectre and glory. (J N Merrill)

Sun pillar. (J Cooley)

n unusually complex halo display was
en from Berkshire on 11 May 1965. Later
nsultation between experienced observers,
ho witnessed the display from different
ositions and at different times, elicited the
ct that 13 separate phenomena were visible.

Haloes are traditionally signs of ap-
roaching rain, and feature in a variety of
hymes. For instance:

ast night the sun went pale to bed
he moon in haloes hid her head.
''will surely rain – I see with sorrow
ur jaunt must be put off to-morrow.'

There is some truth in the rhyme, because
rrostratus, producing haloes, precedes frontal
ain. However, parts of haloes can sometimes
e seen in patches of cirrus which are uncon-
ected with approaching rain, and frontal belts
ften die out without reaching the rain stage.
weather observer interested in the correlation
etween haloes and rain carried out an investiga-
ion near Bristol, between 1 January 1960 and
  March 1971.

Haloes were observed on 80 occasions
uring 66 days. 71 haloes were round the Sun
nd 9 round the Moon; 39 haloes lasted less
han 5 minutes, 11 more than an hour. 20
omplete haloes were seen and 15 upper
emicircles, but no lower semicircles. 20
pper tips were seen and one lower tip.

On only 45 occasions out of 80 did rain
ollow within 48 hours.

rainbow is formed by refraction and internal
eflection in rain drops, so that light emerges
rom the drops along a back-tracking angle of
eviation. A rainbow can therefore only be
een by a person standing with his back to the
un, and the bow is measured not from the
ye, but from the imaginary shadow of the eye
n the distance which is called the 'anti solar
oint'. Only an arc of the circle is visible to
n observer on the ground, because the anti
olar point is on or below the ground, and the
urtain of rain drops is above ground. The
ower the altitude of the Sun, the greater the

arc of rainbow visible. A semicircular bow
would occur as the Sun sets, except that the
light is not then strong enough. A complete
circular rainbow is sometimes seen by pilots
of aircraft, approaching a curtain of raindrops
at a height midway between cloud base and
ground.

The distance of a rainbow from an observer
may be anything from a few yards (when seen
in spray thrown up on a wet road, or in the
spray from a waterfall) to several miles when
seen in rain falling from cloud. The best
coloration in rainbows occurs with large water
drops. When drops are smaller than 0·01 in
(0·3 mm) colour separation is poor.

A primary rainbow is formed when light is
refracted twice and internally reflected once,
emerging with an angle of deviation between
138° at the violet end of the spectrum, and
$139\frac{1}{2}°$ at the red end. The angular measurement
of the primary rainbow from the anti solar
point is $40\frac{1}{2}°$ for the violet colour (inside), and
42° for the red colour (outside).

A secondary bow occurs when there are two
internal reflections within the water drops
before the light emerges at angles between
$233\frac{1}{2}°$ (violet) and 230° (red) from the original
direction. The angular measurement of the
bow from the anti solar point is $50\frac{1}{2}°$ (red) to
$53\frac{1}{2}°$ (violet), and the colours are opposite from
those of the primary bow – red inside and violet
outside. The secondary bow is less bright
than the primary.

Supernumerary rainbows sometimes occur
just inside the primary bow, caused by more
than two internal reflections. Their colours
are poor and the intensity of light is weak.

Rainbows usually have only a fleeting
existence, but at Dover, Kent, on 7 May 1953,
a bow was seen to last for more than 1 hour.
The complete inner and outer bow lasted for
30 minutes, and then the weakening evening
light caused the outer bow to disappear, but
the inner bow lingered slowly for another
half hour.

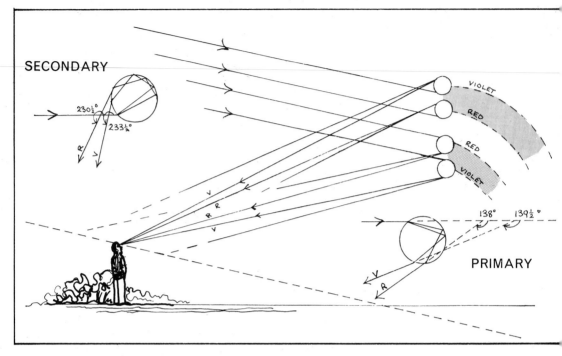

SECONDARY

$230\frac{1}{2}°$
$233\frac{1}{2}°$

PRIMARY

VIOLET
RED
RED
VIOLET

138° $139\frac{1}{2}°$

Method of formation of primary and secondary rainbows.

The most usual time to see rainbows is in the afternoon on days of strong thermal activity. Cumulonimbus are then producing showers, bright periods which intervene permit the Sun to shine on a departing shower and the intensity of light is still strong. Rainbows cannot be seen when the Sun's altitude is higher than approximately 53°, because then the refracted light passes above the head of an observer on the ground.

'The Rainbow's End' is a phrase meaning 'the unattainable', because as soon as one tries to move towards the 'end' the original rainbow seen is displaced by another having a slightly different anti solar point as centre.

Ulloa's bow or fog bow is formed in the same way as a rainbow, except that the Sun shining behind the observer falls on to fog instead of rain drops. The diameter of fog drops is usually less than 0·002 in (0·05 mm),

which ensures that the refracted coloure rays overlap to form a white bow. Only th faintest tinge of colour appears at either en of the white band, red outside and blue insid for a primary fog bow, and blue inside an red outside for a secondary fog bow.

A corona is a series of rings around the Su or Moon, caused by diffraction of light clos to very small water drops. The red light diffracted more than the violet, and the inne ring of light, called the 'aureole' is bluish o the inside and reddish brown on the outsid Sometimes the aureole is all that is seen, bu on other occasions a whole series of ring extends outward beyond the aureole, agai with blue on the inside and red on the outsid The smaller the water drops the larger th corona, and colour separation is best whe droplets are of uniform size. The most spec tacular coronae therefore often occur with new ly formed sheets of stratus or stratocumulu

iridescence is colouring seen in the thin edges of patches of water-drop cloud, and is part of a corona.

Heiligenschein (German, meaning holy areole) is a whitish ring of light surrounding the shadow of an observer's head on dewy grass. It is most frequently seen in early morning, while the Sun's altitude is still low and the grass still wet with dew. Benvenuto Cellini (1500–71), Italian goldsmith and sculptor, was one of the first to describe the phenomenon, ascribing the aureole of light round his head to a mark of religious favour. The mundane modern explanation is that the 'schein' is caused by diffraction of light, in a similar manner to that causing a corona.

Brocken Spectre is a shadow of an observer cast upon fog or low cloud when the Sun is shining from behind. The spectre appears enlarged because the shadow falls through a depth of water droplets. The most usual situation for viewing a Brocken Spectre is when standing on high ground and looking down on valley fog. The name comes from the Brocken summit in the Hartz mountains of Germany. The mountain is in an area which was one of the last strongholds of heathen faiths, and there used to be many superstitions in the neighbourhood about the devil. The uncanny ring of light which often forms round a Brocken Spectre possibly contributed to the superstitions.

glory is a ring of light like a corona, seen round a Brocken Spectre. The reason for its formation is not certain, but it probably results from multiple reflection within tiny drops of water, and then diffraction on the return of light to the eye. A glory can only be seen round an observer's own shadow, but people standing alongside each other can all see each other's shadow. This is therefore one of the few occasions when it becomes obvious that circular optical phenomena are uniquely positioned for each observer.

The Bishop's Ring is a reddish brown ring round the Sun, caused by bending of light round fine dust in the atmosphere. When the Sun is high, the inside of the ring is about 10° and the outside 20°, but the ring enlarges to 30° as the Sun lowers in the sky.

The Bishop's Ring was first observed by a Mr Bishop at Honolulu, on 5 September 1883, after the volcanic eruption of Krakatoa. The heavier particles ejected into the atmosphere sifted out by gravitation, leaving a remainder of tiny particles of nearly the same size, which were capable of producing coloured diffraction. The Bishop's Ring reached its greatest brilliance in the spring of 1884, and gradually declined until June 1886 when it disappeared.

The aurora borealis (northern lights) and aurora australis (southern lights) are spectacular displays of light seen in the northern and southern hemispheres respectively. In latitudes higher than 70° they are seen frequently. In lower latitudes they usually occur during periods of intense solar activity, but displays are often masked by cloud. The lights are caused by electrical solar discharges which are deflected by the Earth's magnetic field and are sometimes organised to appear like waving curtains of light. The colours vary according to the gases present in the atmosphere, and vivid displays may contain all colours of the spectrum. Many displays, however, are less dramatically greyish-white.

People in north Scotland would be able to see aurorae 150 times per annum on average, if it were not for intervening cloud in the troposphere. In fact, Edinburgh may expect to see about 25 displays a year. London is lucky if it witnesses one display of aurora in a year and Malta if it sees one display in ten years.

Aurorae were seen from the Shetland Isles on 203 occasions in 1957, but on only 58 occasions during 1965, these being the record high and low number of displays since reliable observations were started in 1952. The most recent auroral display of spectacular worth in north west Europe occurred on 4–5 September 1958.

Displays were observed in particularly low latitudes on 2 August 1744, at Cuzco, Peru, S. America and on 1 September 1859, over Honolulu, Hawaii, Pacific Ocean.

CHAPTER 17

FORECASTING THE WEATHER

Headquarters of the World Meteorological Organisation, Geneva.

The word 'forecast' was first used by Admiral Fitzroy, Chief Meteorologist to the Board of Trade in Great Britain in the 1850's. The study of weather had been dignified with the name 'meteorology' (after Aristotle's *Meteorologica*, a discourse on atmospheric phenomena) and it was a sensible corollary to create a new image for the more scientific methods of predicting the weather. However, the traditional weather rules, which had evolved over the past centuries and were embodied in rhymes and sayings, did not die out overnight but became known as weather lore.

Weather lore is really single observer forecasting, without instruments and without knowledge of the causes of weather. The word *lore*, tends to give a derogatory impression that the predictive rules of the past are all nonsense.

Some certainly deserve condemnation, but many others can still serve as useful memory aids for people who have no meteorological instruments and yet want to keep one pace ahead of the weather in the local area. There are several erroneous statements which crop up often in weather lore, and many refer to the Moon.

The Moon is an excellent aid to observation at night, but there is no proven connection between the phases of the Moon and the weather which occurs at the same time. The most that can be said is that the Moon influences the sea tides, and that, therefore the unfortunate coincidence of full Moon, high tides and strong winds can cause disastrous secondary effects like storm surges. But the Moon does not create the winds. Neither do upturned crescents of the Moon retain rain in their dishes and produce dry weather on Earth, nor do downturned crescents spill water to Earth as rain. Any dogma which attributes such causative powers to the Moon must be disregarded in the light of modern knowledge. In the past, however, it is understandable that even shrewd weather observers should have explained weather by the phases of the Moon. Virgil (70–19 BC) the Roman poet who embodied much sound advice about the weather in his agricultural treatise *The Georgics* erroneously said '*The Father himself laid down what the Moon's phases should mean, the cue for the south winds dropping. . . .*'

Amongst Virgil's valid statements, however, is:

Nor will you be taken in by the trick of a cloudless
   night
When first at the new Moon her radiance is
   returning
If she should clasp a dark mist within her unclear
   crescent
Heavy rain is in store for farmer and fisherman.

In this instance Virgil does not emphasise so much the phase of the Moon but rather its misty appearance. When a clear Moon gradually becomes blurred it is usually because of a thickening sheet of cloud heralding the advance of a warm front and rain. The misty Moon is the subsequent stage to *'The Moon in haloes hides her head'* indicative of thin ice crystal cloud (p. 207).

The moon focusses attention on a clear sky but has no known effect upon the weather.

The Moon in a cloudless sky is a beautiful sight and often the only reason people look up at the sky at all. Therefore, many weather sayings have attributed the clear sky to the presence of the Moon, specially the full Moon, forgetting that the heavenly body is still there even when obscured from the ground because of cloud. The old couplet *'Full Moon, frost soon'* is therefore wrong because it implies that whenever the Moon is full there is a risk of frost. However, change the emphasis slightly to memorize *'Clear Moon, frost soon'* or *'Clear sky, frost nigh'* and it then serves as a reliable reminder that lack of cloud permits great radiation heat loss from the ground during the night.

When judging the validity of weather lore incorporating mention of the Moon, remember that

'The Moon and the weather
May change together,
But a change of the Moon
Does not change the weather.'

Cloud generally develops in a gradual manner, horizontally or vertically, quickly or slowly and its development can be followed by eye. Many weather prophets have used this fact in their predictive rules, and amongst them was the Shepherd of Banbury, an Englishman about whom little is known. He may have been named John Claridge, he presumably lived in Banbury, Oxfordshire, and his profession of shepherd gave him plenty of time to observe the weather and a great need to predict it. His rules became known by word of mouth and were first published in 1670 under the title *The Shepherd's Legacy*. His observations on cumulus clouds were sound:

'Large like rocks – great showers'
'If large clouds decrease – fair weather'

In other words, if clouds develop extensively upwards they will eventually produce showers; but if large cumulus diminish in size before the expected time of dispersal in the evening then the probable cause is subsidence of the upper air. Providing there is no higher sheet cloud spreading across the sky, the omens are good for improvement in the weather.

Virgil, too, watched the growth of clouds carefully.

'But when towards daybreak the Sun's beams filter between
Thick cloud rayed out like spokes . . . then I fear
Vine leaves will give your ripening grapes but poor protection
Such a storm of harsh hail is coming to rattle and bounce on the roofs.'

He must have noticed that when the air is particularly unstable, cumulus clouds start developing very early in the morning and become gigantic cumulonimbus later in the day.

A popular modern expression relating to the instability of the air is *'Too good to last'*, a verdict on the brilliant blue sky and sharp visibility which deteriorates quickly with rapidly growing cumulus clouds in unstable air.

The only cloud which appears without visual warning, suddenly and *'out of the blue'*, is stratus cloud or lifted fog. A sunny morning may cloud over temporarily as wind stirs fog out of the valleys; or a clear sky at night may become obscured within seconds by thin stratus soon after the cooling air near the ground has fallen to dew point temperature.

A reliable couplet referring to all clouds and any precipitation they bring is

'Long notice, long past;
Short notice, short past.'

It is an obvious statement that weather which advances quickly is travelling at such a speed that it must pass quickly, since there is no abrupt braking system which could operate. It can be a useful memory guide, however, when caught out in rain. The very fact that a heavy shower has crept up without being observed, indicates it must be travelling fast and a short stay in shelter will be worth while. However, a cloud sheet which has been slowly advancing and thickening and only produced rain after several hours will be likely to endure for a long time. Plans may need to be altered or carried out in the rain.

Wind direction data which is included weather lore may prohibit a saying from having universal validity all over the world. European nationalities are reminded of cold and snow by rhymes such as

'The north wind doth blow
And we shall have snow.'

The saying becomes meaningless in the southern hemisphere, where a country like New Zealand expects cold weather with south winds.

Sailors in the North Atlantic coined a catch phrase as reminder that a ridge of high pressure with fair weather and NW wind is often only a temporary intermission between two depressions bringing bad weather on SW wind. They say *'A nor'wester is not long in debt to a sou'wester'*, but the rule can have no validity in the southern hemisphere, where wind changes in opposite manner (p. 77). Similarly *'backing is a bad sign with any wind'* is valid in the northern hemisphere, but has to read *'veering is a bad sign . . .'* in the southern hemisphere.

Sometimes, wind dicta are applicable by coincidence to quite different areas. Hosea, in chapter 13 of his Old Testament Book, writes that

'an east wind shall come up from the wilderness and his spring shall become dry and his fountain shall be dried.'

British people echo the maxim by saying

'When the wind is in the east,
'tis neither good for man nor beast'

Only by chance are the two sayings applicable to either area; east winds bring dry air to the eastern Mediterranean from the desert, and east winds bring dry air to Great Britain from the continent of Europe. The British rhyme reflects not only the dread of drought, but also the particularly cold weather which comes with east wind in the winter.

Precipitation advice is given in many old sayings, and one favourite which endures is
'Rain before seven,
Fine before eleven.'

This is valid in so far as rain belts accompanying depressions usually last about four hours, but there is no significance to the hours of seven and eleven, because depressions are not governed by the hour of day and thermal activity. However, seven and eleven rhyme most excellently and serve subtly to improve the accuracy of the prediction. A rain belt of longer than four hours duration may have already arrived some time before a person gets up in the morning at seven o'clock and first observes the rain, and the four hour prediction will equally well cover the rain belt of five or six hours duration!

'*Too cold to snow*' is a shrewd opinion relating to winter weather. The lowest temperatures occur under clear skies at night in high pressure weather. Snow, while requiring a cold air stream, must fall from cloud and the presence of the cloud suffices to prevent excessive radiation heat loss and very low temperatures.

Sky colour is a predictive factor used in weather lore. The Shepherd of Banbury believed that '*if the sun rise red and fiery – wind and rain*' and it was possibly his saying which initiated other shepherd rhymes, such as

'Red sky in morning, shepherds are warning,
Red sky at night, shepherds delight.'

There is some truth to these sayings, providing one assumes the usual, but not invariable, circumstance of frontal cloud progressing from the west towards the east. A rising Sun in the east can only be seen if unobscured by cloud, and it may then illuminate from beneath a cloud sheet which has approached close to the eastern horizon from the west. In the early morning this is more likely to be frontal cloud than any other type and, therefore, rain and wind are distinct possibilities. In the evening, however, the setting Sun can only be seen in the west if unobscured by advancing sheet cloud. It may then shine on the underneath of broken cloud, which is most likely to be remnants of daytime cumulus in the process of dispersing to leave a cloudless sky.

Animal behaviour features often in weather lore. Virgil says '*rain need never take us unawares for high-flying cranes will have flown to valley*'. Theophrastus (*c.* 300 BC), the Greek philosopher wrote a book of signs containing 200 maxims about the weather. He stated that flies bite harder before a storm and ants run faster as temperature rises, and the latter statement has been proved true. However, all that these statements really say is that animals and insects react to current weather conditions; the human body does that too and is more conveniently to hand as a weather indicator. Neuritis pains often accompany wind change, rheumatic joints stiffen in damp weather, headaches foretell thunderstorms and even pain in a bunion on the foot has moved out of the realm of the music hall joke and become an atmospheric indicator of a highly personal nature. On their own these symptoms cannot foretell weather, but they can most ably reinforce an opinion based on other factors.

Weather lore fails as a memory guide when it is no longer contained in short pithy sentences. This means that serious early attempts to predict for more than about 12 hours ahead yielded dogma which is not worth retaining. For instance, the Shepherd of Banbury said

'When the wind turns to the north east and it continues two days without rain and does not turn south the third day, nor rain the third day, it is likely to continue north east for eight or nine days, all fair; and then to come to the south again.'

It was a shrewd observation which lacked enough theory to be expressed in compact form – north east wind in Great Britain often indicates high pressure and persistent fine weather.

Weather lore fails in content when it attempts to predict for long periods ahead in a few words. It usually generalises from one or a few occasions to propose a regular cyclical behaviour which does not exist. Amongst these traditions is the one that if St Swithins Day, 15 July, is wet it will rain for 40 subsequent days. The story arose in the year AD 971 when the body of Swithin, Bishop of Winchester, was due to be removed to a new resting place within the Cathedral. Since his death in AD 862 he had been buried, at his own request, in the churchyard where the rain might fall from the eaves on to his grave. The rain fell so heavily on 15 July 971 that the re-burial was postponed and when the wet spell continued (perhaps for 40 days) it was taken as a sign that the Saint's last wishes should be respected, and he be left in the churchyard. Statistical analysis has shown that the continuing superstition does not 'hold water'.

Abundant berries in autumn are often quoted as a portent of a hard winter to come. There is no evidence, however, that the berry crop is anything more than a reflection of the weather conditions which prevailed during its formative season – it is *hind* casting rather than *fore* casting.

The advent of the barometer improved the reliability of single observer forecasting because it often gave information of developing pressure systems before there were visible signs in the sky. Admiral Fitzroy's remarks concerning pressure tendency were sound.

'Steady rise indicates fair weather and, in winter, frost'
'A fall of half a tenth inch or more in half an hour is a sure sign of storm.'

Sailors, in particular, relied upon the barometer and coined more easily remembered jingles from Fitzroy's prosaic statements.

'Sharp rise after low
Oft foretells a stronger blow.'
'A greying sky and falling glass
Soundly sleeps the careless ass.'

Multiple observer weather reporting was made possible by the invention of the telegraph in 1836 and enabled more scientific forecasting to forge ahead. From 1855 onwards countries all over the world organised the relay at specified hours of the day of visual and instrumental observations from widely distributed places to central meteorological offices. The dramatic reduction of time lag between

making and receiving a weather observation was crucial to forecasting because the individual factors which constitute weather are always changing.

Mathematical codes were devised so that long wordy descriptions of weather could be converted into concise summaries for even quicker transmission by telegraph. These codes have been amended over the years and have gained international acceptance for use when sending messages by telegraph, telephone, radio or teleprinter.

The modern code for transmitting weather information allocates each item one or more positions within a series of 5 figure groups. Most measurements are given directly in numeral form, descriptive messages are relayed by numerical code.

For instance, the group PPPTT, which is the third group after the station code number gives the last three figures of the barometer reading in tenths of millibars (PPP) and the dry bulb temperature in degrees Celsius (TT).

So the PPPTT group which reads 1241 means that pressure is 1012·4 (corrected to

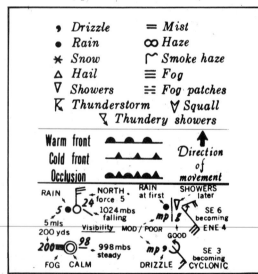

Plotting symbols and examples, as indicated on Met Maps issued by the Royal Meteorological Society.

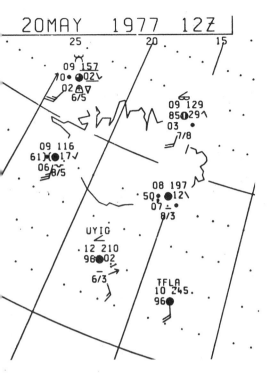

20 MAY 1977 12Z

Weather observations in the Iceland area, plotted automatically by machine. (Meteorological Office, Bracknell)

mean sea level) and air temperature is 13°C.

Cloud descriptions are relayed using one of possible numerals for each group of low, medium, and high category. Past weather is also allocated 9 code figures which are broken down still further into 99 code figures for present weather. Continuous slight rain is 61, but intermittent heavy rain is 64; a hail shower is 90, while continuous heavy snow is 75. Every experienced meteorologist can read each individual message as easily as he can read his own language; what he cannot assimilate is a whole sheet of coded messages which relate to a wide area. Hence, as soon as coded weather messages are received they are converted into symbolical pictures on a map.

Surface observations are plotted on to maps round a station circle located at the place where the observation was made. Each item

in the observation has a fixed position in relation to the circle and, therefore, anyone should be able to go into a meteorological office in any part of the world and read the weather chart, even if the spoken language is incomprehensible to him. A surface weather chart for a country the size of the British Isles can be plotted, analysed and used for forecasting for that area for 12–24 hours ahead, all within one hour of the actual weather observations being made. The time lag was probably the same in the 1860s when surface observations were *all* that the forecasters received.

The first forecasts in Great Britain issued to the press were in July 1861. These were based upon 22 reports received each morning (except Sunday) and 10 reports each afternoon from various parts of Great Britain with a further 5 reports from the continent. The observations were plotted, the isobars were drawn joining places having equal surface pressure and the results were compared with the preceding charts. The forecaster would note how depressions and rain belts had advanced during the period, he would closely scrutinise the weather details for indications that the systems were intensifying or diminishing and, on the basis of that judgement, he would advance the latest pattern by the number of hours ahead for which a forecast was required. The forecasters worked under two major handicaps. They had little information from abroad, or over the Atlantic from which direction most of the weather came, and they had no information about the upper air which was as up-to-date as the surface observations. Nevertheless, the early forecasts were the best available and were welcomed by the public. When Admiral Fitzroy died in 1865, gale warnings and forecasts for the public were stopped on the recommendation of the Royal Society because they thought the current scientific knowledge was inadequate. The public however insisted that inadequate forecasts were better than none and storm warnings to sea ports were soon resumed. They could hardly be called forecasts, because the

Televising a weather forecast from Anglia TV studio.

authorities were simply notified of gale observations and left to make their own deductions.

Forecasts for the public were resumed in 1876 and relayed by notice board, telephone, telegram and press. The first radio gale warnings to ships in the eastern North Atlantic were made in 1911 and shipping bulletins began in 1919.

The first weather forecast to be given by radio for the London area was included in the evening news bulletin from the BBC on 14 November 1922, and district forecasts were sent to local radio stations at Birmingham, Manchester, Newcastle, Cardiff and Glasgow. General forecasts replaced district forecasts in 1924.

In 1932, the Automobile Association in conjunction with the Meteorological Office started a service of weather reports from Heston aerodrome and, in July 1935, this was transferred to special studios at Borough Hill, Northampton, under the direction of the Meteorological Office. Continental reports were included from September 1935, reflecting the growth of private flying.

The first weather chart to be shown on television was on 1 November 1936 from Alexandra Palace, but the 1939–45 World War rendered all weather information secret, and the public was deprived of all forecasting services. As if in compensation, a wavelength was devoted entirely to the weather when

Airmet broadcasts started from Borough Hill in conjunction with the Meteorological Office at Dunstable, on 7 January 1947. Continuous weather information was broadcast from 0700 GMT until 1810 GMT and included reports from 40 aerodromes, forecasts and warnings in continual succession. The service was closed a few years later.

Forecasts on television were resumed again on 29 June 1949 with weather maps and captions being shown and, in 1954, the first live presentation of forecasts were made by professional meteorologists.

There were few spectacular developments in weather forecasting until the late 1930s. Analysis techniques were greatly improved when Bjerknes' theories of air masses and fronts were adopted, but there was still too little information available about the upper air. Three-dimensional weather was virtually being forecast on the basis of two-dimensional information. This was all the more frustrating for meteorologists because one man had devised a mathematical method of forecasting.

Lewis Fry Richardson (1881–1953), English physicist and meteorologist, worked out a scheme by which weather could be predicted by differential calculus using reports from 2000 regularly spaced weather stations over sea and land. His book *Weather Prediction by Numerical Process* was published in 1922 and he himself admitted that it provided a dream for the future and was not a practical proposition at that time. The calculations would have required an army of 64000 mathematicians working every hour of the day all the year and still the weather itself would progress faster than the answers designed to forecast it. Fortunately Richardson lived long enough to be reasonably sure that his particular 'science fiction' was going to come true.

Efficient surveillance of the upper air improved greatly because of the urgent need for accurate forecasts by the Armed Services during the 1939–45 World War. Radio Sonde apparatus, first used in Great Britain in 1937, bleeped regular information to ground stations, overcoming the time lag problem of having to retrieve apparatus before acquiring the data. Special meteorological aircraft flights over the sea at regular intervals and over specified routes probed the atmosphere where surface observations or Radio Sonde were lacking. The acquired information of temperature, humidity and pressure was plotted on to graph paper which to the unaccustomed eye seemed already too crowded with printed curves and lines to be useful for anything else. To the forecaster, however, it gave an instant picture of the vertical cross section of the atmosphere, from which he could detect warm air advancing at high level from several hundreds of miles away and forecast the development of cumulus cloud before even a trace appeared in the sky. The environment was stable if the slope of its curve was steeper than the lapse rate curve printed on the chart; it was unstable if the slope was flatter. The intersections of the environment curve with other fixed lines on the chart gave pertinent information to decide things like cloud base and tops.

Further electronic techniques later enabled instruments in wave-rider buoys on the sea or in remote parts of the world to transmit information to base without human attention, and facsimile machines were invented which transmitted pictures as efficiently as the teleprinter transmitted numbers.

By the end of the 1950s, satellites were orbiting in space and providing photographic evidence of what was happening over the uncharted areas of the world, and forecasters would have been receiving more information than they could handle if the computer had not arrived to process it for them.

John von Neumann (1903–57), the Hungarian-American mathematician, had built during the mid 1940's an electronic computer at Princeton University, USA. Its suggestive name was MANIAC, short for Mathematical Analyser, Numerical Integrator and Computer, and in the first few years during which von Neumann and his team of meteorologists experimented with it, the computer often seemed to live up to its mad name. For 10 years the men worked on the problem of how to feed the computer with digestible material to produce acceptable forecasts of pressure patterns based on Richardson's mathematical formulae, and by the mid 1950's they started to achieve reliable results. For some years forecasters did not trust the computer and in addition plotted their own prognostic charts by traditional methods; but when the machine was consistently more accurate than they were the task was relinquished to computers. The interpretation of the numerical models which the computers produce and the formulation of forecasts for public consumption remain the task of the human forecaster.

The newest computer at the Central Forecasting Office at Bracknell, Berks, an IBM 360/95 is one of the most powerful in the British Isles and is supported by one of the most advanced telecommunications systems in Europe. Since 1972 the computer has been fed with pressure and humidity data relevant to points on a model which has ten vertical levels,

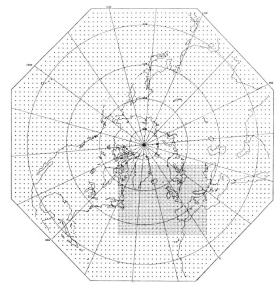

The rectangle and octagon forecast grid points used by the computer at the Meteorological Office, Bracknell. (HMSO)

from 1000 mb to 100 mb, and whose horizontal grid length is 300 km (186 miles). The model relates to the whole hemisphere north of 17° N, and a finer mesh 'window' with grid length 100 km (62 miles) covers north west Europe, Greenland and the North Atlantic as far as Canada. The computer is programmed to advance data according to equations of motion, continuity and thermodynamics in a series of successive steps until it arrives at an anticipated situation for a specified period ahead. It can project ahead for 36 hours for the fine mesh area in a matter of 12 minutes, and a prognosis for 6 days ahead takes only 3 minutes longer.

The accuracy of any computer is only as good as the material fed into it and even the fine grid survey is quite big enough for a vital piece of weather information to be missed. This source of error will probably always remain because it is inconceivable that the whole atmosphere can ever be monitored continually.

Occasionally instrument data is incorrect and must be corrected before being input to the computer. Relatively cheap and expendable electronic thermometers sometimes send back false information, but this can usually be detected amongst other data for the 100 mb level, where temperature usually changes very smoothly. Such rogue readings are corrected for all levels before being fed to the computer. Existing computer programmes seem to have a biased reaction to certain types of weather situation which is not yet fully understood. For instance, the formulae which govern its behaviour do not give enough weight to the power of anticyclones situated over Europe, and the prognostic chart tends to advance rain belts from the west too quickly. Sometimes a forecaster can introduce an extra observation into the data in order to counteract such bias but it needs considerable human skill to judge whether or not to interfere with the computer processes. In January 1977 the computer spelt out a snow situation which forecasters accepted most reluctantly, but which turned out to be quite right.

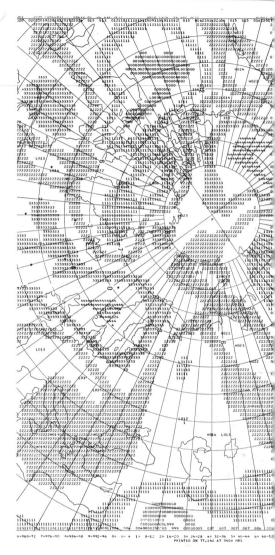

Machines can 'draw' isobars by alternating use of digits and no-digits for ranges of pressure. On this sample chart, 1 = 1008–1012 mb, 2 = 1016–1020 mb etc and the intervening blank spaces represent 1012–1016 mb, 1020–24 mb etc. (Meteorological Office, Bracknell)

The computer is fed its meals of data at midnight and midday, at which hours the maximum amount of upper air data from all over the world is available. At intervening

acsimile Machines transmitting weather charts
t the Meteorological Office, Bracknell.

ours its forecast data, translated into a
umerical picture by an electronic visual
isplay unit, is compared with satellite pictures
f what actually exists. Satellites are merely
uper-efficient observers and in no way fore-
asters.

The accuracy of any forecast, whether it be
prognostic chart from a computer or the
veather interpretation of it by a forecaster,
ecreases with the increase of period for which
he forecast is made. Every slight error in the
nitial data multiplies with every step by which
t is projected ahead. A 24-hour forecast is
ecessarily more accurate than one for 36
ours ahead, 6-day forecasts are reasonably
ood, but 30-day forecasts are still not possible
y numerical forecasting.

Monthly forecasts relate to general features
f the weather only, suggesting that it will be
vetter or drier, warmer or colder than usual,
ettled or unsettled. The forecasts are based
ipon comparison with an analogous sequence
f charts from the past, which the computer
elects according to similarities with the
urrent situation. The progress of the past
equences of weather are then applied to the
urrent weather, adapted for pertinent dif-
erences and a 30 day forecast made. These
orecasts cannot be used for such detail as
vhether a particular day of the month is going
o be wet or dry, but they are much appreciated

by industrial users, such as power stations, ice
cream manufacturers and builders whose plans
can be greatly upset by the weather.

Specialised forecasts are issued now for all
manner of public interests. Frost, snow and
fog warnings go to motoring organisations,
forecasts of rainy or wet spells concern farmers,
and even pigeon racing enthusiasts can get
wind forecasts tailored for their requirements.
Personal briefings about the weather are given
to all aircraft navigators and many commercial
ships avail themselves of a ship routing service.
In Great Britain, a team of Master Mariners
work closely with forecasters at the Central
Forecasting Office at Bracknell to route ships
according to their performance characteristics
and the wind, waves, ice or fog which they may
encounter. The shortest distance does not
necessarily mean the shortest journey time,
as the accompanying hindcast chart indicates.

Forecasts for the general public are issued
at regular intervals of the day via all the media.
Many newspapers publish isobaric charts,
necessarily slightly out of date because of the
time lag due to printing, but nevertheless
extremely helpful to anyone who scans them
with a practised eye. General forecasts are
broadcast at intervals over the radio and on
television, usually in conjunction with news
bulletins; and the more detailed 5-minute
shipping bulletins, from which up to date
isobaric charts can be quickly constructed,

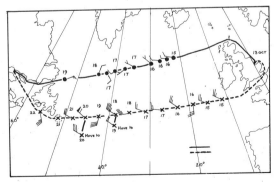

An Atlantic hindcast chart, showing three days
gained by a ship following an advised route. (HMSO)

A forecaster working on weather data at the Central Forecasting Office, Bracknell. (Open University)

re broadcast four times daily in Great Britain. Radio broadcasts are interrupted with warnings of gales or weather hazardous to motoring, and during the summer particularly, various local broadcasting stations give generous time to weather information for yachtsmen. In addition, general forecasts for local areas are tape recorded and are available to the public by telephone.

The efficiency of any forecasting system depends ultimately on the ability of the consumer to understand the information given. Time is always the scarce commodity, and a forecaster cannot supply every locality with the tiny details which make weather slightly different from one place to another. The only viable alternative is for every member of the public to add such detail himself, just as has always been done by farmers and sailors. This has earned them the enviable reputation of forecasting 'better than the professionals', but the skill is no more difficult to achieve by anyone else. Machines may continue to provide increasing information on which forecasts can be made, but nothing is ever likely to substitute for the eyes and logical reasoning of human beings.

APPENDIX

USEFUL INFORMATION FOR THE GENERAL PUBLIC

ATMOSPHERIC PRESSURE-CONVERSION TABLE

Millibars	inches	mm	millibars	inches	mm	millibars	inches	mm
960	28·35	720	990	29·23	742	1020	30·12	765
961	28·38	721	991	29·26	743	1021	30·15	766
962	28·41	722	992	29·29	744	1022	30·18	767
963	28·44	722	993	29·32	745	1023	30·21	767
964	28·47	723	994	29·35	745	1024	30·24	768
965	28·50	724	995	29·38	746	1025	30·27	769
966	28·53	725	996	29·41	747	1026	30·30	770
967	28·56	725	997	29·44	748	1027	30·33	770
968	28·59	726	998	29·47	749	1028	30·36	771
969	28·61	727	999	29·50	749	1029	30·39	772
970	28·64	727	1000	29·53	750	1030	30·42	773
971	28·67	728	1001	29·56	751	1031	30·45	773
972	28·70	729	1002	29·59	752	1032	30·47	774
973	28·73	730	1003	29·62	752	1033	30·50	775
974	28·76	731	1004	29·65	753	1034	30·53	775
975	28·79	731	1005	29·68	754	1035	30·56	776
976	28·82	732	1006	29·71	755	1036	30·59	777
977	28·85	733	1007	29·74	755	1037	30·62	778
978	28·88	734	1008	29·77	756	1038	30·65	779
979	28·91	734	1009	29·80	757	1039	30·68	779
980	28·94	735	1010	29·83	758	1040	30·71	780
981	28·97	736	1011	29·85	758	1041	30·74	781
982	29·00	737	1012	29·88	759	1042	30·77	782
983	29·03	737	1013	29·91	760	1043	30·80	782
984	29·06	738	1014	29·94	760	1044	30·83	783
985	29·09	739	1015	29·97	761	1045	30·86	784
986	29·12	740	1016	30·00	762	1046	30·89	785
987	29·15	740	1017	30·03	763	1047	30·92	785
988	29·18	741	1018	30·06	764	1048	30·95	786
989	29·21	742	1019	30·09	764	1049	30·98	787

Atmospheric Pressure Conversion Table, for those whose domestic barometers read only in inches or millimetres and who wish to compare their readings with the more universally used units, millibars.

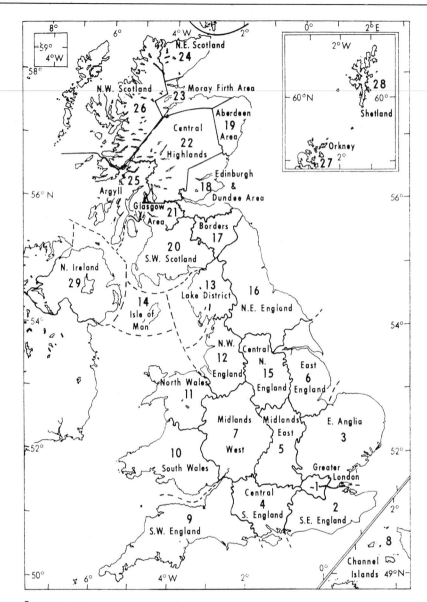

Forecast areas

Full details of Meteorological Office Services are given in the Met.O. Leaflet No 1, called 'Weather Advice to the Community', obtainable from the Director General, Meteorological Office Met.O 18c (Publications), London Road, Bracknell, Berkshire, RG12 2SZ, or from Meterological Offices serving the community.

It is advisable not to start out on any outdoor activity where weather could cause trouble, without first consulting the latest weather forecast.

Meteorological offices serving the community

England and Wales

†	Aberporth, near Cardigan	Aberporth 810117
	Bawtry, near Doncaster	Doncaster 710474
†	Benson, Oxon.	Wallingford 36202
†	Binbrook, Lincs.	Binbrook 527
	Birmingham Airport	021–743 4747
†	Boscombe Down, Wilts.	Amesbury 3331, ext. 2131
†	Brawdy, near Haverfordwest	Solva 528
‡	Glamorgan (Rhoose) Airport	Rhoose 710343
	Gloucester	Churchdown 855566
	Honington, Suffolk	Honington 466
†	Linton-on-Ouse, North Yorks.	Linton-on-Ouse 381
	London Weather Centre	01–836 4311
	Lyneham, Wilts.	Bradenstoke 89283
	Manchester Weather Centre	061–832 6701
†	Marham, Norfolk	Narborough 398
	Newcastle Weather Centre	Newcastle upon Tyne 26453
	Nottingham Weather Centre	Hucknall 3311
	Plymouth, Devon	Plymouth 42534
	Preston, Lancs.	Preston 52628
	St Mawgan, Cornwall	Newquay 2224
†	Shawbury, near Shrewsbury	Shawbury 335
‡	Southampton Weather Centre	Southampton 28844
	Upavon, Wilts	Upavon 286
†	Valley, Gwynedd	Holyhead 2288
†	Wittering, Northants.	Stamford 4802
*	Wyton, Cambs.	Huntingdon 2451, ext. 458

Scotland

‡	Aberdeen (Dyce) Airport	Dyce 722334
‡	Edinburgh Airport	031–334 7777
	Glasgow Weather Centre	041–248 3451
	Kinloss, Morayshire	Forres 2161, ext. 116
‡	Kirkwall Airport, Orkney	Kirkwall 2421, ext. 34
*	Leuchars, Fife	Leuchars 224
	Pitreavie, Dunfermline	Inverkeithing 2566
	Prestwick Airport	Prestwick 78475

Northern Ireland

Belfast Airport	Crumlin 52339

Offices are open 24 hours a day, seven days a week except as indicated:
* Closed Friday evening, Saturday and Sunday.
† Open office hours (Monday to Friday) only.
‡ Open 24 hours per day, but there may be short delays in service in the late evening and during the night.

GENERAL SYNOPSIS AT ..*1200*....HRS *Nov 28 1975*

L 100m N.) Viking 970 → NE
L Plymouth 990 → NE Sweden / 978

GALES SEA AREA FORECAST	WIND, WEATHER VISIBILITY	
VIKING	W 6-8,9 / 4-6	V
FORTIES		
CROMARTY	W 5-7,8	V
FORTH		
TYNE		
DOGGER		
FISHER	W 6-8	9 var 5-6 / NW 6-8 •
GERMAN BT		
HUMBER		
THAMES	9 var 6-8 / NW 5-7 •	V
DOVER		
WIGHT		
PORTLAND	W-NW 5-7,8	V
PLYMOUTH		
BISCAY	W 7-9 / NW 6-8 •	V
FINIST'RE		
SOLE	NW 6-8	V
LUNDY		
FASTNET	NW 4-5 / 5-7	V
IRISH S		
SHANNON	NW 5-6 / 6-8	V
ROCKALL		
MALIN		
HEBRIDES	NW 4-6 / 7-8	V
MINCHES		
BAILEY		
FAIR IS	NW 6-8 / W 4-6	V
FAEROES	W-NW 4-6	V
SE ICELD	N 6-8,9	V

COASTAL REPORTS AT ..*1600*. HRS	WIND	WEATHER & VISIBILITY	PRESSURE & TENDENCY
TIREE	NW 5	22	988 /
SULE SKERRY	W 2	27	984 \
BELL ROCK	W 3	12	987 \
DOWSING	SW 4	11	991
GALLOPER	WN 1	o 5	993 \
VARNE	ENE 3	• 2	989
ROYAL SOV	NE'N 4	o 5	989 \
PORTLAND B	N 6	o 3	990 \
SCILLY	WS 4	5	996 /
VALENTIA	NNE 2	o 13	995 /
RONALDSWAY	W 4	22	991 /
MALIN HEAD	NW'W 6	32	990 \

→ 1500 hrs

Naut miles	0	100	200	300	400	500	600	700

Beaufort force	Warm front - knots	Cold front - knots
8 6 5 4 3 2	40 20 10 5	40 20 10 5

Full details of weather bulletins and gale warnings for shipping are given in the Met. O. Leaflet No 3, available from the Director General, Meteorological Office (Met. 1a), Eastern Road, Bracknell, Berkshire, RG12 2UR.

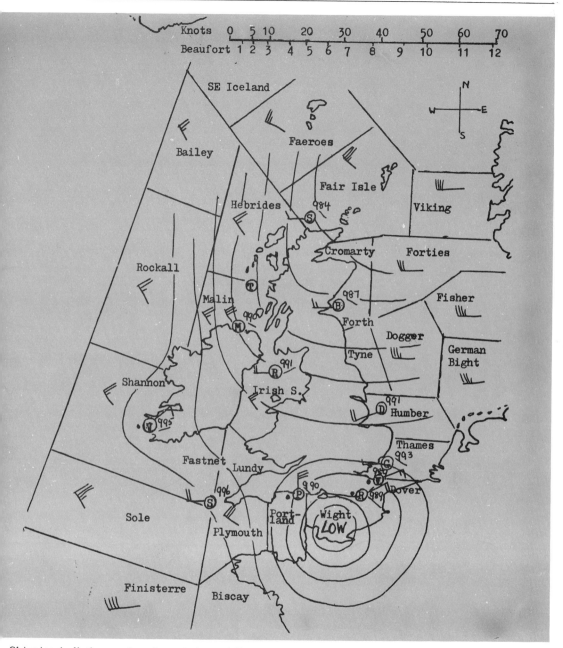

Shipping bulletins are broadcast 4 times daily and last for 5 minutes. The information given can be satisfactorily taken down on to a chart whose format agrees with the order in which the forecast and observations are dictated. An adequate pressure map can then be drawn by a yachtsman at sea, and in the above example was particularly useful in keeping track of a depression moving along the English Channel.

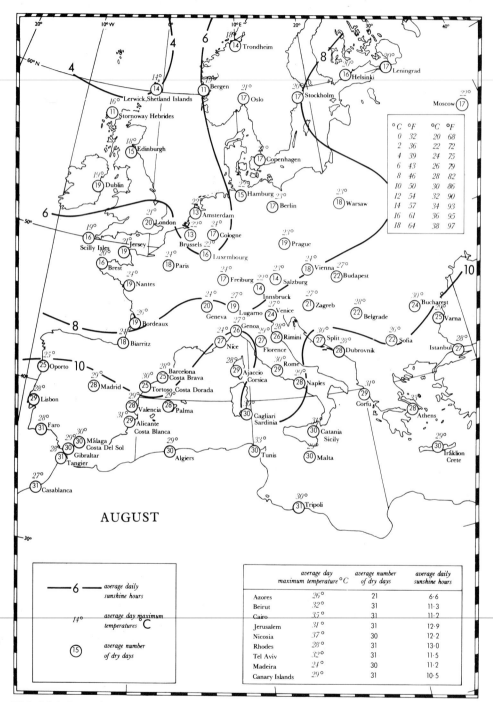

AUGUST

°C	°F	°C	°F
0	32	20	68
2	36	22	72
4	39	24	75
6	43	26	79
8	46	28	82
10	50	30	86
12	54	32	90
14	57	34	93
16	61	36	95
18	64	38	97

	average day maximum temperature °C	average number of dry days	average daily sunshine hours
Azores	26°	21	6·6
Beirut	32°	31	11·3
Cairo	35°	31	11·2
Jerusalem	31°	31	12·9
Nicosia	37°	30	12·2
Rhodes	28°	31	13·0
Tel Aviv	32°	31	11·5
Madeira	24°	30	11·2
Canary Islands	29°	31	10·5

Legend:
— 6 — average daily sunshine hours
14° average day maximum temperatures C
(15) average number of dry days

Helpful information about temperature and rainfall is given in a booklet 'Your Holiday Weather', a London Weather Centre Memorandum No 27, available by post or to callers at any Weather Centre.
Maps similar to the above are given for every month of the year as well as tabulated statistics.

TN 1966 Oct 16/II

Tornado and Storm Research Organisation (TORRO),
Cockhill House, Trowbridge, BA14 9BG, England.

Before completing this form, please refer to the notes in TORRO Publication No. 2/74.

Your Name: G.T. Meaden
Address: Cockhill House, TROWBRIDGE, BA14 9BG, Wiltshire

Telephone no.(business hours): Trowbridge 2872   : (home)

Did you see the phenomenon you are reporting No , or interview eye-witnesses YES ,
or compile your report from newspaper or other written accounts YES ? If the latter,
give full references including, where possible, the name of the writer . .
Oxford Mail 17 Oct 1966 ; Oxford Times 21 Oct 1966; The Times 17 Oct 1966.
In the latter case, indicate whether this writer saw the phenomenon No , or interviewed eye-witnesses .YES, or prepared his account from other or older sources No .
(G.T.M. also visited the site and interviewed eye-witnesses).

A : This report describes the sighting/investigation of {(A_1) TORNADO;} (A_2) FUNNEL
    CLOUD (aloft over land); (A_3) WATERSPOUT; (A_4) FUNNEL CLOUD (aloft over water);
    (A_5) REMARKABLE SHOWER; (A_6) LAND DEVIL; (A_7) WATER DEVIL; (A_8) FIRE DEVIL
    (A_9) OTHER VORTEX; (A_{10}) HAILSTORM.

B : Date of the event 16 Oct 1966 Day of week Sunday . C : Time of day 1620 GMT/BST

    If time unknown, circle as appropriate: before or after dawn/noon/dusk/midnight;
    night/day; early or late morning, afternoon, evening. C_1 : Duration not known

D : Specific location(s) : Barton Estate, Headington (N. of the bypass), Oxford.

D_1: Counties or county : Oxford

E : Strength (consult TORRO Publn 3/74 or leave for TORRO to complete): Force 4 (or 5)

F : Path width affected : Up to 50 metres

G : Path length affected : 1.2 km (between A and F on map)

H : Direction of path : From 200° to 030° (slightly curving to the right)

I : Numbers of humans (2) and beasts (0) injured. (very slight)
    Numbers of humans (0) and beasts (0) killed.

J : Estimated cost of losses to property (£30,000), crops (0), and animal life (0)
    (at 1966 prices)

K : Summary of relevant weather data which occurred before, during and after the
    phenomenon: Heavy rain for a while, which eased just before TN arrived. Described as
    a black cloud 30 yards wide and 200 feet high with wood and corrugated iron swirling
    inside. The Radcliffe Met. Station, 4 km to the W., reported sharp change of wind
    direction at 4.20 p.m. The Oxford Times reported a Radcliffe observer as
    saying the wind spun round from E. to S.W. at the same time as the rain
    came. The day's maximum was 14°C, minimum 9°C, and 24-hour rain 12mm;
    there was no sunshine.

L : Please give a general account of the phenomena which occurred on the reverse of
    this form. In the case of a hailstorm, describe the hailstone sizes, shapes,
    opacity, structure, and number/unit area.

Date this form completed   Signed   G.T. Meaden

Please return to Dr G.T. Meaden at the above address.   TORRO Publn No. 1/74(Rev.75)

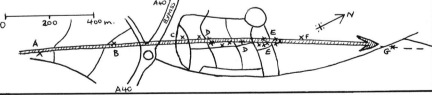

Reports from the public about unusual weather happenings are always welcomed
by the Meteorological Office. Either write direct to the Meteorological Office,
London Road, Bracknell or to the local weather office. Ice meteors found should be
hastily consigned to the deep freeze compartment of a refrigerator and the nearest
Meteorological Office informed. Evidence of tornadoes, hail, water devils etc., will
be welcomed by the Tornado and Storm Research Organisation, set out as above.

INDEX